'Through the Swedish context, Anshelm and Hultman offer provocative accounts of how circulating global discourses about various aspects of climate science-policy shape a spectrum of perceived engagements. This is a compelling tale of how patterns of communicating about climate change are intertwined with our 21st century patterns of practice.'

Max Boykoff, University of Oxford, UK

'If climate change threatens the very core of civilization, why do micro-practices of risk management dominate the policy responses? *Discourses of Global Climate Change* uses discourse analysis to deepen our understanding of climate change politics. This clearly-written, provocative study will enrich the work of policymakers and climate scholars.'

Nancy Langston, Michigan Technological University, USA

'This is an important contribution to understanding the dramatic shifts in global climate debates over the last decade. It links politics and the discourses of climate change in Sweden and internationally. This allows a powerful tool to interrogate the 2009 Copenhagen Climate Summit and illuminate its far-reaching impacts.'

Heather Goodall, University of Technology, Sydney, Australia

'This book provides an exceptionally insightful analysis of the politics of climate change in Sweden, and the predominant discourses they identify illuminate climate change debates worldwide. They highlight limitations of the dominant eco-modernist discourse suggesting that climate change can be handled – via technological innovations, market mechanisms and individual behavioral changes – without fundamentally modifying the current socio-economic system and its commitment to endless growth. Their analysis of the sources of climate change skepticism in Sweden reveals remarkable similarities to the U.S. situation, again showing the wide applicability of their results.'

Riley E. Dunlap, Oklahoma State University, USA

T0300353

Discourses of Global Climate Change

This book examines the arguments made by political actors in the creation of antagonistic discourses on climate change. Using in-depth empirical research from Sweden – a country considered by the international political community to be a frontrunner in tackling climate change – it draws out lessons that contribute to the worldwide environmental debate.

The book identifies and analyses four globally circulated discourses that each call for very different action to be taken to achieve sustainability: Industrial Fatalism, Green Keynesianism, Eco-socialism and Climate Scepticism. Drawing on risk society and post-political theory, it elaborates on concepts such as industrial-modern masculinity and ecomodern utopia, exploring how it is possible to reconcile apocalyptic framing to the dominant discourse of political conservatism.

This highly original and detailed study focuses on opinion leaders and the way discourses are framed in the climate-change debate, making it valuable reading for students and scholars of environmental communication and media, global environmental policy, energy research and sustainability.

Jonas Anshelm is a Professor researching energy politics, environmental history and the political history of ideas at Linköping University, Sweden.

Martin Hultman is a Research Fellow in cultural studies, energy politics and environmental history at Umeå University, Sweden.

Routledge Studies in Environmental Communication and Media

Culture, Development and Petroleum
An Ethnography of the High North
Edited by Jan-Oddvar Sørnes, Larry Browning and Jan Terje Henriksen

Discourses of Global Climate Change
Apocalyptic framing and political antagonisms
Jonas Anshelm and Martin Hultman

Discourses of Global Climate Change

Apocalyptic framing and political antagonisms

Jonas Anshelm and Martin Hultman

Routledge
Taylor & Francis Group

LONDON AND NEW YORK

First published 2015
by Routledge

2 Park Square, Milton Park, Abingdon, Oxon OX14 4RN
711 Third Avenue, New York, NY 10017, USA

Routledge is an imprint of the Taylor & Francis Group, an informa business

First issued in paperback 2016

British Library Cataloguing-in-Publication Data
A catalogue record for this book is available from the British Library

Library of Congress Cataloging in Publication Data
Hultman, Martin.
Discourses of global climate change : apocalyptic framing and political
antagonisms / Martin Hultman and Jonas Anshelm.
pages cm. -- (Routledge studies in environmental communication and media)
1. Climatic changes--Political aspects--Sweden. 2. Global warming--Political
aspects--Sweden. 3. Global environmental change--Political aspects--
Sweden. 4. Climatic changes--Press coverage--Sweden. 5. Global warming--
Press coverage--Sweden. 6. Global environmental change--Press coverage--
Sweden. I. Anshelm, Jonas, 1960- II. Title.
QC903.2.S94H85 2014
363.738'745609485--dc23
2014021402

ISBN 978-1-138-78131-3 (hbk)
ISBN 978-1-138-20133-0 (pbk)

Typeset in Goudy
by Taylor & Francis Books

Contents

Acknowledgements

We have not been alone in finalizing this book, even though it was sometimes lonely in front of the computer. A big thank you goes to Patricia O'Kane and Jim Carrier on the other side of the Atlantic, who made great efforts to revise our English language. Hope to see you around some day! Same goes to Sarah, Louisa and Beth at Routledge. Isak Anshelm retrieved the Swedish data and Maria Anshelm helped us with typewriting. Elin and Kaspar Hultman supported us. Per Gyberg deserves special recognition for inspiring our second chapter.

We both have the good fortune to have supportive, creative and knowledgeable colleagues to work with. At Linköping University, the seminar group Green Critical Forum; and at Umeå University, the assemblage Umeå Studies in Science, Technology and Environment have been vital for developing the analysis presented in this book. Finally, we would like to thank the small community of Bestorp in which we both live.

1   Introduction
Discourses of climate change and global environmental politics

Partaking in the global climate policy debate in the twenty-first century is like stepping into a dimly lit room where people are screaming at each other. Voices bounce off walls and ricochet back towards the centre from different directions. In this cacophony, it is difficult to perceive any sense of urgency, importance or significance. In many respects, it would be rational to hold our hands to our ears, urgently seek out a corner and wait for silence – if it were not for the increasingly clear screams that a fire is burning in the basement and all exits are blocked. This book is written not for those who seek silence but rather for anyone who wants to understand patterns in the arguments; which voices dominate in the room; why the noise level is so high at this time in history; and why the cries seem to subside into a weak murmur just as the fire in the basement gets closer to our room.

Introduction

How can an apocalyptic framing of climate change dominate at the same time that politics is ruled by conservative business-as-usual strategies? This is the main question this book sets out to explore. While there has been a remarkable recognition of climate change across the political landscape, and among researchers and the public, the resulting notion of urgency has not produced comparable political action. Instead, climate change – both before the Stern Review/the Intergovernmental Panel on Climate Change (IPCC)/Al Gore and after Copenhagen – is governed by rather piecemeal and technocratic management of carbon emissions. It is obvious that climate change presents a momentous challenge that is both radical and existential, but paradoxically, this challenge does not provoke equivalent measures. Rather, it generates routine practices and micro-practices of risk management.

Concerns that increasing carbon dioxide emissions, particularly from industry, transportation, and the production of electricity and heat, can lead to profound climate change have been an increasing part of the international political debate since at least the late 1960s (Weart, 2008; Martinsson, 2001). The term "climate change" which has permeated public debate in the past decade, has almost a five-decade history. In 1970, US citizens celebrated the first Earth Day and two years later both the official UN environmental conference and the parallel alternative conference in Stockholm included emissions from fossil fuels as important issues. From the establishment of IPCC in 1988 by two United Nations organizations – the World Meteorological Organisation (WMO) and the United Nations Environment Programme (UNEP) – climate change has been a recurring global political and scientific issue. The Toronto Conference on the Changing Atmosphere in 1988 and The Hague Conference on the Environment in 2001, along with the Green Party's successes in municipal and national elections, increased pressure on governments to take environmental issues and climate change more seriously (Aykut et al., 2012; Knaggård, 2014). In 1989, Sweden became the first country to enact a carbon dioxide tax. Beginning in 1990, a new hegemony arose in environmental politics in the form of an ecomodern discourse. Environmental problems such as climate change were described as being manageable with technology, carbon markets and green consumption. Now the consequences of climate change were being presented in terms of concrete effects on people's lives, and options for mitigation were reduced to individual lifestyle changes. As a result, journalists, politicians and others shaped the issue as a matter of individual morality. Contrary to the political framing of the late 1980s, this ecomodern framing left less room for controversy. NGOs, journalists, the educational system and some scientists promoted lifestyle changes, which translated into greener daily practices (Aykut et al., 2012; Levy and Spicer, 2013; Knaggård, 2014). Dominant politicians, industry leaders and debaters reframed the climate issue as a managerial problem. The term "climate capitalism" has been coined by Newell and Paterson (2010) to describe an economic reorientation of the ecomodern discourse that emphasizes the role of carbon management, as well as trading and galvanizing the resources and political support of key financial actors, including investment banks, traders and accountants. Financial actors – including insurance companies, pension funds and banks – began paying attention to climate risks, particularly the physical damage from hurricanes and business risks created by higher fuel prices or technological obsolescence: so-called "stranded assets". Enthusiasm for carbon markets was instrumental in building a wider coalition by offering strategic flexibility for manufacturers, new market opportunities for financial firms and capital for "developing" countries shaped by flexible mechanisms to lower emissions. Under the Kyoto Protocol, these mechanisms included emissions trading, and the Clean Development Mechanism and Joint Implementation that enabled nations to reduce emissions or remove carbon from the atmosphere in other countries.

Until 2006 the majority of politicians and other elite actors more or less treated climate change as just one of several managerial issues relating to the environment and as something to keep an eye on in the future. This occurred despite grave warnings from environmental organizations, individual researchers and research communities: even as far back as 1990 when the

IPCC published their first report, which stated that this was an issue not to be taken lightly (Knaggård, 2014). All of this history was clearly distilled a couple of years after the millennium. At this point things changed dramatically. From the autumn of 2006 through to 2009, the issue of global climate change was portrayed in apocalyptic terms, accompanied by recommendations for conservative actions to match such dire predictions. In this book we will show how this issue was debated.

During the last ten years or so a growing scientific consensus has emerged about human, or "anthropogenic", influences on the global climate and the significant risks posed to humans and non-human life by the rising levels of greenhouse gases in our atmosphere that are causing climate change. Indeed, there is striking scientific agreement that more greenhouse gases are being created today than before the era of industrialization. Human activities are heating up our planet and causing climate change, according to scientists directly involved in researching the issue. In a quantitative research project Doran and Zimmerman (2009) found that 97 per cent of climate scientists agreed that emissions of greenhouse gases caused by humans, such as methane and carbon dioxide, are contributing to anthropogenic climate change. Our current era of industrialization has even been named the Anthropocene age because of the massive geological changes that humans are causing. Yet, this scientific consensus contrasts with opinions expressed within society. Analysis of mass media and internet communication regarding climate change reveals a contentious debate about the existence and causes of climate change and how to tackle it: a debate that reflects denial, doubt and apathy (Whitmarsh, 2011; Oreskes and Conway, 2010). Framing the issue as a debate between believers and deniers of climate change underestimates the fact that it is a complex mix of values and ideas drawn from science, technology, political ecology, value systems, identities, infrastructures and "need" politics. Climate change is political, therefore different actors with different discourses will be found in society. In this book we will show how climate change has been debated in Sweden in recent years and we will intertwine our findings with the global debate.

This book is therefore not another study of media logic or the role of newspapers in the production of dominant discourses. There are many books and articles with such empirical material and analytic focus (e.g. Boykoff and Boykoff, 2007; Boykoff and Rajan, 2007; Smith, 2005; Cottle, 2009; Boykoff, 2011; Doyle, 2011). Instead, our book is an analysis of the arguments made by different actors in all kinds of printed media, including journals, books and mass media. We argue that if we wish to understand the lack of effective responses from firms and governments, in the face of increasing evidence of a climate crisis caused by anthropogenic greenhouse gases, it is vital that we explore the role climate discourse plays. More specifically, we propose that it is important to make an empirically in-depth analysis combined with theoretical conceptualizations of the contestation between NGOs, business and state agencies over the four core climate discourses of: Industrial Fatalism,

Green Keynesianism, Eco-socialism and Climate Scepticism. This book goes beyond ordinary mass media or political science analysis and examines how global warming, climate change and sustainability were portrayed by leading politicians and commentators in over 3,500 editorials, opinion pieces, political commentaries, books and major feature articles. We also analyse the measures that these actors were required to utilize in order to address these environmental problems.

There are vast numbers of journal articles that cover climate change politics, but very few books that critically analyse a large body of empirical material and unite that analysis with international research. There are a couple of "big picture" books that regard climate change as yet another example of the state of environmental politics. These books posit the climate change debate as part of a larger environmental field of politics. Anthony Giddens' book, *The Politics of Climate Change* (2009), and Ulrich Beck's book, *World at Risk* (2009), are two examples of books in which a well-known theory is applied to climate change. Our aim is not to write that kind of "grand theory" book. Our book combines an abundance of empirical material from political actors with a study of previous research and discusses the accuracy of post-political and world risk society theory. The book by Carvalho et al., called *Climate Change Politics: Communication and Public Engagement* (2012), is an impressive anthology that shows the relationship between climate change and politics in different arenas: we are inspired by it since it also identifies the social movements that are taking part in the process of reshaping the world.

As a whole, the range of study in this field analyses the relationship between climate change, power and environmental politics in late capitalist culture. It is clear that either a mass media approach or a philosophical approach dominates the existing body of work, whereas the inclusion of the political aspects of the climate change debate is investigated in very few books. We strive to extend the analysis by considering the interrelationship between different discourses of climate change and the institutions and practices of environmental politics. Thus, we aim to take a step further in understanding the climate change debate and its influence on environmental politics at the beginning of the twenty-first century. This is done by broadening the analytical and theoretical scope of the scholarship to include a range of climate change discourses and, crucially, the interrelationships between them. The intent of this book is to fill a gap within the current literature on climate change by bringing together the historical and cultural analysis of a large body of empirical material with theoretical discussions about world risk society, post-political conditions and ecomodern utopias.

The intensification of the climate change debate

The year 2006 will forever be remembered as the year when the greenhouse effect was recognized all around the globe as a major crisis in human history. It all began with the collapse of the New Orleans infrastructure and the human – as well as non-human – catastrophes that resulted from hurricane Katrina, which was the deadliest and most destructive Atlantic tropical cyclone of the 2005 season. The aftermath showed people all over America that the US was not wealthy and omnipotent: the consequences of climate change could happen in the heart of even the wealthiest country. Climate change was later identified as the most important term of 2006. Thereafter, it was no longer solely a concern for scientists and environmentalists, but also for the general public, politicians, businesses and the mass media (Avellan 2006; Ekdal 2007, Höijer, 2010; Olausson, 2011). The two internationally renowned environmental debaters from Sweden, Stefan Edman (Social Democrat) and Anders Wijkman (Christian Democrat), proclaimed that climate change had "finally got the place in the debate it deserves" (Wijkman and Edman 2007). Like several other environmental commentators, they pointed to three crucial events that explained the dramatic change in environmental consciousness in industrialized countries. These three were: the economist Nicholas Stern's report on climate change costs; the screening of former Vice President Al Gore's film, *An Inconvenient Truth*; and the publication of the IPCC's fourth report on global climate change. These events garnered much attention globally – in Japan (Sampei and Aoyagi-Usui, 2009), Finland (Lyytimäki and Tapio, 2009; Lyytimäki, 2011), Australia (Kurz et al., 2010), Germany (Reusswig, 2010), as well as in Sweden – where they raised the discussion about climate change to new intensities (Schmidt et al., 2013). It seemed that climate change could be a bandwagon aboard which values, lifestyles and societal structures of consumer democracies were finally revealed as unsustainable (Blühdorn, 2011).

Climate change as a recurrent theme

This newfound focus on climate change was reflected in news reporting all over the world in the first months of 2007, when the consequences of climate change for people and cultures became a recurring theme. One quarter of Bangladesh would be submerged in a hundred years' time, reported Swedish journalists in major media. Bangladesh's difficult struggle against climate-related flooding was described in detail (Holmgren, 2007). The newspaper *Svenska Dagbladet* stated in turn that alpine glaciers would melt within 40 years, while *Aftonbladet* wrote about how Australia was experiencing the worst drought in a thousand years as a result of climate change (Von Hall, 2007; Kadhammar, 2007). Reports of melting ice caps in Greenland, rapidly disappearing glaciers in the Andes and shrinking ice caps in the Arctic followed in quick succession during the first months of 2007. Record summer heat in southern Europe was also interpreted as an effect of global warming. Common to all of these stories was the apocalyptic tone that pervaded them. It was not a question of whether these phenomena could occur or what impact they might have, but that the disasters were occurring right now. They also displayed a profound concern. Similar descriptions are found in Japan, Finland, Australia, the UK, Germany, France and India (Sampei and Aoyagi-Usui, 2009; Lyytimäki and Tapio, 2009; Kurz et al., 2010; Reusswig, 2010; Schmidt et al., 2013).

It is significant that the main daily paper in Sweden, *Dagens Nyheter*, portrayed climate change and the consequences of burning fossil fuels in a long-running and profound series of articles entitled, "Climate Anxiety". *Aftonbladet*, in turn, called upon its readers to sign a petition to stop climate change and regularly announced how many people had signed up (Bjurman 2006). They used clear-cut feedback loops to encourage readers to act. From the autumn of 2006 until the end of December 2009, when the UN conference on climate change was held in Copenhagen, climate change took centre stage in public political debate worldwide (Schmidt et al., 2013). Sweden was no exception. In Sweden all of the parliamentary parties – as well as interest groups ranging from the Confederation of Swedish Enterprise, to the Church – identified ambitious climate actions as a prerequisite for the survival of civilization. But even if they agreed on the need for urgent action against emissions and the threat of climate change, the solutions were far from the same: four very different discourses developed along politically divergent paths.

The increasing tensions and disagreements that these discourses articulated were based on fundamental social questions: what constituted a "good" society? Was economic growth part of the solution or part of the problem? What did an ecologically healthy relationship between politics and the market look like? Had significant changes in lifestyles and consumption patterns in the wealthier part of the world become ecologically necessary, or was it enough to simply have environmental labelling of consumer goods? The actors in Sweden, like others globally, discussed issues such as: what was a globally equitable distribution of the Earth's resources and who was responsible for promoting such a scheme? What roles should technology and science play in the development of measures to address the problem of climate change and the value-based and epistemological problems that were associated with it? What kind of relationship between nature and industrial society should be the basis for the design of climate action to ensure the long-term survival of contemporary civilization?

In this book, we describe four discourses that attempted to answer those questions. The actors who dominated the debate did so with an Industrial Fatalist discourse. Despite the apocalyptic perspective of this discourse, proponents maintained that the climate crisis could still be handled with only marginal changes to industrial capitalist society's fundamental economic and technical structures. This discourse portrayed Sweden as competitive, courageous and a frontrunner in global environmental issues in which other countries did not stand up to the challenge. The Green Keynesian discourse was the second most influential; it portrayed climate change as a symptom of a crisis in the rich industrialized world's economic system. Thus, it included the classic European social democratic confidence in the market as the engine of wealth creation, if the market is properly regulated by strong government institutions. The Eco-socialist discourse, articulated by only a few in Sweden, rested on the assumption that climate change is a symptom of the pathological growth ideology of industrial capitalist society, which needed to be undone. The last discourse, which was articulated by a few elderly men in Sweden, was Climate Scepticism; they denied that emissions with anthropogenic causes created climate change and rejected the need for drastic changes in the organization of Western society.

Environmental politics, as articulated in these discourses, reflected an ideological battle between concrete, fundamental and long-term social values. The question of how the future of society could be organized seemed, for a few years at least, very open to various interpretations. The aim of our book in relation to the existing literature is twofold. First, it is part of a broader trend to refresh the focus on actors in the social study of climate change, thereby making possible a more fine-grained reflection on the political situation. Second, this book contributes more generally to contemporary critical theories of environmental politics by revisiting notions of power, structure, agency and unequal distribution through the lens of climate change. We bring together several different analyses found in other studies. The study of climate change in action enables this by going beyond being an examination of the creation of social orders.

Risk society, post-politics and ecomodern utopia

The well-known German sociologist, Ulrich Beck, proposes a central thesis in which the ability of modern industrial societies to control the risks they produce is heading for an implosion, owing to its nearly limitless success (Beck, 1992). Climate change is caused by unsubdued industrialization with systematic disregard for ecosystems. Climate change is perceived as something serious and calculable that has quantifiable side effects. The increased number of significant self-created risks undermines the operational logic of industrialized capitalist society: control can no longer be maintained. Industrial society is forced to confront its self-produced risks and thus is gradually transformed into a world risk society (Beck, 2009). Beck further argues that a fundamental contradiction arises in contemporary society when it is forced to prioritize self-created mega threats. Large-scale risks inherent in systems, such as climate change, that hold the possibility of self-annihilation and therefore require effective political control, have a social and political explosiveness that sooner or later forces profound social change (Beck, 1997). This situation makes space for the sub-politics happening in the discourses of global climate change that fill this book. Catastrophe can only be made tangible through different forms of communication. Abstractions and modelling of climate change with anthropogenic causes require visualization in order to highlight their apocalyptic consequences. Climate change must be viewed as an ethical problem. The actors who finally develop the necessary macro ethics are social movements in global networks, according to Beck (Beck, 2009).

Another theoretical way of understanding climate change is through a post-political strand of research. The main idea of the post-political concept is that environmental problems (and other prominent societal issues) have been constructed by neo-liberal influenced elites in a consensual way that embraces them as problems for managerial actions and market structures. For a number of years, human geographer Erik Swyngedouw has been one of the most prominent scholars arguing that climate change – as well as other environmental issues – has been constructed in a consensual, non-ideological and post-political way (Swyngedouw 2007, 2010). His main idea is that climate change has been made into part of a "carbon consensus" that frames the issue as tasks of how to reduce carbon emissions, rather than confronting overarching economic and political institutional arrangements that support a fossil-fuel dependent economy. The political controversies are only to be found in the shadows of the overarching presentation of climate change as an apocalypse and the dominating post-political managerial solutions. He argues that climate change is inserted into a story of how to restart capitalism, creating new opportunities for accumulation, overcoming present failures and increasing privatization of resources (Swyngedouw 2007, 2010). The theoretical standpoint is that post-political creation of the climate change apocalypse goes hand in hand with a neo-liberal overtaking of local and global politics; as Gert Goeminne (2010) summarizes it: " [T]he apocalyptic climate scenarios paralyse the political struggle". Ingolfur Blühdorn, a theorist of post-ecological politics, argues that the failure at Copenhagen demonstrates that it is time to recognize the extent to which environmental politics has turned – and is locked – into a politics of unsustainability. A politics of unsustainability is defined, first, by its efforts to secure and defend social practices and socioeconomic structures that are well known to be unsustainable, while allowing the curious simultaneity of an unprecedented recognition of the urgency of radical climate political change, on one hand, and an equally unprecedented unwillingness and inability to change, on the other. Normalization and mainstreaming of environmental crises, as well as political participation by social movements, undermine the sense of alienation and suppresses the vision of a much better, ecologically and socially reconciled society that goes beyond the pathologies of modern consumer capitalism (Blühdorn, 2011). The post-political and post-ecological politics of unsustainability are present especially in the aftermath of Copenhagen. We discuss how to understand this situation in relation to our in-depth case study. Close study of rich empirical material such as ours shows that there is no contradiction between apocalyptic framing and sharp political conflicts. On the contrary, we will, throughout the whole book, argue that our findings illustrate that periods of apocalyptic understanding of climate change are characterized by intense political controversies; furthermore, we will show that the climate issue is one of the few global questions under discussion today that have the potential to open up deep differences in opinion in a society otherwise permeated by a post-political neo-liberal consensus.

Apocalyptic climate scenarios do not according to our analysis paralyse the political struggle: they are actually the prerequisites for making global, political, radical sub-politics possible.

The post-political condition has similarities to the analysis of ecological modernization (Hajer, 1995). In a similar critique to the ecomodern analysis of environmental politics, we argue that the post-political standpoint misses the utopian and emotional way that neo-liberal actors, in our case with regard to the Industrial Fatalist discourse, envision the future. This hegemonic discourse is not only managerial, technocratic, non-ideological or "depoliticized", as Swyngedouw claims (2010); additionally, there is a need to empirically analyse the functions of ecological modernization, especially the way in which it is preoccupied with creating ecomodern conservative utopias that critique prevailing society but at the same time completely disregard alternatives (Hultman and Nordlund, 2013). In these utopias, overall development in society is merely extrapolated from the present to the future, with technological fixes added. The pace of technological change is said to increase, but the social structures remain intact. In this way actors in Industrial Fatalism articulate their vision of the future as an eco-efficient economy operating within the image of Sweden as a frontrunner country. The authoritative and very reassuring image of Sweden as being a unique country in the world, in that it combines lowering carbon dioxide emissions with continuously high growth, is very powerful. Throughout history, this kind of conservative utopia has been characterized by a heavy reliance on technology while detailed descriptions are, paradoxically, notably absent. Instead, the focus is shifted towards the favourable benefits, such as efficient industrial processes, clean (or not) exhaust fumes, the absence of noise and a harmonious state (Hultman and Nordlund, 2013). Whenever Copenhagen is discussed, such ecomodernism is omnipresent. The hegemony of ecological modernization in the form of the post-political situation that is part of Industrial Fatalism also needs to be understood – as it is in this book – as utopian and capable of bringing about powerful emotional images.

The world in Sweden

The empirical foundation of this book originates in Sweden. However, all of the chapters are based on internationally relevant and thorough comparisons with previous research and references to comparative studies. The international political community views Sweden as a frontrunner in dealing with climate change. National politicians from almost all sides also support this view. Sweden is seen throughout the world as a leader in tackling environmental issues and this is an image that Swedish governments, both right wing and left wing, have tried to maintain for a couple of decades now (Eckerberg and Nilsson, 2007; Granberg and Elander, 2007; Sarasini, 2009; Hysing, 2014). Since the late 1960s and the 1972 UN conference on the global environment in Stockholm, Sweden has claimed to be, and has also been widely recognized as, one of the most environmentally progressive countries in the world (Jänicke, 2008). Measures taken against acidification, the regulation of chemicals, the decrease of emissions related to industrial production, bans on biocides, the implementation of high carbon taxes and the phasing out of fossil fuels has given Sweden the reputation of being a leader in the fight against environmental degradation (Lundqvist, 2004; Lidskog and Elander, 2012): an image that has become culturally established. For example, President Obama legitimized his visit from the US in September 2013 with the argument that Sweden is a leader in both climate politics and energy technologies. Sweden is hence an internationally interesting nexus around which to build an analysis of the worldwide debate on climate change. In many parts of the world, Sweden is still also thought of as a social democratic utopia (McCarthy and Prudham, 2004; Tranter, 2011) despite two decades of neoliberalism (Hysing, 2014). In conclusion, we argue that it is important to understand that Sweden seems to be a country where politicians can deal with climate change in a transitional way: or at least there is a possibility that this might happen. Levy and Spicer (2013) also point out the need for studies that do not have a US–UK focus in order to open up the horizons for dealing feasibly with climate change. During the period studied the debate was open to these ideas. A transition seemed possible, but nothing concrete came out of it owing to the particular formation of the discourses of global climate change.

All parliamentary parties during this period, as well as interest groups ranging from the Swedish Enterprise Organisation to the Swedish Church, identified ambitious climate action as a prerequisite for the survival of industrial civilization and the transition to another form of society. Because of the apocalyptic nature of the climate change debate this could have been the moment in time when an alternative green socialism defined the future. But the consensus over climate change research was not matched by political action. Instead, ecological modernization, part Industrial Fatalism and part Green Keynesianism prevailed, emphasizing solutions such as green technology, carbon dioxide markets, innovations, taxes and new infrastructure. This was a common set of solutions all over the world (Dryzek, 1997; Hajer and Versteeg, 2005; Dobson, 2000).

Method

The aim of this book is to analyse the climate change debate as it played out on a glocal scale and how global events and science are mediated and recreated in local contexts. Using the database Artikelsök, we compiled a comprehensive collection of about 3,500 newspaper and magazine articles from 2006 to 2009 to answer our research questions on the discourses of global climate change. The database contains information about what is published in all national newspapers and all major regional newspapers as well as the vast majority of magazines that are relevant in this context. It is important to emphasize that the material includes editorials, opinion pieces, political commentaries and major signed feature articles. Ordinary news reporting is only included as background context in the survey; this exclusion distinguishes our empirical material from most other studies in the field which focus primarily on shorter texts written mainly by journalists. Our data also includes about 20 debate books that were found using the Libris database. The keywords used in all searches were climate change*; *greenhouse effect, global warming*; climate policy*; *climate negotiations, climate action*; *climate, climate adaptation*; carbon*; carbon reduction*; and related synonyms.

Once the material was compiled and arranged chronologically, we repeatedly read through it to sort out the parts that we considered relevant to the political aspects of the climate debate in Sweden. We then read the selected individual texts closely to identify their central premise and coded them accordingly. Thus, for example, one hundred articles that suggested flexible mechanisms, carbon taxes or personal allowances as solutions to the climate problem were identified. Such focal points were identified for all of the articles in the collection; these were then correlated to reveal regular and consistent patterns. In this book we have explored the analytical possibilities of our data in great depth. All of our excerpts and examples cannot fit in this text but can be examined in more detail in Anshelm's Swedish book, *Kampen Om Klimatet. Miljöpolitiska strider i Sverige 2006–2009.*

The focal points of the articles have been interpreted to represent specific and coherent discourses that struggle to give meaning to a particular aspect of the world, or to stake out a specific territory in the debate on climate change. A discourse is not limited to simply "talk" but is also viewed as a socially constitutive phenomenon that influences and structures social conduct and social perceptions (Fairclough, 1992). After the first analysis was carried out and we were able to produce an overview of the material, we found that the following four areas were of particular interest for our study: a description of the fundamental problem; the historical construction of the relationship between industrial, economic, political and atmospheric conditions; proposals for action; and responsibility. Each discourse represents about 20–30 interconnected formations. Although the individual discourses have been established based on the analysis of both individual and large groups of texts, they do not represent composites of ideas nor are they a product of chance. They are based, instead, on the repeated and systematic readings of extensive empirical material and observation of discursive patterns and the repeated use of various examples. In other words, a discourse is identified by the particular metaphors and catchphrases that are habitually deployed (Hajer and Versteeg, 2005).

Content

Our book examines and discusses four different discourses that articulate global climate change. They will be analysed together with previous research in the first four chapters and then in relation to each other as part of the global climate meeting in Copenhagen in 2009. The book ends with a discussion, inspired by Ulrich Beck and Eric Swyngedouw, about how to understand environmental politics in relation to global climate change.

In chapter two, we discuss how climate change was surrounded by apocalyptic worries but still construed as a modern problem of actors articulating an Industrial Fatalist discourse. This meant that only marginal changes were proposed to industrial capitalist society's fundamental economic and technical structures. We will discuss the understanding of climate change politics as a competition and how Sweden was portrayed as competitive and a courageous frontrunner in a global environmental race. Sweden was a country said to lead by example; its leadership was permeated by a fundamental belief that international agreements between states would make it possible to regulate greenhouse gas emissions and thereby manage climate change risks. This type of image is not restricted to Sweden, as we will demonstrate; all over the world, politicians and actors involved in the climate change debate try to pose as the most environmentally friendly (Carvalho, 2007; Boykoff, 2011). The conviction that all nations have a common interest in combating climate change, despite their diverse cultural and economic conditions, is based on the idea that scientific consensus allows for a rational political handling of the problem while conserving industrial modernity. Law, economics, science and technology are said to solve the problem with only marginal changes to industrial capitalist society's fundamental economic and technical structures, according to actors articulating the Industrial Fatalist discourse. Therefore, significant changes to industrial society's way of life, economic growth, use of natural resources, production of energy and goods, transportation, flow of materials, or any other aspect of industrial society's metabolism, are unnecessary: even contra productive.

In this chapter we will argue that Industrial Fatalists portrayed climate change as a new crisis phenomenon because it was a global, irreversible and long-term problem that required a complicated coordination of international efforts that had never been seen before. International negotiation was portrayed as being critical for the world to be saved from global climate collapse and its devastating consequences. Nevertheless, the proposed solutions were the same as those employed to solve other environmental problems; they were described in unilaterally optimistic terms, not as being in opposition to a continuation of industrial modern society. This dominant discourse suggested instead that the problem would be solved by utilizing more adapted technology such as nuclear power, technology exports, intensified research, economic growth, the use of market mechanisms, better informed consumer choices, and internationally coordinated regulatory frameworks. It argued that there was absolutely no need to reconsider industrial civilization's basic relationship with the natural world. Within this discourse it was understood that the climate crisis was merely a temporary disturbance in civilization's industrial modernization process.

In chapter three, we will cover the Green Keynesian discourse, which was the second most influential. It has a long tradition in Sweden building upon the social democratic idea of the green welfare state from the mid-1990s. It contained the classic social democratic confidence in the market as the engine of wealth creation, but only if the market is properly regulated by strong government enforcement to reduce inherent dysfunctions. This discourse is also prominent in other western European states in which Social Democrats have or have had leading political roles (Jackson, 2011). The proponents of this discourse describe the threat of climate change not as an isolated management problem, but as a symptom of a self-generated institutional crisis in the ecological system of the rich industrialized world. This crisis could not be met solely with a "business as usual" attitude, that is, a reliance on new technologies, nuclear power, market mechanisms, enlightened consumer choices and international negotiations as proposed by Industrial Fatalists. Green Keynesianism took a rather profound stance regarding an industrial capitalist mode of action. System changes, behavioural changes and fundamental value changes were necessary to meet the threat of climate change. Proponents argued that economic models must be reformed, growth concepts reclassified, ecological considerations internalized, a gentler approach to nature developed, and demands for global justice respected, even to the point of becoming, with time, an intrinsic part of climate-change politics. Changes of this kind could not be left to the market, which is why policies responsible for promoting them were of great importance in the Green Keynesian discourse.

The policies suggested in the Green Keynesian discourse included atoning for the rich world's ecological debt to poor countries by making extensive cuts in carbon emissions in rich countries while providing aid to poor countries to help them develop without excessive carbon emissions. In Sweden, as well as throughout the world, this required comprehensive changes in energy, transport and production strategies including renewable energy, rail mass transit, energy efficiency benefits and taxes, and bans to discourage carbon emissions. The Green Keynesian discourse emphasized the importance of binding international agreements, but the difficulties in achieving such agreements were instead used as an argument for accelerating national adaptations to climate change in order to demonstrate its feasibility. The proponents of the discourse also declared that reductions in Swedish emissions must be implemented in the long run, for example by setting up new transportation, energy efficiency and consumption patterns. They argued that it was better to start early and make the reductions gradually rather than pushing for change at the last minute and being forced to make changes hastily. This discourse was nourished by a belief that a fundamental restructuring of society in a climate-friendly direction by political decision-making is possible, and that the economic system can be kept more or less intact.

In chapter four, we will discuss the ideas of Eco-socialism. In many parts of the world Sweden is still thought of as a social democratic, almost socialist, utopia (McCarthy and Prudham, 2004; Tranter, 2011), despite two decades of neo-liberalism and ecomodernization, not unlike that which has occurred in other countries to the same degree, or an even greater extent as exemplified with the marketization of the school system, train infrastructure and energy providers in some areas. Because Sweden is thought of as having good preconditions for progressive environmental politics, it seemed that a green democratic socialism could blossom when climate change was on the agenda (Barry, 1999; Dryzek et al. 2003; Kronig, 2010). Interestingly though, this was not to be the case. In this chapter we analyse the few debaters who actually articulated Eco-socialist ideas. Their discourse was at the margin of the Swedish debate during those years when climate change was described as having apocalyptic dimensions, but some of their standpoints, for example climate justice, reached the centre of the debate. Climate justice refers to principles of democratic accountability and participation, ecological sustainability and social justice, and their combined ability to find solutions to climate change. This chapter will discuss how the green socialism discourse rested on the assumption that climate change is a productive force that not only allows for change in the pathological growth ideology of industrial capitalist society, but also unmasks unjust global exchange relationships. The Eco-socialist discourse evoked the image of climate science as a fixed point, an authority, which compels extensive and immediate changes in basic economic structures, relationships, lifestyles, transport and energy systems, and forms of production in contemporary capitalist society. Earth was seen as an ecological interdependent network of humans and non-humans. The impetus for radical social change no longer comes from the social sciences, but from the journals of Nature and Science, and from the indigenous people of the world that are affected by climate change in everyday life. Hopes were linked to an alliance between a scientific elite and local opposition groups with strong commitments to the global environment, and a joint effort to persuade established political communities to use their state apparatus to tackle climate change. Essentially, this was a global climate change movement from below, demanding a transition and leading the way.

In chapter five, we will display the discourse of Climate Sceptics in Sweden who did not agree with the majority of the scientists regarding the anthropogenic cause of climate change, nor the need to expedite drastic changes in the organization of Western society. With only one exception this group consisted of elderly men with influential positions either in academia or large private companies. We discuss how they describe themselves as marginalized, banned and oppressed dissidents, forced to speak up against a faith-based belief in climate science. We examine their strong beliefs in a market society, great mistrust of government regulation and a constructivist position against climate science that contradicts their sturdy belief in engineering and natural science rationality. Denouncing the theory of global warming is not a new phenomenon. In the US, the link between scepticism on climate science and conservative think tanks has been proven in an array of studies (Leggett 2001; Oreskes and Conway, 2010). The previous research on Climate Scepticism in the US (and to some extent in the UK) provides a good picture of who they are and what they claim. Research tends to focus on media coverage of climate change in press articles; very few studies of mediated climate change address the articulated arguments in a detailed and focused manner. In this chapter we will qualitatively analyse the arguments put forward by Climate Sceptics and connect the analysis to historical changes. We do this by utilizing gender theories on masculinity and research into the history of ideas. We contend that Climate Sceptics in Sweden can be understood as being intertwined with a modern industrial masculinity that argues as if the society they had built was being challenged. Climate Sceptics tried to save the modern industrial structures of which they were a part and they defended its values. Here, gender analysis moves beyond previous research by understanding this discourse not only as an ideologically based outcry against science and politics but also a recognition of identities, historical structures and emotions.

Chapter six will cover the months leading up to the meetings in Copenhagen in December 2009 as well as the time afterwards. This chapter details Sweden's role and examines different practices of climate change politics around the world. This chapter illustrates the clash between different discourses and how they changed in relation to each other when new issues entered the debate. Here we combine analysis and previous research on the climate change debate in an international setting: the 2009 United Nations Climate Change Conference (COP 15). We also extend the analysis beyond Copenhagen by including a history of what happened after that meeting.

The book ends with a discussion about the climate change debate inspired by concepts such as the risk society, post-politics and ecomodern utopia. This discussion shows the different ways our analysis can be used to deepen the understanding of current environmental politics.

References

Anshelm, J. (2012). Kampen om klimatet, Stockholm: Pärspektiv Förlag.

Avellan, H. "Årets ord: klimatförändring", *Sydsvenska Dagbladet* 30/12 2006.

Aykut, S. C., Comby, J. B. and Guillemot, H. (2012). Climate change controversies in French mass media 1990–2010. *Journalism Studies*, 13(2), 157–74.

Barry, J. (1999). *Rethinking Green Politics*. London: Sage Publications.

Beck, U. (1992). *Risk Society: Towards a New Modernity*. London: Sage Publications.

Beck, U. (1997). *The Reinvention of Politics: Rethinking Modernity in the Global Social Order*. Cambridge: Polity Press.

Beck, U. (2009). *World at Risk*. Cambridge: Polity Press.

Bjurman, P. "Ett mycket bra initiativ. Kofi Annans ord till Aftonbladets läsare", *Aftonbladet* 11/11 2006.

Blühdorn, I. (2011). The politics of unsustainability: COP15, post-ecologism, and the ecological paradox. *Organization and Environment*, 24(1), 34–53.

Boykoff, M. T. (2011). *Who Speaks for the Climate? Making Sense of Media Reporting on Climate Change*. Cambridge University Press.

Boykoff, M. T. and Boykoff, J. M. (2007). Climate change and journalistic norms: A case-study of US mass-media coverage. *Geoforum*, *38*(6), 1190–204.

Boykoff, M. T., and Rajan, S. R. (2007). Signals and noise. *EMBO reports*, *8*(3), 207–11.

Carvalho, A. (2007). Ideological cultures and media discourses on scientific knowledge: re-reading news on climate change. *Public Understanding of Science*, *16*(2), 223–43.

Carvalho, A. and Peterson, T. R. (2012). *Climate Change Politics: Communication and Public Engagement*. Cambria Press.

Cottle, S. (2009). Global crises in the news: Staging new wars, disasters and climate change. *International Journal of Communication*, *3*, 24.

Dobson, A. (2000). *Green Political Thought*. London: Routledge.

Doran, P. T. and Zimmerman, M. K. (2009). Examining the scientific consensus on climate change. *Eos, Transactions American Geophysical Union*, *90*(3), 22–23.

Doyle, J. (2011). *Mediating Climate Change*. Ashgate Publishing, Ltd.

Dryzek, J. (1997). *The Politics of the Earth: Environmental Discourses*. Oxford: Oxford University Press.

Dryzek, J. S., Downes, D., Hunold, C., Schlosberg, D. and Hernes, H. K. (2003). *Green States and Social Movements: Environmentalism in the United States, United Kingdom, Germany, and Norway*. Oxford: Oxford University Press.

Eckerberg, K. and Nilsson, M. (eds). (2007). *Environmental policy integration in practice: Shaping institutions for learning*. London: Earthscan.

Ekdal, N. "Davos, i väntan på Texas", *Dagens Nyheter* 26/1 2007.

Fairclough, N. (1992). *Discourse and Social Change*. Cambridge: Polity Press.

Giddens, A. (2009). *The Politics of Climate Change*. Cambridge: Polity Press.

Goeminne, G. (2010). Climate policy is dead, long live climate politics! *Ethics, Place and Environment*, *13*(2), 207–14.

Granberg, M. and Elander, I. (2007). Local governance and climate change: reflections on the Swedish experience. *Local Environment*, *12*(5), 537–48.

Hajer, M. and Versteeg, W. (2005). A decade of discourse analysis of environmental politics: achievements, challenges, perspectives. *Journal of Environmental Policy and Planning*, *7*(3), 175–84.

Höijer, B. (2010). Emotional anchoring and objectification in the media reporting on climate change. *Public Understanding of Science*, *19*(6), 717–31.

Holmgren, M. "Här är klimatförändringen en kamp på liv och död", *Dagens Nyheter* 14/1 2007.

Hultman, M. (2013). The making of an environmental hero: A history of ecomodern masculinity, fuel cells and Arnold Schwarzenegger. *Environmental Humanities*, *2*, 83–103.

Hultman, M. and Nordlund, C. (2013). Energizing technology: expectations of fuel cells and the hydrogen economy, 1990–2005. *History and Technology*, *29*(1), 33–53.

Hysing, E. (2014). A green star fading? A critical assessment of Swedish environmental policy change. *Environmental Policy and Governance* *24*(4), 262–74.

Jackson, T. (2011). *Prosperity Without Growth: Economics for a Finite Planet*. London: Routledge.

Jänicke, M. (2008). Ecological modernisation: new perspectives. *Journal of cleaner production*, *16*(5), 557–65.

Kadhammar, P. "Dödens hetta", *Aftonbladet* 25/1 2007.

Knaggård, Å. (2014) What do policy-makers do with scientific uncertainty? The incremental character of Swedish climate change policy-making. *Policy Studies*, 25(1), 22–39.

Kronig, J. (2010). *Climate Change: The Challenge for Social Democracy*. London: Policy Network.

Kurz, T., Augoustinos, M. and Crabb, S. (2010). Contesting the 'national interest' and maintaining 'our lifestyle': A discursive analysis of political rhetoric around climate change. *British Journal of Social Psychology*, 49(3), 601–25.

Leggett, J. (2001). *The Carbon War: Global Warming and the End of the Oil Era*. London: Routledge.

Levy, D. L. and Spicer, A. (2013). Contested imaginaries and the cultural political economy of climate change. *Organization*, 20(5), 659–78.

Lidskog, R. and Elander, I. (2012). Ecological modernization in practice? The case of sustainable development in Sweden. *Journal of Environmental Policy and Planning*, 14(4), 411–27.

Lundqvist, L. (2004). *Sweden and Ecological Governance: Straddling the Fence*. Manchester University Press.

Lyytimäki, J. (2011). Mainstreaming climate policy: the role of media coverage in Finland. *Mitigation and Adaptation Strategies for Global Change*, 16(6), 649–61.

Lyytimäki, J. and Tapio, P. (2009). Climate change as reported in the press of Finland: From screaming headlines to penetrating background noise. *International Journal of Environmental Studies*, 66(6), 723–35.

Martinsson, M. (2001). *Ozonskiktet och risksamhället: en studie av den svenska politiska diskussionen rörande ozonskiktet 1968–1992*. Linköping University.

McCarthy, J. and Prudham, S. (2004). Neoliberal nature and the nature of neoliberalism. *Geoforum* 35(3), 275–83.

Newell, P. and Paterson, M. (2010). *Climate Capitalism: Global warming and the Transformation of the Global Economy*. Cambridge University Press.

Olausson, U. (2009). Global warming – global responsibility? Media frames of collective action and scientific certainty. *Public Understanding of Science*, 18(4), 421–36.

Olausson, U. (2011). "We're the ones to blame": Citizens' representations of climate change and the role of the media. *Environmental Communication: A Journal of Nature and Culture*, 5(3), 281–99.

Oreskes, N. and Conway, E. (2010). *Merchants of Doubt: How a Handful of Scientists Obscured the Truth on Issues from Tobacco Smoke to Global Warming*. New York: Bloomsbury Press.

Reusswig, F. (2010). *The new climate change discourse: A challenge for environmental sociology* (pp. 39–57). Netherlands: Springer.

Sampei, Y. and Aoyagi-Usui, M. (2009). Mass-media coverage, its influence on public awareness of climate-change issues, and implications for Japan's national campaign to reduce greenhouse gas emissions. *Global Environmental Change*, 19(2), 203–12.

Sarasini, S. (2009). Constituting leadership via policy: Sweden as a pioneer of climate change mitigation. *Mitigation and Adaptation Strategies for Global Change*, 14(7), 635–53.

Schmidt, A., Ivanova, A. and Schäfer, M. S. (2013). Media attention for climate change around the world: A comparative analysis of newspaper coverage in 27 countries. *Global Environmental Change*, 23(5), 1233–48.

Smith, J. (2005). Dangerous news: Media decision making about climate change risk. *Risk Analysis*, 25(6), 1471–82.

Stern, N. (2006). *The Economics of Climate Change*. Cambridge University Press.

Swyngedouw, E. (2007). Impossible/Undesirable Sustainability and the Post-Political Condition. In Krueger, J. R. and Gibbs, D. (eds) *The Sustainable Development Paradox*, pp.13–40. New York: Guilford Press.

Swyngedouw, E. (2010). Apocalypse forever? Post-political populism and the spectre of climate change. *Theory, Culture and Society*, 27(2–3), 213–32.

Tranter, B. (2011). Political divisions over climate change and environmental issues in Australia. *Environmental Politics*, 20(1), 78–96.

Von Hall, G. "Glaciärerna smälter. Alpglaciärer kan vara borta 2050", *Svenska Dagbladet* 24/1 2007.

Weart, S. R. (2008). *The Discovery of Global Warming* (Vol. 13). Harvard University Press.

Whitmarsh, L. (2011). Scepticism and uncertainty about climate change: dimensions, determinants and change over time. *Global Environmental Change*, 21(2), 690–700.

Wijkman, A. and Edman, S. "Våga ompröva tillväxttänkandet", *Svenska Dagbladet* 11/1 2007.

2 The discourse of Industrial Fatalism
Keeping the promise of modernity intact

Introduction

In the words of Ulrich Beck, the dominant climate change and climate miti-gation discourse in Sweden during the time period covered by our study can be described as "Industrial Fatalism" (Beck, 1995). Confronted with the question of how the climate challenge might be handled, the answer is that it can only be done according to the logic of linear modernization. This means that the same purposeful rationality, claims of control and risk management that have guided the relationship to nature in industrial modernity must be adopted to handle the climate crisis. The actors that shape this discourse in Sweden during the study period are mainly representatives of the four political parties in the Liberal–Conservative government coalition, the orga-nizations of trade and industry, and parts of the labour movement and the daily newspapers, the latter almost totally dominated by a liberal political orientation. Globally this discourse dominates as well. In the US, Levy and Spicer (2013) have called a similar combination of actors and values a "cli-mate apocalypse imaginary". In the UK, Rogers-Hayden et al. (2011), Lovell et al. (2009) and Swyngedouw (2010) identify the same tendency. A similar trend of dominating actors and values is also found in France (Aykut et al., 2012).

Historically, technological determinism has a long tradition in Sweden; it has dominated energy and environmental politics for long periods of time. From the middle of the 1950s, Swedish energy and environmental policy was firmly aimed at industrial and large-scale energy transformations, first in the form of hydropower, then in form of nuclear power (Össbo and Lantto, 2011; Anshelm, 2000). When a number of environmental problems (includ-ing biocides, DDT and air pollution) that had the potential to undermine the modern industrial production system surfaced in the 1960s, the dominant political parties and environmental groups in Sweden all agreed that it was possible to resolve these problems with the help of modern industrial solu-tions, such as nuclear power (Anshelm, 2000). Until the early 1970s, there was an almost complete domination of faith in these energy sources, espe-cially among elite actors, first in large-scale hydropower then in nuclear power, as Sweden sought economic growth and a rationalization of production to manage energy and environmental policy requirements. Industrial modernization was simultaneously presented as a cause of environmental problems and a prerequisite to overcoming them (Anshelm, 2010).

In the 1970s and early 1980s there was criticism of modern industrial society's flaws and shortcomings in Sweden, as well as around the world. Modern industrial logic was no longer able to handle a number of global environmental problems, such as acidification and anthropogenic climate change (McNeill, 2003; Hornborg et al., 2007). In contrast to the dominant practices and ideas, a number of Swedish public intellectuals formulated a vision that included small-scale technologies, the decentralization of power, renewable energy sources and a critique of economic growth as a measure of prosperity. These visions, seriously discussed throughout the 1980s, were evident in public opinion, the election of Green Party members to the parliamentary assembly, mass-media debate, new regulations and small-scale renewable energy projects (Hultman, 2014). An intense clash with far-reaching implications occurred as environmental politics were reshaped by the influence of industry, which promoted an ecomodern discourse. By the beginning of the 1990s, the ecomodern discourse became dominant (Hultman and Yaras, 2012). At the beginning of the climate debate 2006 antagonism was once again enacted in which particular positions that had previously been resolved re-emerged (Hysing, 2014).

For the Industrial Fatalist discourse which came to dominate the debate, climate change was conceived as a scientific, technological, economic and legal management problem, albeit of unprecedented proportions. This way of performing ecomodern discourse was already understood by Hajer (1995) who wrote that ecological modernization could be executed and understood both as institutional learning and a technocratic project. Industrial Fatalism, as we will see, is an example of shaping climate change into a technocratic project, especially with regard to proposing, planning and subsidizing new nuclear plants.

Climate change as a matter of concern even for Industrial Fatalists

When Lord Nicholas Stern, an established and world-renowned economist, published a voluminous report, "The Economics of Climate Change", at the end of October 2006, it generated widespread attention from media around the world, including Sweden's (Stern, 2006). Fifty years of climate concern became part of the international debate as the voices of environmental organizations, individual researchers, research communities and the Intergovernmental Panel on Climate Change (IPCC) were finally heard. The editorial pages of major newspapers *Dagens Nyheter* and *Sydsvenska Dagbladet* stated, in reference to Stern's report, that it was time to break the link between greenhouse gas emissions and economic growth (Ekdal, 2006;

Ohlsson, 2006b). This close dependency was established in the beginning of the period of industrialization, when coal was used instead of slave man-power. Today fossil fuels such as coal, oil and gas account for around 85 per cent of the energy used and sold. The total amount continues to rise today with shale gas and tar sand as the newest forms of exploited fossil fuels. The basic argument in Stern's report was that strong action against climate change needed to be taken immediately. This was the only possible way to stabilize carbon dioxide emissions and ensure they were at an acceptable level by 2050. Unless drastic action was taken, floods and droughts would afflict many of the world's countries and nearly 200 million people would be turned into climate refugees by the middle of the twenty-first century. This apocalyptic scenario led the authors of the report to argue that one per cent of global gross domestic product needed to be spent as soon as possible on measures to stabilize carbon emissions. New technologies, economic and policy instruments, and green growth were suggested as solutions (Stern, 2006).

While Stern's report was discussed in newspaper editorials and on debate pages, Al Gore's film, *An Inconvenient Truth*, which premiered in Sweden on September 8 2006, left a significant impression on the global public (Höijer, 2010). Gore, who toured as an established and, in many respects, conservative statesman dressed in a suit and tie could hardly be suspected of representing subversive interests. However, through his consistent work with global issues, Gore had become one of the celebrities of the environmental move-ment, a status his new film reinforced (Boykoff and Goodman, 2009). He had a reputation as a family man, he referred to fellow politicians as family members and he used a caring language that meshed with important global issues (Gordon, 2004; Dowling, 2010). He was described in the Swedish as well as the UK mass media as someone who had presented an issue that could, and should, be addressed by industrial capitalist society (see, for example, Bennet et al., 2006; Boykoff, 2008).

In early February of 2007, the IPCC's fourth climate report further edu-cated the Swedish public and politicians about global warming. The UN panel issued its sharpest warning to date, based on the combined research of thousands of studies. This warning created a lot of attention all over the world, including in India (Billett, 2010), the UK (Lorenzoni and Hulme, 2009) and France (Aykut et al., 2012). Over 2,000 scientists from more than 100 countries concluded that climate change was probably accelerating faster than previously assumed. This change was expected to result in temperature increases of between 2 and 4.5 degrees Celsius over the next hundred years, and a rise in sea level of between 2 and 6 metres in the same period. Sea ice over the Arctic was in danger of disappearing in the summer, the Greenland ice sheet was melting faster than expected and the Gulf Stream was weaken-ing. Droughts and floods in many parts of the world were predicted to become even worse. These and similar scenarios had been described in earlier UN climate reports, but what was new in 2007 was that the IPCC stated, with 90 per cent certainty, that these changes were due to human emissions of carbon dioxide and other greenhouse gases. Virtually all major Swedish newspapers commented on the report in editorials and these were accompanied by extensive debate and news articles. The consensus pervading these articles, with few exceptions, was that it was no longer responsible or justifiable to continue the discussion on whether or not climate change was taking place or whether such change was anthropogenic. This consensus gave way to profound discussions and constructive suggestions about solutions. Across the board, people in Sweden asked for powerful and morally responsible political action. Thus, the IPCC report contributed greatly to establishing climate change as the most important environmental issue in contemporary public discourse.

To illustrate this, when Conservative Party leader Fredrik Reinfeldt, who at this time headed the opposition, was in the midst of the 2006 election campaign, he delivered a key speech during Almedalen week in Gotland that did not include the environment as a priority issue. Reinfeldt's speech in the summer of 2006 provides a valuable illustration of the dramatic change about to overtake the climate debate. During Almedalen, Reinfeldt declared that environmental issues could be handled with suitable measures and was really nothing much to worry about. On becoming prime minister (2006–2014), Reinfeldt was repeatedly criticized for this statement and forced to recant and change his position (Ehn, 2007; Kjörnsberg, 2007; Nordin, 2007). The Liberal–Conservative coalition won the election in Sweden that autumn. The fact that as late as the summer of 2006 Reinfeldt could treat the most severe environmental issues of our generation so lightly, and that this position did not raise storms of protest, testifies both to the political standpoint of political parties in Sweden, as well as to the power and speed with which climate change conquered the Swedish political conversation later in the autumn of 2006. Climate change was not an issue in the general election campaign and consequently only mentioned in a minor passage of the new Liberal–Conservative Swedish government's legislative program (Regeringsförklaringen, 2006). Only a few months later, climate change became the crucial issue for the future of all humans and non-humans around the world. Each parliamentary party said they would prioritize it. When Reinfeldt spoke during Almedalen two years later, in the summer of 2008, he declared that his opinion about environmental issues, especially climate change, had changed radically. He stressed now that the upcoming 2009 Copenhagen negotiations on global climate change meant that we all faced "one of mankind's most important decisions" and that it was Sweden's task to "show leadership and take the initiative". This radically changed position could be interpreted as personal enlightenment: he stressed in the speech that he had learned to "respect" that human behaviour in large regions of the world was unsustainable, that he understood the global warming threat and that it required political decisions to manage it (Reinfeldt, 2008). Another interpretation is that Reinfeldt, who was spearheading the Liberal–Conservative government action against the Swedish welfare system in a post-political way, was forced to accept that climate change made it necessary to take a political stand on environmental issues. The apocalyptic framing of climate change at this time made it necessary to talk about the good of society, responsibility for future generations and the need to prevent climate catastrophe. The post-political situation was, with the help of the apocalyptic representation of climate change, turned into an antagonistic dispute over what future society should look like, which could not be ignored.

Climate change once again on the political agenda

The year 2006 marked the point when the greenhouse effect was recognized all around the globe as the symptom of a major crisis in human history. Climate change was identified as the most important term of 2006 and a concern not just for scientists and environmentalists but also for the general public, politicians, businesses and the mass media. Three crucial events were responsible for changing the tenor of the debate: economist Nicholas Stern's report on climate change costs; the screening of politician Al Gore's film, *An Inconvenient Truth*, and the publication of the IPCC's fourth report on global climate change. Researchers and the environmental movement had provided the arguments for a long time (Anshelm, 2004); Stern and Gore repackaged the arguments into a format that had a greater impact; and everyone in Sweden now asked for powerful and morally responsible political action.

This newfound focus on climate change was reflected in global news reporting during the first months of 2007; the consequences of climate change for people and cultures was a recurrent theme. In Sweden coverage included reports of flooding, melting of glaciers, drought and record summer heat. The apocalyptic perspective was a common thread that ran through all of these stories. It was not a question of whether these phenomena could occur or what impact they might have, but that climate change disasters were already occurring. News articles in Sweden and around the world displayed a profound concern for the future during the first half of 2007 (Sampei and Aoyagi-Usui, 2009; Lyytimäki and Tapio, 2009; Kurz et al., 2010; Reusswig, 2010; Schmidt et al., 2013).

The great attention that climate change was given in the media in the autumn of 2006 forced the new Liberal–Conservative government to change its stance on environmental and climate issues. Less than six months after Prime Minister Fredrik Reinfeldt declared in Almedalen that the environment was not a political priority, Environment Minister Anders Carlgren and Minister for EU Affairs Cecilia Malmström stated that Sweden together with the EU should play a leading role in efforts to reduce carbon emissions (Carlgren and Malmström, 2006). The aforementioned events, environmental campaigns and the realization that in autumn 2009 Sweden, in its EU presidency role, would have a major responsibility in the renegotiation of the Kyoto Protocol in Copenhagen, led the new government to posit climate change as an important issue. The new government also positioned themselves as the principal international representatives of responsible and progressive climate politics. In early 2007, Reinfeldt called the EU's decision to reduce carbon dioxide by 20 per cent, increase renewable energy to 20 per cent of the total energy mix and improve energy efficiency by 20 per cent, "historic". He said he was proud to have helped formulate this decision, which demonstrated that the EU was prepared to show the way for other countries. He also announced that Sweden was ready to make further efforts, once the burden had been spread among individual states (Björklund, 2007). In May 2007, Reinfeldt visited the United States to discuss climate issues with George W. Bush. It was reported that "the government has decided to make climate issues a prime topic during the Swedish presidency of the EU in autumn 09" (Albons, 2007). The Conservative Party secretary now proclaimed the party as the one to actually "deal with environmental issues" (Schlingman, 2007). This was also confirmed by the prime minister after a year in office; when explicitly referring to the Stern report, he declared that Sweden must "raise ambitions in climate politics" and continue to be an international pioneer in the field. He promised that he would "do everything possible" to reach an agreement on a new international climate regime in the years leading up to the Copenhagen climate conference (Reinfeldt, 2007). Reinfeldt's volte-face subsequent to September 2006 illustrates the transformative influence of climate change on the political debate the year after the Liberal–Conservative government came into power. It was no longer possible to downplay environmental and climate issues. On the contrary, there was widespread public agreement that action to address climate change must be taken, although there were still considerable disagreement about which actions to take. In this chapter we follow the arguments articulated by proponents of the Industrial Fatalist discourse.

New large-scale technology as the solution

Within the discourse of Industrial Fatalism, the primary answer to the question, "How do we handle the severe unintended consequences that the industrial system generates?" is arrived at through intensified large-scale technological development and more efficient innovations. Prime Minister Fredrik Reinfeldt, Environment Minister Andreas Carlgren, and their political colleagues emphasized that mitigation of climate change should first be performed by creating and exporting "climate-friendly" technology along with international rules that promote this technology (Carlgren, 2006a; Carlgren and Malmström, 2006). Carlgren even identified great business opportunities for Swedish industry given global demand for CO_2 efficient technology (Carlgren, 2006a; Claesson, 2005; Baltscheffsky, 2007a). Carlgren and Reinfeldt explicitly stated that their government intended to make Sweden a frontrunner in international climate negotiations and at the same time a world leader in "rapid technology production and export efforts" (Reinfeldt and Carlgren, 2006; Rasmusen and Reinfeldt, 2007; Schlingman, 2007). Norwegian researchers Knut H. Alfsen and Gunnar Eskeland investigated the matter for the Swedish Treasury Department in 2007 and drew the same conclusion. They added that Sweden should invest in developing its nuclear energy because this energy source does not increase greenhouse gases significantly (Alfsen and Eskeland, 2007). The government's representatives emphasized that climate solutions must be addressed in a global context, but that Sweden could choose the energy source it considered most suitable. This can be interpreted as a sign that the threat of climate change made it possible for politicians, who had previously advocated the retention or expansion of nuclear power, to support their climate positions with non-negotiable environmental arguments. Nuclear power came to be revalued in light of the climate threat. The discourse of Industrial Fatalism postulated that the management of self-generated global environmental risks created new markets for economic growth, advantages for Swedish corporations in international competition and a need to revise international rules. However, this discourse did not call for any reconsideration of industrial society's relation to nature. Climate change was just another reason to pursue GDP growth. The reaction could be understood as a reflex, since it was evoked directly and without any doubt, and served the cause of system conservation. The core of the argument was that self-inflicted environmental risks caused by grand-scale technology had to be managed with the help of improvements in that same grand-scale technology. Every new unintended consequence was conceived of as a business opportunity or a temporary deviation that could be handled with the help of minor corrections of the industrial socio-technical system. This was the prevailing opinion in the Swedish Liberal–Conservative government and it was heavily supported by editorials in major newspapers (Ekdal 2006, 2007).

Swedish business organizations responded in the same way. They declared themselves capable and willing to play a leading role in the development of climate-friendly technology. Volvo's managing director argued that it had become necessary to construct new technological systems to mitigate climate change, but explicitly warned about changes in socio-economic structures that could lead to severe consequences for Swedish industry (Sievers, 2007). Climate change was understood as something to be handled within existing structures and production systems. Spokespersons for the national organization for trade and industry urged the environmental movement to focus on technologies that could solve the problem. Without political obstacles, technology could deliver the necessary solutions by itself, as if by an invisible hand (Fölster and Resvik, 2007). These actors were especially blunt when articulating their deterministic beliefs in the blessings bestowed by technology. The solution to technological problems was by definition new technology – not very different from the technology in systems that caused the problems – in other words, a conservative ecomodern utopianism. A fundamental, unrestricted and under-problematized confidence in goal rationality and progress characterized the reaction to the dangers that industrial civilization had brought upon itself.

New nuclear power plants

Nuclear power was the most important technology: an argument not unique to Sweden. It also dominated the discussion in the UK, for example (Lovell et al., 2009), and France (Laurent, 2009). As Rogers-Hayden et al. showed, the hegemonic discourse in the UK presupposed that a new generation of nuclear power plants had become necessary to decrease carbon emissions. Prime Minister Gordon Brown was pushing nuclear power as the solution (Rogers-Hayden et al., 2011). In Sweden, several editorials, which warned of alarmism and prophecies of doom, and instead confessed to Industrial Fatalism, used the horrors of climate change to legitimize new investment in nuclear power despite the Swedish parliament's decision to phase out this technology. Voices that had previously advocated expansion of nuclear power once again made use of the climate change argument to support technology from the late 1980s. Others claimed that they were reconsidering nuclear power in light of the disasters that climate change might create. As early as 1980, Liberal and Conservative political parties, Swedish industry and labour unions linked to large industries had all proclaimed nuclear power as a prerequisite for dealing with climate change (Anshelm, 2000). The same arguments were now reused to the point that 2006–2009 coincided with what has been called the "nuclear renaissance" by proponents, a global effort to promote nuclear power as the solution to climate change (Rogers-Hayden et al., 2011). Proponents proclaimed repeatedly that it would be impossible for Sweden to reach the goals it had for decreasing emissions without using nuclear power and that the country even had moral obligations to use its ability to produce electricity that was free of carbon dioxide and export it to Europe. The exploitation of Sweden's scientific and technological competence in nuclear energy was portrayed as a gesture of solidarity with the rest of the world. Nuclear power was depicted as the only possible alternative to fossil fuels and thereby necessary in order to avoid "the worst disaster of all, a collapse of the global climate" (Ohlsson, 2006a, 2006b). Once again fossil fuels or nuclear power were described as the only choices available, even though nuclear power produced less than 5 percent of the world's electricity (Anshelm, 2000). In a major Swedish daily newspaper, an editorial cited the internationally renowned environmental pioneer James Lovelock; he had declared that the choice lay between "nuclear power and a crash-landing for civilization". Coming from the father of the Gaia hypothesis, these words had a special power. Editorials in *Dagens Nyheter* favoured nuclear power, a totally different stand to the one that the paper had espoused in the 1980s. Lovelock's words and authority were used to emphasize the indisputable need for nuclear energy (*Dagens Nyheter*, 2006). The chief editor, who later on became a prominent Climate Sceptic, argued for large investments in new nuclear power stations and the export of electricity from these facilities at the same time as he accused Swedish media of pursuing doomsday journalism – without admitting that it was exactly this kind of journalism that provided him and those who shared his opinions with their best argument (Bergström, 2006). Several editorials declared that Sweden had no choice but to invest heavily in nuclear power. The renaissance of this previously discarded energy source was presented as unavoidable. At this point the paper echoed the arguments of representatives of Liberal and Conservative parties, labour unions and business organizations, as they had been doing since the beginning of the 1990s (Anshelm, 2000). At the beginning of 2008, the education minister from the Liberal party, a longstanding supporter of nuclear power, declared that climate goals made it necessary to immediately drop the prohibition on building new nuclear reactors. There was a demand for four new reactors, and ten existing reactors needed to be replaced. According to the minister, the devastating problems of global warming could only be mitigated through a major increase in the use of electricity in systems for heating and transportation, and this could only be obtained from nuclear energy. Once again, politicians and citizens were said to have no choice if global disaster were to be avoided, but now it was the government itself that advanced this argument (Björklund, 2008).

The pattern was the same in the larger labour unions that had been strongly pro-nuclear and supportive of industrial modernization. Editorial writers in the labour unions' collaborative (LO) magazine and the head of LO's economic policy unit took the position of the Liberal Party and warned that without new nuclear plants, high electricity prices and expensive carbon emission charges would reduce Swedish industrial competitiveness internationally and the standard of living nationally. That argument was seen as an answer to climate change and gave LO's energy position increased legitimacy (Bildström, 2008). As in years past, when the future of nuclear power was being debated, LO and business associations worked together. The chief economist at the Confederation of Swedish Enterprise was even more enthusiastic about nuclear power in light of the climate threat (Fölster, 2009). This came as no surprise since this had been the standpoint of Swedish business organizations and representatives for more than three decades (Anshelm, 2000). During the spring of 2009 there were signs that the government was using climate change as an argument for stopping the phase-out of nuclear power and permitting the construction of new reactors. In July the government passed a bill which included new investments in nuclear power. Thus, in less than three years nuclear power had been transformed from being a parliamentary impossibility, owing to the left–green government that was in power until 2006, into an integrated part of the new Liberal–Conservative government's energy and environmental politics from

2007 onwards; the discourse of Industrial Fatalism now dominated the parliament.

A request for voluntary climate-intelligent consumption

Another important element in the discourse of Industrial Fatalism was an effort to change consumer behaviour. In the autumn of 2006, major newspapers published articles that informed individuals what they should and should not buy. Consumer information and recommendations for the benefit of the climate were frequently published. News articles were directed at families and individual citizens. The primary message was that every activity impacts the climate and that consumers must be educated about the consequences of their purchases of everything from food to transportation. By changing their behaviour, consumers could exercise influence over the supply of products and services in favour of the climate through the market economy. The strong belief in the enlightened consumer who would make rational choices, thereby creating an invisible hand of change, was very evident in the Industrial Fatalist discourse. If every individual could decrease his or her personal emissions, Sweden's total contribution to global warming could be cut considerably. Hence personal responsibility for the global problem and the possibility of the individual to make a difference were underscored (Ennart, 2006).

This individualization was in line with the argument of government representatives – namely, that individual responsibility and personal behaviour was the key to the problem. The Industrial Fatalist discourse did not include the need for structural changes or reductions in total production and consumption. Policymakers assumed that the changing demand of enlightened consumers would change production. Political regulation, in the form of taxes, fees and prohibitions, for example, was therefore not warranted. Environment Minister, Andreas Carlgren, declared that the government would take the initiative to facilitate climate labelling of foods in order to "ensure that Swedish consumers have the opportunity to do good for the climate" (Carlgren, 2007). But there was no legislation involved; the Liberal–Conservative government let consumers and producers deal with the issue on their own. The only way to change consumption patterns was to create better-informed consumers: anything else was impossible. That was the credo of Industrial Fatalism (Västerteg, 2007). When the individual consumer was proclaimed a substantial power over the environment, s/he also became responsible for the environment. Many of the politicians who interpreted climate change as a matter of individual decision appealed to citizens' individual consciences and their responsibility to future generations. It is illustrative that the Christian Democrats' programme for municipal climate policy almost exclusively focused on how to make it easier for individuals, businesses and organizations to change their behaviours, and hardly at all on the system or structural changes (Hägglund, 2008).

The individualization of the global environmental problem, which was also happening in France and the UK at the same time, was in line with solutions advocated by the political parties in office (Aykut et al., 2012; Swyngedouw, 2010). They emphasized the morality of making correct consumption choices – without reducing consumption itself. Since personal behaviour and responsibility were described as key to the problem, there was no need for structural socio-economic changes or any decrease in total consumption or production volumes, according to actors articulating the Industrial Fatalist discourse. Green consumerism, it was assumed, would lead to changes in production, and accordingly, political regulations in the form of prohibitions were not needed. The role of politics, from the perspective of the Swedish government, according to the spin-doctor behind the Conservative Party, was to create "incentives for companies and individuals to act in a friendly manner in relation to the environment" (Schlingman 2007).

The concept of consumer power might, at first sight, appear irreconcilable with Industrial Fatalism since it denotes an individual's power to change society. During the 1970s and 1980s, parts of the environmental movement, especially those connected to liberal political parties, used the concept of turning consumption into political action and to create the contours of a totally different society where economic growth was not structurally determined (Anshelm, 2000). Beginning in the 1990s consumer power was changed to mean choices within a capitalistic system, not part of a transition out of it. The total amount of goods was no longer questioned (Anshelm, 2004). Today, the concept is used by Liberal–Conservative political parties in office, spokespersons for business organizations and even environmental organizations to stress that it is through consumption behaviour that individuals ought to exert influence on the production of goods and services in an environmentally sound manner.

There is no alternative to economic growth

According to the discourse of Industrial Fatalism, only minor corrections were needed within the dominating socio-economic order to deal with global climate change. The answer to the crisis created by industrial modernization was more industrial modernization, but with ecological conditions taken into consideration. There was no crisis of the system, only marginal dysfunctions that could be managed through innovations, new knowledge, improved information, enlightenment, and so on. Undiminished economic growth was a precondition for this system change. Hence, all appeals for decreased growth or changes to the economic relations of exchange were condemned by actors in the Industrial Fatalist discourse as immediate threats to the mitigation of climate change.

The discourse of Industrial Fatalism rested on the notion that there was no alternative to intensified technological innovation and economic growth;

even questioning this notion was depicted as harmful. This could be viewed as a sign that these actors were unsure about their own views and therefore had to dismiss even the idea that another world was possible. Criticism of economic growth was said to be counterproductive since growth was held to be a precondition for mitigating climate change. Environmental concern now became the strongest reason for continuing business as usual. Restrictions on economic development in Sweden would be totally ineffective since the large economies of the world would never accept any limitations, according to Industrial Fatalism. Editorials in Sweden's two major daily newspapers stated, with explicit reference to the Stern report, that it had become necessary to cut the connection between CO_2 emissions and economic growth, but the latter must not be hampered. Sweden had to take a step forward and assent to progress, not go backwards towards defeatism. This message was spelled out continuously in the editorials of the major Liberal daily newspapers, the conclusion being that Sweden did not have to give up its "freedom" and that climate mitigation did not "have to hurt", thanks to the country's hydropower and nuclear power assets. There was no need for "large cuts in our lifestyle", "impositions", "sacrifices", or "self-imposed burdens" (e.g. Ekdal, 2006; Ohlsson, 2006a). This lack of alternatives was emphasized as soon as somebody mentioned that slowing down economic growth might be worth considering. As an opinion piece in *Dagens Nyheter* characteristically concluded: "The road must lead forward[s] not backwards; it is new and more intelligent technology that is the solution to the problem, not horse carriages and earth floors" (Ekdal, 2006). Editorials in several Swedish newspapers warned of political solutions that would mean "gigantic sacrifices in the form of restricted growth and welfare, even a return to ancient poverty and plainness" (*Uppsala Nya Tidning*, 2007; Nordebo, 2008).

These warnings were uttered despite the very small proportion of Eco-socialists who wanted system change not climate change, which begs the question whether it was environmentalists, citizens, or themselves the polemical writers were trying to convince. The governing political parties repeatedly pushed the idea of "environmental challenges as an economic lever for growth, enterprise and jobs" (Reinfeldt et al., 2007), an idea that reaffirmed Sweden as a prime example of a country that was preserving both the environment and its high growth rate (Reinfeldt, 2007). If the right economic incentives were provided, policy innovations would follow both in Swedish small businesses and in global industry. It was assumed that new markets and demand for green technologies would occur in supportive political climate coupled with research and business policies. Climate change, in other words, was not only a threat but also an opportunity, and a way to strengthen Sweden's international economic competitiveness, according to the Liberal–Conservative government. It was assumed that countries that could export climate-friendly technologies early in the crisis would be rewarded in the long run. This market approach supported claims that Sweden had already proved itself to be one of the few countries to reduce its carbon footprint while maintaining economic growth

(Sievers, 2007; Ekdal 2006). The notion that Sweden had reduced its CO_2 emissions considerably since 1990 and at the same time had substantially increased its economic growth proved that these were compatible goals (Ohlsson, 2006a). At the end of 2007, Prime Minister Fredrik Reinfeldt and other ministers claimed that Sweden had "broken the connection between economic growth and increased emissions" (Reinfeldt et al., 2007). Sweden was thereby presented as a role model in the decoupling of growth and environmental protection. With the UN conference in Bali at hand, the environment minister, Andreas Carlgren, declared that Sweden had been able to break this link and that other countries should strive to do the same thing. At the conference he maintained that between 1990 and 2006 Sweden had decreased its CO_2 emissions by 8.7 per cent and had achieved economic growth of 44 per cent (Carlgren and Malmström, 2006; Olsson and Johansson, 2007). *Dagens Nyheter* stated that at the conference Sweden had shown, in a "statistical way", the road to successful climate politics, which combined CO_2 reduction with economic growth – and that this combination could be replicated (*Dagens Nyheter*, 2007). Even the general secretary of the Swedish Society for Nature Conservation argued, in contrast with his other values, that the country had demonstrated it was "possible to mitigate climate change without giving up established material well-being" (Axelsson, 2007a, 2007b).

Sweden as an environmental role model

As already noted, a very important part of the discourse of Industrial Fatalism was the conviction that Sweden had a special role to play in international mitigation of climate change (Lidskog and Elander, 2012). Sweden was described as an ecomodern utopia in which economic growth could go hand in hand with tough environmental restrictions (Hultman and Nordlund, 2013). This characterization grew out of national confidence regarding technological development and a high degree of moral and political self-righteousness (Olausson, 2010).

The portrayal of Sweden as a role model of industrial modernity, showing the way out of the darkness of the climate crisis and putting out the fire in the basement, was an obligatory feature whenever the government described its goals and measures to counteract global warming. By the end of 2006 it was a cornerstone of the Swedish government's political proclamations on climate change. As early as November 2006, Environment Minister Andreas Carlgren declared: "With broad cooperation we will be able to turn Sweden into a role model for a modern society built on renewables in harmony with the climate conditions of the earth" (Carlgren, 2006).

The positioning of Sweden as a frontrunner in the race to tackle climate change was used by government representatives in two distinct contexts. First, it denoted that the country was part of an international competition, where it strived to wear "the leader's shirt" and to "take the lead" (Carlgren and Malmström, 2006). This metaphor implied that it was an advantage for Sweden to rapidly and forcefully take measures against climate change. Early changes in the national energy system, the development of carbon-free technology and transformations in production processes were depicted as steps that could position the country favourably in the global economic market, since all countries would, sooner or later, have to go through the same process. Moreover, it would engender international respect and recognition for Sweden. Sweden would stand out as a progressive, courageous and successful country that did not hesitate to take on serious challenges. The second meaning of the metaphor portrayed an ambitious Sweden eager to exercise leadership through the power of being a good example, in the role of a guide to the future. The prime minister and his allies declared several times that Sweden should be a "prototype", "leading country", "good example", or had the obligation to "show leadership and take the lead" (Reinfeldt et al 2007; Reinfeldt 2007, 2008; Olofsson et al., 2009). The government declared that Sweden's ability to combine low emissions with economic growth ought to convince other countries that emission decreases do not jeopardize national economies, but are actually a prerequisite for continued industrial and economic development. In this fashion, between 2006 and 2009 the government, with heavy support from the daily press, created a narrative about Sweden as a frontrunner in international climate politics. Sweden was depicted both as a country that eagerly pushed the EU to work in favour of more ambitious international agreements and at the same time voluntarily made considerable national efforts with the explicit purpose of showing the world that they were feasible. The national climate goals were said to be more ambitious than those prescribed in international agreements; several minor measures were presented as exemplary. In this spirit, goals were announced for the country's transport system to be fossil-fuel independent by 2030, and for half of the energy supply to be shifted to renewables by 2050 (Reinfeldt and Carlgren, 2006; Reinfeldt, 2007). The statements were characterized by a self-confidence and conviction that Swedish undertakings considerably exceeded what other countries were attempting. The trade minister made this statement in early 2009: "The government's agreement is the most ambitious in the world" (Mellgren, 2009).

This claim was not questioned in daily newspaper opinion pieces. Government climate declarations were supported almost without objection (*Östgöta Correspondenten*, 2008; *Vestmanlands Läns Tidning* 2007a; *Expressen*, 2008). However, when the European Commission presented its energy and climate package in January 2009, a less clear-cut picture appeared. For Sweden, the EC's proposal meant cutting CO_2 emissions by 17 per cent by 2020 and increasing renewables to 49 per cent. As regards the principle behind the proposal – "improvement in relation to bearing capacity" – Sweden was assigned a comparatively large contribution. Major labour and business organizations opposed this. They argued that countries such as Sweden, that had already made considerable efforts, were being punished by new harsh demands. Yet the levels proposed by the Commission were well in line with the Swedish government's own frontrunner goals (Lönnaeus, 2008; Björklund, 2008). This did not stop the Swedish trade minister from objecting. She declared that it was unreasonable to ask countries that had led climate efforts to carry the heaviest load (Hördin, 2008). Prime Minister Reinfeldt put forward a similar argument, but declared that Sweden had no intention to do "so much that other countries that had done less could escape from doing their share" (Bondesson, 2008). The environment minister also questioned the EU's assertion that only 3 per cent of member states' emission cuts could be accomplished through flexible trading measures outside Europe (*Expressen*, 2008; *Aftonbladet*, 2008). Accordingly, when the Commission at last announced its proposal, Sweden's reaction was hardly enthusiastic, although government ministers declared that Sweden was willing to assume its responsibility, provided that other countries did the same. This time, what was heard was not the voice of political visionaries but of negotiators.

The successful portrayal of the "brave country up north" combined with the European Commission directive led to warnings that overambitious undertakings by the Swedish government would be severely harmful to domestic industry. As the frontrunner picture was cemented, editorials and business organizations raised the question whether further measures in Sweden would make any meaningful contribution to the mitigation of climate change, since the country was so much ahead of the rest of the world. If the government had plans to invest more in combating climate change, the investment ought to lower CO_2 emissions in countries that lagged behind. Characterizations such as that, well in line with the discourse of Industrial Fatalism, called for a government response.

The climate politics are too ambitious

In December 2006, when Fredrik Reinfeldt and Andreas Carlgren declared that by 2020 the government would reduce greenhouse gas emissions by 30 per cent from 1990 levels, the Confederation of Swedish Enterprise promptly objected and expressed concern that Sweden's international competitiveness would be "hampered" (*Expressen*, 2006). Other corporate interests followed suit and declared that Sweden should promote competition-neutral international regulations, and not unilaterally formulate ambitious objectives which could damage Swedish industry. Sweden's share of global greenhouse gas emissions was said to be negligible, thus unilateral cuts in Sweden would be inconsequential. It was necessary to "avoid getting into a bidding war on the national climate goals" (Grahnquist, 2007; Österlund, 2007). These voices did not challenge the fundamental need for action on climate change, but only the idea that Sweden should be an international model and frontrunner. The leader of the Confederation of Swedish Enterprise even argued that cutting emissions in Sweden would increase global emissions. If the Swedish energy-intensive industries were forced to move overseas, production would re-emerge in other countries where the rules for greenhouse gas emissions were more liberal. If Sweden used less oil it would instead be used in other countries without carbon taxes. Belief in the idea of positioning Sweden as a global guide was low among the representatives of the business community (Fölster, 2008). One of the industry's most influential leaders, who later became a Climate Sceptic – Sverker Martin Löf, chairman of SCA (a Swedish company manufacturing hygiene and forest products) and vice president of the Confederation of Swedish Enterprise – said that Swedish measures would be futile as long as the major emitting countries did not take the same measures. This meant that Swedish climate politics could cause "significant harm to Swedish large-scale industry" (Karlsson, 2008).

These proposals from Swedish Enterprise leaders and other representatives of Swedish industry were met with great sympathy in the editorial pages of Swedish daily newspapers, as well as the business press and among economics writers. The Industrial Fatalist discourse had many interpreters; now some of them turned against the Liberal–Conservative government's climate policies. They asked the rhetorical question: why would the Swedes take on the role of playing the "blockheads of Europe?" (*Sydsvenska Dagbladet*, 2008). Sweden should refrain from imposing significantly greater restrictions than other countries. Allowing national prestige to dominate at the expense of Swedish companies and the welfare of its citizens, when Sweden contributed only 0.2 per cent to global greenhouse gases, was nothing but a harmful policy that increased opportunities for more environmentally damaging activities abroad.

In a similar argument, editorial writers at *Dagens Nyheter* asserted that these policies were a gamble when Sweden could not control international development and the global agreements necessary to reduce greenhouse gases. The newspaper noted that climate politics was associated with significant costs and that it should not be guided by any "bad conscience". An international "game" could result in a situation where one country's reduction allowed for greater emissions from other countries, a risky game in which less scrupulous countries could "exploit the situation and attract Swedish industries" (Schück, 2008a, 2008b). The spectre of Swedish climate politics that rested on credulity, idealism and morality in a world characterized by self-interest, cynicism and calculation was raised. This was problematic. Liberal and neo-liberal commentators claimed that Swedish politicians needed to acquire a more realistic view of their importance and a more accurate picture of how international politics work, and needed to downplay symbolic politics. This was the view of the most influential Swedish newspaper (Wolodarski, 2008; Roos, 2008), especially in 2008, and its views were aimed at both the government and its opposition. This kind of message was also conveyed periodically in editorial pages of newspapers outside the metropolitan area after 2008 (Nordström, 2008; *Borås Tidning*, 2008, 2009;

Vestmanlands Läns Tidning, 2008a; *Sydsvenska Dagbladet*, 2009). Even though Swedish political leaders emphasized Sweden as a climate-protection role model, Prime Minister Fredrik Reinfeldt at the same time summed up the situation in these words:

> Climate change is serious. Humanity's emissions affect the Earth with huge negative consequences. We can do something about it, but it requires political leadership. Sweden accounts for only 0.2 percent of the world's greenhouse gases. We can do a lot but our national efforts lead to no greater global impact if they are not followed by efforts to unite the world to joint action.
>
> (Reinfeldt, 2009)

No matter how various actors assessed the opportunity to become an international role model, domestic climate policies were evaluated differently. For those who doubted that Sweden really could play such a role, national goals appeared meaningless. Several economic researchers and the Liberal–Conservative newspapers' editorial writers argued that further emission reductions in Sweden would be expensive and completely useless.

The standpoint of becoming an international leader on climate control increasingly met with resistance from industry representatives. Even though the majority of voices agreed that Sweden was on the frontline and that this was something to be proud of, several actors expressed worry that eagerness to be "best in class" jeopardized future economic growth. This opinion echoed that of Climate Sceptics, as we will analyse later. If industry could develop and export environmentally sound technology, this effort should not be obstructed by overly ambitious climate goals. Business organizations declared that the government ought to work in favour of international rules that were market-neutral rather than one-sided formulas that might harm Swedish industry. Sweden's share of global CO_2 emissions was insignificant and, accordingly, one-sided cuts within its borders were more or less meaningless. Most industry supporters did not question the need to tackle global warming. However, they did warn that Sweden should not be in the vanguard of climate protection at the expense of economic development, employment and even its own environment (Grahnqvist, 2007; Österlund, 2007; Fölster, 2009). Some of them even declared that decreases in emissions within Sweden increased global emissions. If Swedish industry was forced to leave the country in order to stay profitable, production would be relocated to countries where environmental regulations were far more liberal (Fölster, 2009). In the summer of 2008, the major labour organization joined forces with business organizations and stated that climate politics should not be carried out as "a domestic political beauty contest", and that all political efforts should be directed towards international negotiations (Lundius et al. 2008a, 2008b).

Proposals like these were endorsed by editorials in daily newspapers and the business press. The discourse of Industrial Fatalism accommodated these voices. Some actors questioned the intelligence of allowing national prestige to ruin Swedish industry and the welfare of its citizens (Linder, 2006; *Svenska Dagbladet* 2007a, 2007b). Continued "self-mortification" and "welfare losses" were uncalled for. Additional restrictions were inefficient. Nothing would be gained from going beyond Sweden's existing efforts and other flexible mechanisms were available which did not harm Swedish industry (Linder, 2006, 2007).

Flexible mechanisms: turning emission cuts into climate aid and export possibilities

In 2007, economists working on behalf of the financial department published several reports concerning climate politics. The conclusions of these reports reached the public through debate articles written by economists and distributed by major daily newspapers. The message was that resources that the government planned to use to reduce CO_2 emissions in Sweden that exceeded the prescribed EU levels would generate considerably more emission cuts if they were used to develop smart technology that could be exported (Alfsen and Eskeland, 2007; Brännlund, 2007; Carlén, 2007; Klefbom, 2009). Norwegian researchers Knut H. Alfsen and Gunnar Eskeland argued that Sweden should invest in technological development, preferably nuclear, rather than further reduce its already low national emissions of greenhouse gases during the next fifteen years (Alfsen and Eskeland, 2007). Resources that Sweden planned to use to reduce emissions beyond the Kyoto Protocol and the EU burden-sharing agreement would provide significantly greater reductions in global emissions if used to develop technologies that could be exported, according to the two researchers. Swedish economist Runar Brännlund, who was working in the Expert Group for Environmental Studies, came to the same conclusion after a review of research in the field. He claimed that the idea that high GHG reductions and high carbon-charges would enhance Swedish productivity was totally wrong. Such regulations did not promote the development of new environmentally friendly technologies to the extent assumed; their main effect was to negatively affect productivity in energy-intensive sectors. Brännlund concluded that better trade-offs between costs and benefits should be made (Brännlund; 2007). At the time, this was a common argument in countries with the highest emissions. Flexible emissions opened a global market for powerful nations and industrial sectors that feared losing their competitive advantage to emerging competitors such as India and China. These mechanisms fitted smoothly with the rise of climate change as an issue for corporate social responsibility and pressure on firms to overhaul their emissions (Bailey et al., 2011). In late 2007 the economist Björn Carlén, also from the Expert Group for Environmental Studies, found it futile to set more stringent emission targets at home. Instead, Sweden should focus on increased participation in international emissions trading, which would free up resources for technology development and emission reduction abroad: "Swedish climate politics with the ambition to achieve global emissions reductions in the near future requires action outside of Sweden" (Carlén, 2009). These economists all argued that there were important reasons to reconsider the focus on a national emission policy based solely on cuts. Ambitious goals to lower national emissions were labelled as "symbolic politics". Sweden ought to refrain from this and instead concentrate on the international trade of Swedish-made emissions technology. Sweden had to use the flexible mechanisms within the Kyoto Protocol that allowed it to buy emission cuts made by other countries and count them as part of Sweden's national share. Under the Protocol, it mattered little where the cuts were made (Carlén, 2007; Klefbom, 2009).

Several Swedish economists and financial writers agreed with the politics that had already been practiced from 1993 onwards by the Liberal and Conservative parties (Knaggård, 2013). Flexible markets encapsulate the ecomodern "have-your-cake-and-eat-it-too" logic that reconciles economic growth with environmental protection (Bailey et al., 2011). Bengt Kriström, an economics professor and the Director of the Government Commission on Sustainable Development, described the situation as follows: "If one invested SEK it would give ten times as much emission reduction if invested abroad. There are from an efficiency perspective, neither environmental [n]or common sense reasons, to invest that SEK in Sweden" (Kriström, 2008; e.g. Eklund, 2009). The economists argued that the most effective Swedish climate action should take place outside the country. Local efforts, such as subsidies for renewable energy and rail investments, would be the least effective. A climate politics aimed at reducing national emissions was therefore, according to the National Institute of Economics, completely unproductive (Schück, 2008b). Even the Swedish Energy Agency and the Swedish Environmental Protection Agency formulated a climate strategy that advocated that a large proportion – 50 per cent – of the Swedish emission reductions be achieved through investments in other countries. This would help Sweden reduce greenhouse gas emissions by 30 per cent by 2025, without significant economic impact (Baltscheffsky, 2008).

The policies advocated by the Treasury department's Expert Group on Environmental Studies were very much in line with the Industrial Fatalist discourse. We argue, in fact, that the image of Sweden as frontrunner and the concrete politics of the Liberal–Conservative Industrial Fatalist discourse had a special correlation. The Expert Group for Environmental Studies' reports and opinion pieces concluded that Swedish energy-intensive industries should not suffer emission standards to the detriment of competitiveness and, further, that domestic emissions targets were meaningless and national climate action was a waste of resources. Instead, it was proposed that government investments in new technology, especially nuclear power, should be carried out and Swedish emissions targets should be met by investing abroad, where the cost benefits were much greater. With such a perspective, no conversion of the energy, transport and industrial production was needed. Sweden was already a leader, so not until the rest of the world reached the country's emissions of greenhouse gases would it be rational to reduce emissions domestically. This was a politics of "business as usual". It is worth noting that none of the Expert Group, or their like-minded actors, discussed whether a conversion of the national energy and transportation systems, for example, would in the long run prove to be necessary, or when it might be advantageous to initiate this change. Instead the only emphasis was on being cost-effective in the short term. Their perspective was based strictly on neo-liberal market economy principles and solutions which required as few changes as possible to contemporary Swedish industrial structures. It is important to emphasize that the flexible mechanism is a market construct in which corporations, countries and local communities operate inside a value-exchange system in which nature-cultures become interdependent on a new regime. This may seem like "business as usual", but in reality this is a game changer that re-creates nature-culture relationships all over the globe to fit the emission levels of a few industrialized nations (Arora-Jonsson, 2011).

The group of hired economic experts actually constituted an avantgarde of Industrial Fatalism, trying to convince the government to take several steps further in the appointed direction. With explicit references to the economists, several leading writers also concluded that climate politics that focused on domestic policy should be revised and investments made where the pay-off was highest. The use of flexible mechanisms was a way of safeguarding the export industry, economic growth and the common welfare. This was certainly an attractive solution since everybody would be winners, including "developing" countries and the climate. Moreover, climate politics that did not rest on moral arguments and a bad conscience was welcomed within the Industrial Fatalist discourse (Linder, 2007; Wolodarski, 2008; Ström, 2009). By taking advantage of the Kyoto Protocol's flexible mechanisms, a recurring message was that Sweden, to a much greater extent than before, could achieve its ambitious emission reduction targets without harming Swedish industry's international competitiveness, domestic economic growth or civic welfare. This was obviously a very appealing solution, because everyone would win, including "developing" countries and the climate. This version of climate politics did not include any historical environmental injustices, moral questions about the relationship between humans and nature, or any type of appeal to the conscience. It was articulated in metaphors like this:

> Climate change needs fewer subtle moralists and a few more hard-boiled economists. Cleaning our own house might seem good. But when the

marble in front of our entrance is polished and the dirt lies in drifts on a neighbour's porch, it is perhaps better to take the broom over there.

(Ström, 2009)

The implication was that Sweden should help others who had not behaved so well. This was also of course another kind of morality, not so much self-reflexive as a form of moral colonialism. That it was also shaped by the proposed use of flexible mechanisms as a help to others – and not as a way to escape domestic emissions cuts or a more cost-effective way to achieve national climate goals – possibly made it more attractive for those who did not belong to the economist corps. This way of thinking about and utilizing flexible mechanisms was in opposition to the idea of Sweden as a technological frontrunner, and it introduced a widening contradiction inside the Industrial Fatalist discourse. This contradiction was handled by modifying the image of the frontrunner to include being best at using flexible mechanisms and achieving emission reductions somewhere other than home.

Early in 2008, several representatives of the Liberal–Conservative political parties in office appeared to have taken lessons from the economists engaged by the financial department. Accordingly, they argued that Sweden should invest in the development of low-carbon technology adapted for "developing" countries. These investments abroad were repeatedly used to legitimize "more realistic goals at home" (Björklund, 2008; Hamilton, 2008). When the EU proposed that by 2020 Sweden should have decreased its emissions of greenhouse gases to 17 per cent less than 2005 levels, the national political reactions that followed were similarThe EU allowed a sixth of the national share to be attained through investments abroad, but the Swedish government declared that the share ought to be considerably larger, since such investments resulted in ten times the emission reduction (*Göteborgs-Posten*, 2008). When the government passed a climate bill a year later, it stated that a third of CO_2 reductions in Sweden should be obtained by investments in other EU-countries or in "developing" countries (Mellgren, 2009). The share of Swedish emission reductions that was planned through flexible mechanisms had steadily grown since 2007. According to the judgement of editorials in daily newspapers, this was an expression of wise and well-considered politics; meanwhile, the environmental movement's call for more radical measures was dismissed as irresponsible (Carlsson, 2009). As Bailey et al. have shown, flexible mechanisms harmonized well with the neo-liberalism of several governments; the political demands for national economic growth; the economic interests of industrial organizations; and the will to preserve material standards of living (Bailey et al., 2011). Despite a declared ambition to present a progressive position the Swedish government argued for extended use of flexible mechanisms because it was beneficial to large and influential groups of actors in Sweden; apparently the government did not realize that this stance was inherently contradictory. The Reinfeldt government continued to claim moral superiority over Copenhagen. The narrative of Sweden as a morally righteous, successful, progressive and rational nation implied obligations for other countries. The idea of Sweden as a frontrunner made it impossible to take another position when the issues of climate mitigation were raised, even when the discourse of Industrial Fatalism denoted that Sweden had done more than enough already. Therefore, the only legitimate strategy for harmonizing this narrative with national economic growth was, first, to show that the problem was located in other places (abroad) and second to demonstrate that Sweden had done everything in its power to come to terms with the problem.

Towards Copenhagen; other countries and other people are the problem

The climate debate in Sweden between 2006 and 2009 demonstrates how the role of one nation became problematic in the global climate crisis. What role can or should a single nation play? In Sweden the frontrunner narrative was a key element: the portrait of great technological competence, beneficial economic conditions and high moral ground gave the country a special position in international negotiations, according to the Industrial Fatalist discourse. By autumn of 2006, Fredrik Reinfeldt and Andreas Carlgren declared that Sweden, scheduled to assume the presidency of the EU in 2009, had set its sights on bringing about a new international climate agreement to replace the Kyoto Protocol at the UN conference in Copenhagen (Reinfeldt and Carlgren, 2006). Against this backdrop, the government intended to push the EU to adopt ambitious binding emission targets and establish the EU as "the platform to change the direction of the really big emitters, such as the US and China" (Carlgren and Malmström, 2006). Because the EU only accounted for 14 per cent of global greenhouse gas emissions, it set a high standard. However, according to Reinfeldt, it was necessary that countries such as China and India follow suit and that a binding agreement be signed in Copenhagen in 2009. In late 2007, before the upcoming UN conference in Bali, Reinfeldt declared the following:

> My hope is that Bali will be the start of negotiations on a new international climate agreement to replace the current Kyoto Protocol. Such an agreement must take place if we are to include those countries that are major emitters and it must contain binding commitments on emission reductions. And it is my goal that we, in the fall of 2009, when Sweden have the presidency of the EU, will do everything possible to reach agreement on a new international climate regime.
>
> (Reinfeldt, 2007)

The Swedish environment minister described the Copenhagen climate summit as a last chance to save the process that was initiated in Kyoto. According to actors within the Industrial Fatalist discourse there was no doubt that the fundamental problem was related to getting the US, China and India to accept binding emissions targets. The notion that the EU was the only power that could accomplish this was deeply rooted among Swedish politicians and in the Swedish daily press (Avellan, 2007). Overall, journalists portrayed Sweden as a frontrunner with other countries lagging behind and in need of enlightenment (e.g. Olausson, 2010). The Swedish chief negotiator at the meeting in Bali determined that it was time for the US, China and other major emitters to reveal how far they were willing to go to mitigate climate change. As a result, the talks in Bali were interpreted as a stepping stone to a big agreement in Copenhagen in 2009 (Munck, 2007). Initially, Swedish reporting from Bali was pessimistic when the EU's proposal to set binding emission targets was rejected. Environment Minister Carlgren predicted a disappointing result, which would not be in line with what climate problems demanded. Similar reviews were published in several news and editorial pages. The US was accused of hindering and preventing binding agreements and threatening the ability to deal with climate change (*Dagens Nyheter*, 2007; *Expressen*, 2007; *Aftonbladet*, 2007). In the end the United States committed to binding emission limits to be specified and agreed to equal requirements for rich and poor countries, to be negotiated in Copenhagen in 2009. Carlgren concluded that the meeting had become a "huge success" (Baltscheffsky, 2007b). The researcher Bo Kjellén noted that the United States were now going to participate fully in the ongoing negotiations, finally making this a global issue (Kjellén, 2007). Sweden's role as lead negotiator in Copenhagen 2009 was now thought to be inevitable.

EU as the saviour of industrial civilization

In Sweden's daily newspapers, especially in the editorials, the EU was described as the only actor capable of taking the lead when it came to implementing ambitious international rules for climate mitigation within the frames of the existing system of industrial capitalism (e.g. Olausson, 2010). Only the EU could manage the tasks of writing emission goals and regulations, introducing a system for emission rights and creating incentives for industries and households to change their behaviour. In January of 2008, when the European Commission decided to implement an energy and climate package – which included a 20 per cent reduction in emissions of greenhouse gases, an increase of 20 per cent in renewable power and an increase in energy efficiency of 20 per cent – it was interpreted as a significant global initiative. The 20-20-20 decision was depicted as a "milestone" in climate politics. Every Swedish newspaper described the decision as necessary for further international climate negotiations. It also underscored the strength of the Commission in standing up to lobbying campaigns from energy-intensive industries and the protests of member states. The EU was the actor that could show the way in negotiating global greenhouse gas levels (Bondesson, 2008).

This was confirmed when, after just one year in office, the prime minister stated that Sweden must "raise its climate political ambitions" and continue to be an international pioneer. He promised to do "everything in his power" to make an agreement on a new climate regime possible (Reinfeldt, 2007). When Sweden assumed the EU chairmanship in July 2009, Reinfeldt and Carlgren made what can be interpreted as programme declarations. Reinfeldt declared that it was a priority to marshal member countries in an effort to reach a binding climate agreement that all countries of the world could accept (Reinfeldt 2009; Carlsson 2009). Carlgren expressed himself in more visionary terms when he stated:

> The most important task for the EU in the short run is to reach a strong climate agreement in Copenhagen. There is no alternative – there is no plan B. The political leaders of the world under the Swedish chairmanship of the EU have to give a full political answer to what science has shown to be necessary.
>
> (Carlgren, 2009)

Describing climate change as an apocalypse from which we could still be saved was at the core of the Industrial Fatalist discourse worldwide (Methmann and Rothe, 2012; Levy and Spicer, 2013). The apocalypse was represented as the end of accelerating development. What was at stake was the very end of time itself, which had to be deferred through political intervention. Using apocalyptic as a metaphor changed the logic of climate risk: it presented the climate change challenge as a comic (in the meaning of the greek drama) apocalypse with only one possible solution: the technocratic arrangement of ecological modernization management (Foust and O'Shannon Murphy, 2009). The dominant Industrial Fatalist discourse assumed that climate change was in principle a resolvable problem, the solution to which would also positively affect many other issues without risking the future of modern industrial society. This opened up opportunities for political antagonism, even though the solution that Industrial Fatalism actors proposed was of an ecomodern conservative nature. Thus, technology became indispensable, especially nuclear technology, carbon sequestration, biofuels or other so-called "clean" technologies. Whatever it took to avoid climate change, technology would do the job.

The USA as the climate gangster

Industrial Fatalists described the US as the EU's opposite. Daily Swedish newspapers characterized the US as a brake during international climate negotiations. It was said that President George W. Bush refused to sign all binding agreements with regard to the lowering of CO_2 emissions and other regulations that might conflict with "the American way of life" (Karlsson, 2007). However, the Swedish government saw a possible way to exercise influence over climate politics through the EU. In the autumn of 2006, the prime minister and the environment minister declared that Sweden, as the chair of the EU, intended to work for a continuation of the Kyoto Protocol (Reinfeldt and Carlgren, 2006). Accordingly, the government strived to push the EU to take on ambitious and binding emission goals. Furthermore, the EU was understood to be a "platform for negotiations about changes of the ways of the major emitters, for example, the US and China" (Carlgren and Malmström, 2006).

In May 2007, Prime Minister Reinfeldt visited the US in order to discuss climate politics with George W. Bush, and *Dagens Nyheter* stated that "the government had decided to make climate issues a prioritized political subject during the Swedish EU chairmanship in the autumn of 2009" (Albons, 2007a, 2007b; Schlingman 2007). The EU and the US were depicted as being in sharp contrast. The progressive role, the forceful action and the international leadership of the EU contrasted with the passive and irresponsible position held by the US. In this way it was possible to portray the EU as the only actor in the rich industrialized world that was really prepared to take action to save civilization from self-inflicted annihilation. Up until the meeting in Copenhagen the US was held to be the worst culprit in terms of climate change. The Swedish daily press depicted the US as an international environmental villain, a power of darkness, whereas the EU was depicted as the only bringer of hope for a new international climate regime. In this narrative, there was one hero and one bad guy.

Discussion

The discourse of Industrial Fatalism was permeated by the belief that it was possible to mitigate climate change through international negotiations and agreements on CO_2 emission caps. This belief was founded on the idea that this global threat would force all countries of the world to cooperate. It assumed that, in spite of their different cultural and economic preconditions, all countries should have a mutual interest in avoiding a global climate collapse and that scientific consensus would facilitate rational political management of the problem. Trust in the rationality of the international processes of negotiations and planning implied that only marginal changes in fundamental economic and technological structures of industrial capitalism were necessary. Law, economy, natural sciences and technology would solve the crisis. Especially important, was that long-standing arguments for nuclear power were now reutilized to coincide with the "nuclear renaissance", as it was universally nicknamed by its proponents (Rogers-Hayden et al., 2011). Nuclear power was depicted as the only possible alternative to fossil fuels.

Within the Industrial Fatalist discourse climate change would create some minor costs (and also profits), but would not require significant changes to lifestyles, consumption volumes, economic growth, use of natural resources, systems of energy and transport, processes of production, flows of material or the metabolism of industrial society in any respect. This is why it was expected that all parties would act with the same rationality in international negotiations. In this discourse it was assumed that international agreements were an efficient way to regulate CO_2 emissions. A global consensus based on the solid ground of natural science was supposedly within reach.

However, the threat of climate change was in some respects depicted as a new crisis phenomenon because it is global, irreversible, and seemingly perpetual, and thus requires complicated and unparalleled international coordination. For this reason it is portrayed in apocalyptical terms even within the discourse of Industrial Fatalism. Statements such as "the next international negotiation is the last chance to save the world" recur. In spite of this, the solutions recommended are the same as for the other environmental problems: new and more efficient technology, export of smart technology, intensified research, economic growth, use of market mechanisms, better-informed consumption behaviour and coordinated international regulations. In other words, at the time, the dominating discourse on climate change in Sweden was characterized by what Erik Swyngedouw has called a "post-political condition" (Swyngedouw, 2010). All requests to rethink the fundamental relationship between nature and industrial society were immediately discarded as totally impossible and leading to backwards development. Rogers-Hayden et al. describe the UK's characteristics of Industrial Fatalist discourse in this way:

> In sum, the hegemonic climate change discourse centres around considering it as an environmental issue linked to technological solutions that 'save the planet'. DEFRA's limited remit and other variations on perspectives of climate change partly underpinned this discourse. This construction reinforces the focus on decarbonising energy as a desirable goal. Newly built nuclear power stations therefore appear to be a 'natural' solution.
>
> (Rogers-Hayden et al., 2011)

If environmental problems in general, and climate change in particular, constitute a self-inflicted institutional crisis that extorts a change of industrial modernity, this was not something the discourse of Industrial Fatalism observed greatly. Rather, the crisis is conceived as a scientific, technological, economic and legal management problem, among others, albeit with unprecedented proportions. Hajer (1995) noted that the dominating discourse of ecological modernization could be performed and interpreted both as institutional learning and a technocratic project. Industrial Fatalism is an example of the technocratic project, especially when new nuclear plants are proposed, planned and subsidized. Any sign of doubt that established methods for problem-solving should prove to be inadequate or counterproductive cannot be detected. When doubts of these kinds are expressed in counter-discourses they are immediately rejected. To conclude, the Swedish government on the one hand claimed to be a good example regarding national measures for decreasing CO_2 emissions, and on the other hand declared its commitment to an Industrial Fatalism that left little or no room for political reform or changes of the national systems of production and consumption. It is new technology, economic growth and market mechanisms that have to do the job. In the 1950s and 1960s, owing to the goal of energy self-sufficiency, Sweden invested heavily in hydropower and nuclear power, and later on in bioenergy; as a result, the country has low emissions today. This is only the case, however, provided that the emissions related to the vast consumption of goods produced abroad are not taken into consideration, and that ecological footprints are generally disregarded. Sweden's place as a climate-protection frontrunner is based on dammed rivers, large assets in industrialized forests and heavy investment in nuclear power. Moreover, Sweden exported low-carbon technology and imported high-carbon consumer products in order to maintain the national standard of living, enhance economic growth and decrease emissions. Some call this progressive national politics that leads the way in the global fight against climate change and towards climate-change mitigation. Others would, as the coming chapters will show, simply call it hypocrisy.

References

"EU måste ändra klimatstrategi", *Aftonbladet* 17/12 2007.
"Stäng smitvägarna från miljöansvaret", *Aftonbladet* 24/1 2008.
"Högt pris för Sverige", *Borås Tidning* 26/11 2008.
"Straffa inte glesbygden", *Borås Tidning* 11/3 2009.
"Vägen framåt i klimatfrågan", *Dagens Nyheter* 3/12 2006.
"Bali bara början", *Dagens Nyheter* 15/12 2007.
"Bra klimat för Sverige", *Expressen* 19/12 2006.
"Bakhalt på Bali", *Expressen* 16/12 2007.
"Så ska det låta", *Expressen* 24/1 2008.
"Etanol är inte framtiden", *Göteborgs-Posten* 16/2 2008.
"En milstolpe för Europa", *Östgöta-Correspondenten* 24/1 2008.
"Sveriges ansvar handlar också om kärnkraft", *Svenska Dagbladet* 3/2 2007a.
"Utan kärnkraft ingen klimatpolitik", *Svenska Dagbladet* 10/3 2007b.
"Europas dumskallar", *Sydsvenska Dagbladet* 5/3 2008.
"Klimatet: Världen kan inte vänta", *Sydsvenska Dagbladet* 11/3 2009.
"Det är inte för sent att lösa klimatproblemet", *Uppsala Nya Tidning* 29/12 2007.
"Det är nödvändigt att EU agerar kraftfullt", *Vestmanlands Läns Tidning* 24/1 2008a.
"Centern skärper tonen i klimatfrågan", *Vestmanlands Läns Tidning* 17/11 2008b.
Albons, B. "Med klimatmål i sikte", *Dagens Nyheter* 9/5 2007a.

Albons, B. "De vill ta ett gemensamt grepp om klimatet", *Dagens Nyheter* 16/5 2007b.

Albons, B. "USA sade nej till halvering av utsläppen", *Dagens Nyheter* 8/6 2007c.

Alfsen, K. and Eskeland, G. S. "Investera i kärnkraften för att rädda miljön", *Dagens Nyheter* 16/3 2007.

Anshelm, J. (2000). *Mellan frälsning och domedag. Om kärnkraftens politiska idéhistoria i Sverige 1945–99.* Symposium.

Anshelm, J. (2004). *Det vilda, det vackra och det ekologiskt hållbara: om opinionsbildningen i Svenska naturskyddsföreningens tidskrift Sveriges natur 1943–2002.* Print and Media, Umeå universitet.

Anshelm, J. (2010). Among demons and wizards: The nuclear energy discourse in Sweden and the re-enchantment of the world. *Bulletin of Science, Technology and Society, 30*(1), 43–53.

Arora-Jonsson, S. (2011). Virtue and vulnerability: Discourses on women, gender and climate change. *Global Environmental Change, 21*(2), 744–51.

Avellan, H. "Kallt huvud och varma sanningar", *Sydsvenska Dagbladet* 27/10 2007.

Axelsson, S. "Den gröna julen", *Expressen* 25/12 2007a.

Axelsson, S."Så slipper vi oljeberoendet", *Expressen* 27/12 2007b.

Aykut, S. C., Comby, J. B. and Guillemot, H. (2012). Climate change controversies in French mass media 1990–2010. *Journalism Studies, 13*(2), 157–74.

Bailey, I., Gouldson, A. and Newell, P. (2011). Ecological modernisation and the governance of carbon: a critical analysis. *Antipode, 43*(3), 682–703.

Baltscheffsky, S. "Tuffa beslut krävs för att avvärja klimathotet", *Svenska Dagbladet* 5/5 2007a.

Baltscheffsky, S. "Hopp om genombrott på Bali", *Svenska Dagbladet* 15/12 2007b.

Baltscheffsky, S. "Utlandsåtgärder ska rädda klimatmålen", *Svenska Dagbladet* 29/6 2008.

Beck, U. (1995). *Ecological Politics in an Age of Risk.* Cambridge Polity Press.

Bennet, C., Ekman, B. and Johansson-Hedberg, B. "Vår livsstil måste ändras", *Svenska Dagbladet* 25/9 2006.

Bergström, H. " Medier tappar huvudet inför klimathotet", *Dagens Nyheter* 9/12 2006.

Bildström, M. "Hög tid att planera för ny kärnkraft", *LO-Tidningen* 6/3 2008.

Billett, S. (2010). Dividing climate change: global warming in the Indian mass media. *Climatic Change, 99*(1–2), 1–16.

Björklund, M. "EU hoppas pressa omvärlden med uppgörelsen om energin", *Dagens Nyheter* 10/3 2007.

Björklund, J. et al. "Sverige måste bygga fyra nya kärnkraftverk", *Dagens Nyheter* 11/1 2008.

Björklund, M. "Sverige ska minska sina utsläpp rejält", *Dagens Nyheter* 24/1 2008.

Bondesson, K.-J. "Stort steg för klimatet", *Göteborgs-Posten* 24/1 2008.

Boykoff, M. T. (2008). The cultural politics of climate change discourse in UK tabloids. *Political geography, 27*(5), 549–69.

Boykoff, M. T. and Goodman, M. K. (2009). Conspicuous redemption? Reflections on the promises and perils of the 'celebritization' of climate change. *Geoforum, 40*(3), 395–406.

Brännlund, R. "Det kostar för svensk ekonomi att driva en tuff miljöpolitik" *Göteborgs-Posten* 17/9 2007.

Carlén, B. "Sveriges klimatpolitik måste läggas om genast", *Dagens Nyheter* 14/12 2007.

Carlgren, A. "Sverige ska bli förebild", *Östgöta Correspondenten* 29/11 2006a.

Carlgren, A. "Utsläppen av växthusgaser ska minska med 30 procent", *DN* 18/12 2006b.

Carlgren, A. "Klimatmärkt mat smart val", *Svenska Dagbladet* 8/7 2007.

Carlgren, A. "Sverige driver EU till täten", *Uppsala Nya Tidning* 3/6 2009.

Carlgren, A. and Malmström, C. "Så ska klimatskutan vändas", *Svenska Dagbladet* 7/12 2006.

Carlsson, G. "Vi satsar en dryg miljard på miljösäkrat bistånd", *Dagens Nyheter* 7/1 2009.

Claesson, C. G. "Sverige långtifrån värsta utslöppsboven", *Göteborgs-Posten* 17/12 2005.

Dowling, R. (2010). Geographies of identity: climate change, governmentality and activism. *Progress in human geography*, 34(4), 488–95.

Ehn, T. "Reinfeldt upptäcker klimathotet", *Borås Tidning* 24/3 2007.

Ekdal, N. "I det långa loppet är vi alla föda", *Dagens Nyheter* 19/11 2006.

Ekdal, N. "Det enkla valet mellan två onda ting", *Dagens Nyheter* 4/2 2007.

Eklund, K. (2009). *Vårt klimat.* Stockholm: Norstedts Akademiska Förlag.

Ennart, H. "KRAV redovisa transportutsläpp", *Svenska Dagbladet* 20/11 2006.

Foust, C. R. and O'Shannon Murphy, W. (2009). Revealing and reframing apocalyptic tragedy in global warming discourse. *Environmental Communication*, 3(2), 151–67.

Fölster, S. "Miljöpartiet ökar utsläppen", *Östgöta Correspondenten* 18/3 2008.

Fölster, S. "Mer kärnkraft och färre bomber", *Östgöta Correspondenten* 13/1 2009.

Fölster, S. and Resvik, B. "Välj rätt växthuspolitik", *Sydsvenska Dagbladet* 3/5 2007.

Gordon, C. (2004). "Al Gore's our guy": linguistically constructing a family political identity. *Discourse and Society*, 15(5), 607–31.

Grahnquist, H. "Lösningen ligger i globala spelregler", *Östgöta Correspondenten* 21/6 2007.

Hajer, M. A. (1995). *The Politics of Environmental Discourse: Ecological Modernization and the Policy Process.* Oxford: Clarendon Press.

Hamilton, C. B. "En tung ekonomisk belastning", *Västerbottens-Kuriren* 6/4 2008.

Höijer, B. (2010). Emotional anchoring and objectification in the media reporting on climate change. *Public Understanding of Science*, 19(6), 717–31.

Hördin, L. "Nu prövas samarbetet", *Helsingborgs Dagblad* 22/1 2008.

Hornborg, A., McNeill, J. R. and Alier, J. M. (eds). (2007). *Rethinking Environmental History: World-system History and Global Environmental Change.* Lanham: Rowman AltaMira.

Hultman, M. (2013). The making of an environmental hero: A history of ecomodern masculinity, fuel cells and Arnold Schwarzenegger. *Environmental Humanities*, 2, 83–103.

Hultman, M. (2014). *Den inställda omställningen. Svensk energi-och miljöpolitik i möjligheternas tid 1980–1991.* Sala: Gidlunds Förlag.

Hultman, M. and Nordlund, C. (2013). Energizing technology: expectations of fuel cells and the hydrogen economy, 1990–2005. *History and Technology*, 29(1), 33–53.

Hultman, M. and Yaras, A. (2012). The socio-technological history of hydrogen and fuel cells in Sweden 1978–2005; mapping the innovation trajectory. *International journal of hydrogen energy*, 37(17), 12043–53.

Hysing, E. (2014). A Green Star Fading? A Critical Assessment of Swedish Environmental Policy Change. *Environmental Policy and Governance*, 24(4), 262–74.

Karlsson, L-I. "Bush och Kina bromsar ny klimatpolitik", *Dagens Nyheter* 18/5 2007a.
Karlsson, L.-I. "Hoppom utökat klimatavtal", *Dagens Nyheter* 3/12 2007b.
Karlsson, L.-I. "Larmen om klimathot är inte övertygande", *Dagens Nyheter* 14/6 2008.
Kjellén, B. "Äntligen är klimatet en global fråga", *Uppsala Nya Tidning* 28/12 2007.
Kjörnsberg. S. "Politiken måste ge alla en chans att ta sitt miljöansvar", *Borås Tidning* 25/7 2007.
Klefbom, E. "Doldisen som sätter agendan", *Miljöaktuellt* 2009:2.
Knaggård, Å. (2014). "What do policy-makers do with scientific uncertainty? The incremental character of Swedish climate change policy-making." *Policy Studies, 25*(1), 22–39.
Kriström, B. "Vi kan göra mer till en lägre kostnad", *Uppsala Nya Tidning* 3/8 2008.
Kurz, T., Augoustinos, M. and Crabb, S. (2010). Contesting the 'national interest' and maintaining 'our lifestyle': A discursive analysis of political rhetoric around climate change. *British Journal of Social Psychology, 49*(3), 601–25.
Laurent, E. (2009). Bleu, Blanc … Green? France and Climate Change. *French Politics, Culture and Society, 27*(2), 142–53.
Levy, D. L. and Spicer, A. (2013). Contested imaginaries and the cultural political economy of climate change. *Organization, 20*(5), 659–78.
Lidskog, R. and Elander, I. (2012). Ecological modernization in practice? The case of sustainable development in Sweden. *Journal of Environmental Policy and Planning, 14*(4), 411–27.
Linder, P. J. A. "Värna ett mänskligt livsklimat", *Svenska Dagbladet* 19/11 2006.
Linder, P. J. A. "Gör klimatpolitiken ännu mer gränslös", *Svenska Dagbladet* 12/9 2007.
Lönnaeus, O. "Norden får bära tyngsta bördan i EU:s miljöplan", *Sydsvenska Dagbladet* 23/1 2008.
Lorenzoni, I. and Hulme, M. (2009). Believing is seeing: laypeople's views of future socio-economic and climate change in England and in Italy. *Public Understanding of Science, 18*(4), 383–400.
Lovell, H., Bulkeley, H. and Owens, S. (2009). Converging agendas? Energy and climate change policies in the UK. *Environment and Planning C: Government and Policy, 27*(1), 90.
Lundius, A. et al. "Sverige behöver kärnkraften", *Svenska Dagbladet* 8/7 2008a.
Lundius, A. et al. "Klimatpolitik utan låsningar", *Svenskt Näringslivs hemsida*, 25/8 2008b.
Lundqvist, L. J. (2004) 'Greening the People's Home': The Formative Power of Sustainable Development Discourse in Swedish Housing. *Urban Studies* 41(7), 1283–301.
Lyytimäki, J. (2011). Mainstreaming climate policy: the role of media coverage in Finland. *Mitigation and Adaptation Strategies for Global Change, 16*(6), 649–61.
Lyytimäki, J. and Tapio, P. (2009). Climate change as reported in the press of Finland: From screaming headlines to penetrating background noise. *International Journal of Environmental Studies, 66*(6), 723–35.
McNeill, J. R. (2003). *Something New Under the Sun: An Environmental History of the Twentieth-Century World.* New York: W.W. Norton and Company.
Mellgren, F. "Regeringen investerar utomlands", *Svenska Dagbladet* 12/3 2009.
Methmann, C. and Rothe, D. (2012). Politics for the day after tomorrow: The logic of apocalypse in global climate politics. *Security Dialogue, 43*(4), 323–44.

Munck, A. "På randen till en katastrof", *Svenska Dagbladet* 18/11 2007.

Nordebo, O. "Klimatfrågan och den gröna optimismen", *Västerbottens-Kuriren* 19/7 2008.

Nordin, L. "Falsk klimatpolitik – regeringen sparar mer än den satsar", *Borås Tidning* 29/9 2007.

Nordström, N. "Politiker, lär av Wigforss", *Göteborgs-Posten* 19/3 2008.

Ohlsson, P. T. "Inte utan kärnkraft", *Sydsvenska Dagbladet* 19/11 2006a.

Ohlsson, P. T. "Det blir svettigt värre", *Sydsvenska Dagbladet* 16/12 2006b.

Olausson, U. (2010). Towards a European identity? The news media and the case of climate change. *European Journal of Communication*, 25(2), 138–52.

Olofsson, M., Borg, A. and Carlgren, A. "Vi höjer nu skatten rejält på koldioxid och diesel", *Dagens Nyheter* 10/3 2009.

Olsson, A.-C. and Johansson R. "Miljöhotet blev en het fråga", *Borås Tidning* 28/8 2007.

Össbo, Å. and Lantto, P. (2011). Colonial Tutelage and Industrial Colonialism: reindeer husbandry and early 20th-century hydroelectric development in Sweden. *Scandinavian Journal of History*, 36(3), 324–48.

Österlund, L: "Lösningen för miljön ligger i konkurrens på lika villkor", *Borås Tidning* 8/12 2007.

Rasmussen, A.-F. and Reinfeldt, F. "20 procent av energin ska vara förnyelsebar år 2020", *Dagens Nyheter* 8/3 2007.

Reinfeldt, F. "Sverige kan visa vägen i det internationella klimatarbetet", *Göteborgs-Posten* 23/9 2007.

Reinfeldt, F. "Speech in Almedalen" 11/7 2008.

Reinfeldt, F. "Europa måste ta klimatansvar", *Svenska Dagbladet* 9/5 2009.

Reinfeldt, F. and Carlgren, A. "Utsläppen av växthusgaser ska minska med 30 procent", *Dagens Nyheter* 18/12 2006.

Reinfeldt, F., Olofsson, M., Björklund, J. and Hägglund, G. "Nu måste resten av EU börja ta sitt klimatansvar", *Dagens Nyheter* 5/12 2007.

Reusswig, F. (2010). The new climate change discourse: A challenge for environmental sociology. In *Environmental Sociology* (pp. 39–57). Springer Netherlands.

Rogers-Hayden, T., Hatton, F. and Lorenzoni, I. (2011). "Energy security" and "climate change": Constructing UK energy discursive realities. *Global Environmental Change*, 21(1), 134–42.

Sampei, Y. and Aoyagi-Usui, M. (2009). Mass-media coverage, its influence on public awareness of climate-change issues, and implications for Japan's national campaign to reduce greenhouse gas emissions. *Global Environmental Change*, 19(2), 203–12.

Schlingman, P. "Det är vi moderater som driver miljöfrågorna", *Göteborgs-Posten* 11/6 2007.

Schmidt, A., Ivanova, A. and Schäfer, M. S. (2013). Media attention for climate change around the world: A comparative analysis of newspaper coverage in 27 countries. *Global Environmental Change*, 23(5), 1233–48.

Schück, J. "Svenskarna tar på sig en meningslös börda", *Dagens Nyheter* 7/3 2008a.

Schück, J. "Klimatförslag sågas. Konjunkturinstitutet kritiskt till transportskatter", *Dagens Nyheter* 3/6 2008b.

Sievers, J. "Så här fixar vi klimatarbetet", *Östgöta Correspondenten* 1/3 2007.

Stern, N. (2006). *The Economics of Climate Change*. Cambridge University Press.

Ström, P. "Alternativet är kol", *Dagens Nyheter* 17/1 2009.

Swyngedouw, E. (2010). Apocalypse forever? Post-political populism and the spectre of climate change. *Theory, Culture and Society, 27*(2–3), 213–32.

Västerteg, C. "Ekonomisk tillväxt och miljöhänsyn går att kombinera", *Borås Tidning* 5/6 2007.

Wolodarski, P. "Kärnkraften räddar Sveriges klimatbokslut", *Dagens Nyheter* 11/1 2008.

3 The Green Keynesian discourse

Introduction

In Sweden, as well as across the globe, the Industrial Fatalist discourse dominates the global climate debate. The second most dominant discourse is what we call "Green Keynesianism". Green Keynesianism was the most widespread of the discourses that opposed Industrial Fatalism in the global climate debate. The Green Keynesian discourse is characterized by deeper reflections on how side effects of industrial society should be handled. Where Industrial Fatalism urges that the problem could be managed through new large-scale technical solutions, market solutions and international agreements, Green Keynesianism raises questions about society's technical, political and economic foundations. Climate change is described in the Green Keynesian discourse not as an isolated management problem, but rather as one of many symptoms of a more serious institutional ecological crisis, which requires not only a change of the relationship between industrial civilization and nature, but also a change in the global distribution of resources and the dispersal of the ecological footprint created by the world's inhabitants. It is noteworthy, however, that Green Keynesianism relies on the same systems of science, economy and values typical of ecological modernization that permeate Industrial Fatalism. This sameness and difference has already been researched by Hajer (1995) who wrote that ecological modernization could be implemented both as a technocratic project, as in our analysis of Industrial Fatalism, and institutional learning – here in the form of Green Keynesianism. During the period studied, Green Keynesian discourse had a significant power disadvantage vis-à-vis Industrial Fatalism, a position that manifested itself mainly as criticism. Those articulating this discourse in Sweden were environmental organizations: the Green Party, the Left Party, Social Democrats, and some scientists and political intellectuals whose ideas could be read in the daily press, opinion pages and in journals.

Green Keynesianism has a long history in Sweden and internationally. During the 1990s, a new hegemony arose within energy and environmental politics. This happened in Sweden but also in countries such as the Netherlands, the United Kingdom and Germany (Hajer, 1995). This is recognized in:

(1) the changing roles of science and technology; (2) the increasing importance of market dynamics and economic agents; (3) transformations in the role of the nation state; (4) modifications in the position, role and ideology of social movements; and (5) changing discursive practices and emerging new ideologies. Mol and Sonnenfeld write that in the ecologically modern discourse, science and technology are not only judged for their role in the emergence of environmental problems, but also highly valued for their potential in curing and preventing them. The nation state is at the same time changed from a regulatory body to a cultivator of environmental innovations (Mol and Sonnenfeld, 2000). The green welfare state, in which Green Keynesianism has its roots in Sweden, was shaped during 1996–1997 and was based on a classic Social Democratic philosophy of faith in scientific progress, economic growth, new technologies and new products in order to solve contemporary environmental problems over a 25-year period (Lundqvist, 2004). Along with the increasing importance of market dynamics and economic agents that had powered the change, the state, research institutions and social movements also began to change as a new ideology of public partnerships emerged. Social movements morphed from green activism to reformism right up until climate change was put on the political agenda as a problem for human civilization (Mol and Sonnenfeld, 2000; Anshelm and Hansson, 2011).

Stop talking and start acting

The questioning of Sweden's Liberal–Conservative government's willingness to pursue rigorous climate policies was a common theme within Green Keynesian discourse. Intellectuals, environmentalists, environmental organizations and political parties urged the government to "stop talking and start acting". The government was criticized for trying to "bury the issue in studies" in order to postpone necessary steps, or to make as few changes as possible in line with industry's economic interests (Sternlycke, 2007; Edman, 2007b).

Opposition political parties made the same criticism. Green Party representatives accused the government of investigating instead of taking action, of failing to unravel the politically motivated decisions of the previous government and of making infrastructure investments that increased carbon emissions. Green Party spokespersons argued that the government's emissions targets were "as full of holes as Swiss cheese" (Domeij, 2007). The Left Party leader, Lars Ohly, dismissed Reinfeldt's actions as "media manoeuvres" and declared that the government's climate initiative – a council and a committee – did not reduce emissions of greenhouse gases at all. He accused the government of trying to avoid taking any national climate action (Ohly, 2007; Ohly et al., 2007). The Social Democrats' former environment minister, Lena Sommestad, noted that the government refused to listen to the environmental movement's "scathing criticism", that it put concrete targets on hold and that it had lapsed into passivity. This meant that the necessary transformation of energy and transportation was hampered significantly. What was missing in the Industrial Fatalist discourse, according to Sommestad, was not knowledge of the climate problem or what should be done, but the political will to implement far-reaching structural changes in society (Sommestad, 2007a, 2007b). In a surprising but revealing alliance, Conservative Party member Mats Svegfors and Green Party member Håkan Wåhlstedt spoke in a joint opinion piece about the "dominating politicians' inability to implement and coordinate action in response to the government's own speech on climate change" (Svegfors and Wåhlstedt, 2007). The sharpest criticism of the Liberal government's climate politics came from the Green Party. Their leading representatives claimed to be amazed by the "arrogance" the government showed when claiming it had done enough or even too much to reduce greenhouse gases, even though Swedes, per person, contributed significantly more greenhouse gas than the global average. Consequently, they found the government's climate politics amounted to "sabotage" against the globe, its politics "being frozen in ice" (Eriksson and Bolund, 2007; Eriksson, 2009).

Green Party member Jonas Eriksson accused the government of wanting to "avoid taking the measures that Sweden required by blaming others" (Eriksson, 2009). He argued that the government operated at the lowest possible level of ambition, below the EU average in terms of investments both in renewable energy and energy efficiency. Representatives of the Left Party and the Social Democrats made similar criticisms, albeit not with the same clarity (Ohly, 2007; Pekgul, 2008).

In 2007, the government's inability to implement uncomfortable, concrete climate policies also became a topic of discussion in the Swedish daily newspapers' editorial pages, especially those leaning towards left-Liberal. The Social Democratic *Aftonbladet* claimed that the government continued to "live with closed eyes" and that it was not enough to "only talk" (*Aftonbladet*, 2007a, 2007b). Even pro-government newspaper editorials took up the issue, raising objections and calling for a review of climate politics. This could be interpreted as the government's failure being perceived as a real problem, even among its Liberal supporters. Leading writers of *Dagens Nyheter* warned that it was not sufficient to merely give "vague reference to international agreements" (*Dagens Nyheter*, 2007). *Sydsvenska Dagbladet* noted that politicians should not avoid "unpleasant decisions" (*Sydsvenska Dagbladet*, 2007). *Helsingborgs Dagblad* complained it was troublesome that the Liberal government politics was characterized by "postponing urgent decisions" (2007). And *Västerbottens-Kuriren* pointed out that international agreements could not compensate for the absence of "our own active environmental policy" (Lönnaeus, 2008; Olofsson, 2007). The push for powerful measures thus came from very different directions. The government's actions were questioned widely in the Green Keynesian discourse.

New technology alone does not solve the climate issue

Voices within the Green Keynesian discourse questioned the idea that new climate-friendly technologies would solve the problem of the global climate crisis. Since the problem was, fundamentally, global and local consumption, new technical solutions without structural changes to production systems and consumption behaviours would not be enough. Relying on technology to solve climate change was interpreted as an expression of an unwillingness to discuss the issue of civilization's technological, economic and political foundations. Bo Ekman, chairman of the internationally renowned Tällberg Foundation, noted that any new technology creates unpredictable side effects. This meant that even if climate-friendly technologies were developed, they could not be a quick fix without changes in the patterns of over-consumption. Behavioural changes and new technologies needed to be developed together "because human behaviour is the biggest threat". Climate problems were a consequence of how richer countries' consumption, lifestyles, infrastructure, energy and production systems. This meant that system changes became necessary, and these could not be replaced by technological solutions with unforeseen long-term consequences. What was needed was greater humility and a better understanding of the causes of climate change (Ekman, 2006, 2007).

The Green Party and Social Democrats declared that it was not reasonable to believe that it would be possible to maintain existing patterns of living in a rich world through new technology. A group of internationally renowned, Social Democrat women – Margot Wallström, Gro Harlem Brundtland and Mary Robinson – argued that an exaggerated and one-sided faith in techno-logical solutions was detrimental to the handling of the climate problem: "With only technological innovation, we can never achieve a sustainable low-carbon economy. Technology cannot eliminate poverty, respect human rights, guarantee equality, stop climate change or build a sustainable society. It is only we, as human beings, who can accomplish this" (Wallström et al., 2008). Somewhat unexpectedly, this view was shared by Volvo's former chairman, Pehr G. Gyllenhammar, who questioned the Liberal–Conservative government's promise that new technologies could solve the climate pro-blem. He called technological optimism an empty expression of hope that diverted the attention away from what needed doing; this was a "painless" way to cope with the problem. Instead, the government should "set much more stringent requirements for the industry", according to Gyllenhammar (Rognerud, 2008).

Nuclear power as an alibi solution

If nuclear power in the Industrial Fatalist discourse was presented as a tech-nological saviour for widespread ecological threats, it was dismissed in the Green Keynesian discourse as an outdated technology, a deceptive solution purporting to manage a large and complex problem in a simple and merci-less manner. A spectrum of environmental organizations and opposition political parties challenged those who wanted to prepare for a climate-driven nuclear renaissance.

The General Secretary of Greenpeace-Sweden, Lennart Daléus, explained on several occasions in 2006 and 2007 that hopes for nuclear power were based on the misconception that nuclear power was a major source of energy globally and that uranium would always be available. His long experience with the Swedish energy debate, in which he was one of the leading people on the renewable side, prompted him to speak up again and again (Anshelm, 2000). In fact, he explained, nuclear power is a very marginal contributor to energy consumption globally, accounting for only around 6 per cent of world energy use. A tenfold increase in the figure would require that 4,000 nuclear power plants be built within two decades, which Daléus found totally unrealistic and beyond planetary resource boundaries. Nuclear power was not a realistic alternative, instead renewable energy and energy efficiency improvements could "save the climate without harming the economy" and avoid the choice between Scylla and Charybdis (Daléus, 2006; Robért, 2007). According to the spokesperson on energy issues for Swedish Greenpeace, Martina Krüger, the world did not need nuclear power, since 70 per cent of the world's electricity needs could be met by renewable energy sources combined with energy efficiency. Given this, Krüger argued that the threat of climate change was used as a "pretext for expansion of nuclear power" by those who had long advocated it. Nuclear power was a solution that sought its problem, and found it in the climate threat, as evidenced by the total absence of a comprehensive analysis of global energy and climate change. Even if nuclear power would have been an unproblematic technology in ecological terms, it would not have reduced global greenhouse gas emissions to any significant extent. Krüger also emphasized that nuclear power carried very high risks associated with uranium mining, reactor operations, waste storage and nuclear proliferation, risks that would hardly be reduced if the technology spread across the globe (Krüger, 2008).

Among political parties, it was primarily the Green Party that led the charge to stop the development of what they considered an obsolete technology. The person in charge of energy issues, Per Bolund, accused the Conservatives and the Liberal Party of using climate change to propagate nuclear power, something he found somewhat bizarre because the technology had so many inherent problems. Did the Swedish government really want countries such as Iran, North Korea and Belarus to have nuclear power and thus access to nuclear weapons? If not, then you could hardly advocate a global spread of nuclear power. Nuclear power, in terms of capacity, was far too limited; with 4,000 new reactors, uranium would run out. This growth would also create a need for safe reactor operation and waste storage locations. Moreover, it took far too long to build nuclear power plants: at least fifteen years. Policymakers could not wait that long to deal with climate problems. Plus, compared to renewables, nuclear technology was unreasonably expensive. In the end, it was not sustainable because it required the use of finite natural resources and risked delaying investments in renewable energy sources. Like other Green Party members, Bolund found that nuclear

power would never be able to save the climate. It could hide the real problems in a national arena, but the equation could not be reconciled on a global
scale (Bolund, 2007). In a rhetorical comment, the Left Party leader, Lars
Ohly, and others asked the public to choose between an "active or radioactive"
climate solution (Ohly et al., 2007). Leading Green Party spokespersons rose
on several occasions in 2008 and 2009 to register these objections and
claimed that "Nuclear could be phased out" and "Nuclear power is for those
who given up" (Wetterstrand, 2008, 2009; Eriksson and Özdemir, 2008). But
their arguments never caused any real debate; the Industrial Fatalist discourse
dominated the nuclear power debate totally and this may also indicate its
strong position overall in the climate-change debate.

The central focus on nuclear power by the Industrial Fatalist discourse
was interpreted within the Green Keynesian discourse as a sham solution,
not a valid policy measure. It was criticized as a non-solution, the consequences of which would thwart and delay real solutions, such as the
development of renewable energy and energy efficiency. Nuclear power,
though cherished by the Liberal–Conservative government, trade unions and
business organizations as a solution to the problem of global emissions of
greenhouse gases, was strictly a national solution. It was an expansion of
nuclear power in Sweden that the Industrial Fatalists advocated, but they did
not discuss at all how this expansion would solve the global climate
problem.

Like their counterparts in the UK and France, but not the US, Green
Keynesian actors in Sweden depicted climate change as a consequence of
unsustainable lifestyles and consumption patterns (Rogers-Hayden et al.,
2011; Laurent, 2009; Levy and Spicer, 2012). Nuclear power could not be a
solution to the real problem, which was the unsustainable use of natural
resources. According to Green Keynesianism, a shift to nuclear from fossil
fuels would only transfer the problem.

Fewer market solutions, more democratic politics

In the previous chapter we saw how the Industrial Fatalist discourse presupposed that market mechanisms could be used to manage climate change.
Setting a price on carbon would contribute to the development of new climate-
friendly technologies, emissions trading would lead to decreased emissions and
educated consumers would ask for climate-friendly goods, thereby affecting
production. The safeguarding of market principles was described as absolutely necessary: anything else was intolerable. The Stern Review, however,
identified climate change as the biggest market failure ever, a clear sign of the
market's inability to deal with externalities, such as environmental impacts
(Stern, 2006). The reporting of Stern's analysis spread worldwide and led
partly to a larger movement towards opening up the climate debate to a
discussion about alternate solutions (Sampei and Aoyagi-Usui, 2009; Lyytimäki
and Tapio, 2009; Kurz et al., 2010; Reusswig, 2010). This inability of markets

to solve climate change is a starting point in the Green Keynesian discourse. It leads to recurrent demands for increased political control of the market.

Well-known journalist and author, Göran Rosenberg, noted, for example, that self-interest could not be reconciled with the public interest when it came to climate change, and that market forces would not work in this context. Short-term and individual preferences conflicted with long-term survival and common goals. Rosenberg did not interpret climate change as a market failure but instead said it was "the result of the market coming to replace politics in contexts where the market does not work". He concluded that it was necessary to reduce the market's impact on climate issues and improve political support for long-term responsibility (Rosenberg, 2007). Similar thoughts were heard from Bo Ekman, who declared that it was impossible to rely on "free market self-interest" when it came to creating a sustainable society. Politicians' reluctance to choose between short-term growth and ecological sustainability posed a dilemma. Although it was possible to understand politicians' hopes that the market economy would quickly generate technical solutions, so that political intervention in the economic system could be avoided, Ekman argued that this was not a realistic or sustainable approach. A greater political accountability for global issues had become increasingly inevitable (Ekman, 2007).

Stefan Edman, a nationally recognized environmental debater, claimed to have a concrete explanation for why market solutions did not lead in the right direction. The climate benefits that new technology created were soon subsumed by increasing consumption. This so-called rebound effect had been widely researched (Stern, 2006), which indicated "a disastrous zero-sum game with the climate" (Edman, 2007b). The only solution Edman could see to this problem was that politicians discipline the market and curb over-consumption. Along with environmental historian Sverker Sörlin, Edman urged actors within the Industrial Fatalist discourse to reconsider the "naively simplistic view of the relationship between growth and climate policy" (Edman and Sörlin, 2008; see also Lindstedt, 2006; Norberg, 2008). Along with Anders Wijkman – European Parliament member, member of the Royal Swedish Academy of Sciences and the vice president of the Club of Rome, as well as the Tällberg Foundation – Edman also questioned the usual concept of growth and acknowledged the need to reform economic models. For too long, the ecological dimension had been excluded from economic models. Climate change was considered by Edman and Wijkman to be the clearest sign that the ecological crisis could not be solved with new technology alone. The reform of economic models was essential, otherwise there would be no real change possible. Although the ecological crisis could temporarily be handled, new crises would occur as a result of reductionism in economic models. They did not reject economic growth, but claimed that its content needed to change and become much less material-intensive in nature, in order to discourage the over-consumption of natural resources (Edman and Wijkman, 2007; Wijkman, 2007). Edman even asked if our consumption was compatible with a healthy climate (Edman, 2007a, 2007b) and the Tällberg Foundation declared that the current model of growth and prosperity had reached the "end of the road". However, they all still thought that Sweden and the EU had an opportunity to create a model that in the long run would be able to "combine growth with sustainability", a measure that the threat of climate change necessitated (Ekman et al., 2007).

Environmental debaters received support from some innovation researchers and economists. Christian Berggren, Staffan Jacobsson and Staffan Laestadius argued that climate problems could not possibly be solved only by individuals being encouraged to change their consumption habits, or the hope that the market would solve the problem. What was needed was a political act. The government should: "[T]ake a comprehensive approach to energy, industrial, fiscal and environmental policies to drive the transformation of Sweden". A good start would be to raise carbon taxes, plus energy and vehicle fuel taxes. Only far-sighted and ambitious political reform efforts could help meet the climate challenge. Passively waiting for market mechanisms to sort out the matter was a simple, but hopeless attitude (Berggren et al., 2007). Christian Azar, a professor of sustainable energy, was on the same path and in his book *Makten över klimatet* [Influence over climate change] (Azar, 2008), he stressed that not a single major environmental problem had ever been solved by voluntary changes in human behaviour. In 2009 Azar was chosen as the most influential person in the environmental debate in Sweden; in 2010 he was given the José Vasconcelos World Education Award for his contribution to making science understandable. If the importance of individual responsibility and action were exaggerated, Azar said, the need to handle global climate change through powerful policymaking would be missed (Azar, 2008). These researchers' arguments coincided at this point with both the Green Party and Left Party representatives (Wetterstrand and Svensson Smith, 2008; Holm, 2008). Even Liberal newspapers criticized the market's inability to account for externalities and the urgent need for control and enforcement frameworks (*Dagens Nyheter*, 2006; *Göteborgs-Posten*, 2007; *Expressen*, 2008b). Among all these voices, no one questioned the market as an economic system: rather, they focused on market principles that did not work, and the government's unrealistically high hopes that market mechanisms could solve global environmental problems.

The failure of carbon dioxide trading systems

One of the market mechanisms that the Liberal–Conservative government put their trust in was trading rights for carbon dioxide emissions, a system that was subjected to a thorough criticism among environmental groups and commentators from the Green Keynesian discourse. The EU was criticized for mismanaging emissions trading by distributing free allowances to industries such as forestry, mining and steel, instead of auctioning them off as originally intended. The EU failed to withstand the pressure of European industry, which, according to critics, had bizarre consequences. The problem was that the allocation of allowances was based on these industries' own data on how much carbon dioxide they produced. According to critics, this resulted in a generous surplus of allowances. Large European companies managed to negotiate a surplus of allowances, which, when sold, could "generate multi-million dollar profits in doing nothing". The system was criticized because it did not lead to any reductions in carbon emissions, and actually benefited those who generated the greatest emissions. This meant that "free money" was given to industries that emitted high levels of carbon (*Expressen*, 2008c; *Aftonbladet*, 2008e; *Sydsvenska Dagbladet*, 2009; Baltscheffsky, 2007). Azar and former environment minister Lena Sommestad demanded that "all companies needed to be restricted by carbon regulations", in complete agreement with the Energy Agency and the Environmental Protection Board, who proposed that both the EU and the Swedish government reduce emission allocations significantly. If they did not do this, trading could never contribute to reductions in carbon dioxide emissions (Azar, 2007; Sommestad, 2007). Greenpeace was even more critical and called emissions trading an utterly ineffective "fiasco" which gave the forestry, mining and steel industries "freedom to increase emissions" without any incentive to invest in climate-friendly technologies (Fröberg, 2007; Flood, 2009). Although none of these critics rejected the idea of emissions trading, they highlighted how the Swedish government and the European Union had to admit the contradiction between the industry's short-term interests and long-term public interest, and act accordingly. Industries must be forced to reduce carbon dioxide emissions, not be expected to do so voluntarily, and the system of emissions trading should be adjusted accordingly.

The myth of Sweden as frontrunner

As detailed in the previous chapter, the Liberal–Conservative government claimed that under its leadership Sweden had evolved into an international climate protection frontrunner. This picture was challenged by the Green Keynesian discourse. First, the Green Keynesians argued, government officials had adorned themselves with borrowed plumage thanks to relatively low Swedish emission levels resulting from an energy system switch (in the 1980s and 1990s) in the housing sector from fossil fuels to nuclear power. Sweden could therefore be given credit in international negotiations (Engström, 2009). Second, it was argued that Sweden's frontrunner claim was largely imaginary, as the emission calculations were based on misleading statistics in per capita terms (Finnveden et al., 2008. Berggren et al., 2007).

Actors speaking within the Green Keynesian discourse questioned both the government's confidence in the pace of technological solutions and its hopes for market solutions. The government's politics was based on false claims and a distorted self-understanding. Green Keynesians requested that instead there should be politics for a sustainable society. The image of

Sweden as a climate politics pioneer was inaccurate and subjected to a thorough critique. As explained by professors Berggren, Jacobsson and Laestadius, Sweden had not managed to decouple itself from the long-running negative relationship between economic growth and carbon emissions, despite the government's claims at the UN Conference in Bali (and at all COP conferences since then). The government's calculations excluded the emissions from aviation and shipping to and from Sweden, for example. If this traffic was included, Swedish carbon dioxide emissions equalled levels of fifteen years before. According to the authors the talk of decoupling was a huge "myth" dedicated to portraying Sweden as an ethical nation – both nationally and internationally – in the fight against climate change. Instead of spreading the image of Sweden as an international leader and demanding that other countries emulate this good example, they said the government should raise climate ambitions at home by for example reducing the fuel consumption of new cars sold in Sweden to the European average. The claim that Sweden was ahead of other countries in Europe was a distorted self-image that only justified a passive political stance on climate issues (Berggren et al., 2007).

The idea of Sweden as a model nation in terms of climate-protection was deconstructed further in 2007, when scientists and environmental commentators began to call attention to the emissions caused in other countries as a result of the outsourced production of goods consumed in Sweden. The increasing consumption of goods produced in China and India, for example, raised Chinese and Indian emissions, but not Sweden's. This transfer enabled the Swedish ecological footprint and the Swedish contribution to the greenhouse effect to grow, while the government could claim to have broken the link between economic growth and emissions. It all looked like a "lie" or a "scam", according to actors representing the Green Keynesian discourse. The Swedish government moralized over other countries' emissions, despite the fact that Swedish consumers took advantage of those emissions produced elsewhere. It was time to "expose the decoupling myth" (Grenholm, 2008; Wejryd, 2008; Johnsson, 2008; Lillemets, 2009; Engström, 2009). If Sweden's imports and Swedish-owned industry emissions throughout the world were counted, Sweden would, according to the World Wildlife Fund, be among the very worst countries when it came to carbon emissions. Statistics professor Anders Grimvall testified that the emissions caused by Swedish citizens abroad meant that it was quite possible that the total amount of carbon dioxide per Swede had increased. It was clear that emissions had not decreased (Sievers, 2008).

All these voices agreed that Swedish emissions of carbon dioxide were generally underestimated and that Swedish climate politics rested on misconceptions. According to the Swedish Archbishop, Anders Wejryd, this led to a completely passive stance and business-as-usual policies. Citizens in Sweden lived largely under the delusion that Swedes released CO_2 at the global average, or less. In fact, the Swedish population emitted 50 per cent more carbon gases per person than the global average. This revelation demanded both individual and political accountability, according to Wejryd. Swedes should not blame other countries and people outside Sweden for climate change, which would be a case of "the pot calling the kettle black" (Wejryd, 2008). Given this background, requiring a 40 per cent reduction (compared to 1990 levels) in domestic emissions by 2020 was "reasonable", even if it was hardly enough to turn Sweden into an international role model. Representatives of the Green Party and the Left Party shared this goal, and found the government's ambition to decrease the emission by 30 per cent within the borders of Sweden and 8 per cent in other countries, with the help of flexible mechanisms shameless (Asteberg, 2009).

Sweden as a true role model within the current system

Sweden could still become a climate-protection role model, according to participants in the Green Keynesian discourse. In the fall of 2006, representatives of the environmental movement argued that Sweden actually was in an extraordinarily good position – and had a moral obligation – to take a leading role in the global transformation necessary to reduce greenhouse gases. The healthy economy, the high degree of technological knowledge, the large assets of carbon-free energy sources, the sparse population and the political culture of cooperation were interpreted as an excellent foundation for ambitious climate politics. The country could show the rest of the world that forceful efforts to combat climate change were totally consistent with high levels of welfare and economic and technological development (Ekman, 2006; Axelsson, 2007). Thus, the idea that climate change could turn into a business opportunity was also very much a fundamental part of the Green Keynesian discourse, albeit in a slightly different guise. As argued by the Swedish Society for Nature Conservation (SSNC) at the beginning of 2007, the government should not have considered it a sacrifice to cut domestic carbon emissions, rather it should have recognized the long-term economic benefits of being oil-independent. Countries that were first to invest in using their supply, production and consumption to move in a climate-friendly direction would be rewarded with good export opportunities and a generally favourable economic situation; other countries would be required to do the same in the future (e.g. Axelsson, 2007).

Around the same time, Swedish Greenpeace called the assertion that big cuts in carbon emissions would threaten the economy a widespread fallacy. Just increasing energy efficiency by 50 per cent would have significant economic benefits for households and businesses, which meant that large emission reductions were fully compatible with economic prosperity: it was good business to reduce emissions (Daléus, 2006). According to the SSNC, who had taken an ecomodern stance for almost twenty years, it was important for environmental organizations to convince the public and politicians that there was no contradiction between climate-related considerations and economic growth; in the long run, climate improvement was a prerequisite for growth (Anshelm, 2004; Axelsson, 2007). The Green Party and Social Democrats said that strengthened international economic competitiveness, increased opportunities for export of green technologies and a substantial number of new jobs would result if strong climate action was taken (e.g. Karlsson, 2007; Åkesson and Werner, 2007; Eriksson and Valtersson, 2008).

Swedish Liberal–Conservative government double standards in climate politics

In early 2007, environmental organizations, other non-profit organizations, individual debaters and the political opposition strongly criticized the government's climate politics, claiming that Sweden was not taking responsibility for global climate change. The government was accused of shifting responsibility to other countries and future generations and avoiding necessary measures to reduce carbon emissions, for example in energy-intensive industries and the transport sector. Representatives of SSNC, the Swedish Church, the Swedish United Nation Association and Swedish engineers criticized the government for not having any proposals to discuss with regard to combating climate change, for settling for the existing nuclear and hydropower low-carbon emissions and for hoping that the climate problem would resolve itself without new ideas (Wejryd, 2007). In late 2008, the three aforementioned organizations handed the prime minister a petition signed by more than 40,000 people, who demanded that the government enacted more ambitious climate policies (Axelsson et al., 2008b; Lönnaeus, 2008). These and other organizations, individual commentators and political opponents criticized three policies: first, that Swedish emission targets were defensive in nature; second, that these targets could be met through flexible mechanisms; and third, for fending off tighter EU standards while, at the same time, criticizing other EU countries for not taking responsibility.

The SSNC's general secretary Svante Axelsson and others saw "a new attitude to climate change" in Sweden. He found it very disturbing that Prime Minister Reinfeldt repeatedly emphasized that Swedish emissions, from a global perspective, were very small, almost negligible, and that Sweden had already done so much that further action would be relatively inconsequential. What Axelsson discerned was an uncooperative government taking actions that were contrary to citizens' demands (Axelsson, 2007; Pettersson et al., 2009). When, in the autumn of 2007, the Liberal-Conservative government's scientific board on climate change declared that Sweden did not have to reduce its greenhouse gas emissions by more than 20–25 percent of 1990 levels to meet EU requirements, SSNC chairman Mikael Karlsson objected. Since the EU goal for 2050 was an 80 per cent cut, the government's proposal would postpone major cuts and leave the responsibility for them to future generations. Once again, the Industrial Fatalist discourse, with its trust in new technologies and market mechanisms, was being advanced: this time by the government's scientific board. This trust in new technology was not shared by Karlsson, who found the recommendations that Sweden should back off and not take the lead, in order to speed up international work on protecting the climate, unworthy of Sweden. He noted that Swedish climate politics would "break down" a few years into the 2020s if ambitious measures were postponed (Karlsson, 2007).

In the same vein, the Archbishop, Axelsson and others explained that Sweden still lacked a climate emission goal and that the Liberal–Conservative government was postponing the issue. Given this, they advocated a parliament decision that emissions would be reduced by at least 40 per cent by 2020, and that these cuts would be implemented at a steady pace. In addition, they proposed that Sweden should contribute to equal cuts in "developing" countries (Wejryd et al., 2007). In the climate petition that the SSNC, the Swedish Church and the Swedish United Nations Association initiated, this goal was clear-cut and accompanied by this call: "Politicians assume your responsibility to the climate – Act Now" (Axelsson et al., 2008b). In 2008, and on the same grounds, authors, journalists and researchers began to criticize the Liberal–Conservative government over climate policy. In May, the social movement Climate Action was created. In an appeal in *Aftonbladet* under the heading "Act Now!", 59 researchers, writers and journalists expressed their frustration over government inaction and proposed comprehensive climate budgets to reduce greenhouse gas emissions in Sweden by an average of 4 per cent per year. This would reduce emissions by 90 per cent by 2050. In addition, Climate Action proposed that reductions should be distributed "fairly" so that those who consume the most fossil fuels would be responsible in proportion to their emissions (*Aftonbladet*, 2008d; Alizadeh, 2008). On the cultural pages in various newspapers the government was criticized by individual debaters for not even bothering with a cut of 20 per cent; across the EU, few countries were doing as little as Sweden to reduce emissions. It was time to pay Sweden's "environmental debt" (Malm, 2008; Andersson, 2008). The tone of environmental organizations, other non-profit organizations and individual environmental commentators was sometimes rancorous. Their powerful demands called for a basic reconsideration of environmental politics. The idea was that the government should immediately begin to prioritize climate change and other environmental issues, because time was short and the responsibility to avoid ecosystem collapse almost unlimited. Considerable indignation was aroused by organizations and individuals who perceived that the government remained passive and was avoiding policies that might conflict with company interests, relying instead on new technologies, markets, changes in individual consumption choices and international agreements to solve the problem. The parliamentary opposition parties aligned themselves with this emerging movement. A few months into 2008, the three opposition parties "demanded 40 per cent reductions in emissions" in Sweden by 2020. Like SSNC the leading representatives of these political parties argued that a steady rate of improvement was necessary if Sweden were to cut its emissions by 75–90 per cent by 2050 (Ohly et al., 2008).

Flexible mechanisms as a modern indulgence

While the level of ambition of the Liberal government's emissions targets was criticized, so too was the method it chose to achieve them. From 2007 onwards, the government's intention to achieve a proportion of the national emissions target by investing in other countries and using flexible mechanisms became the subject of intense debate. The SSNC claimed, for example, that the government's way of achieving emission reductions in countries like India and China shifted the focus from the fact that Sweden's own emission levels were unsustainable. To maintain the Swedish emissions level while shifting reductions to "developing" countries was cheating, according to the SSNC. First, an ambitious reduction programme in Sweden did not rule out investments in other countries: rich countries should do both. Second, Sweden's contribution to reducing global emissions of greenhouse gases would be very limited regardless of whether the investments were made in Sweden or abroad. Hence, the SSNC concluded that Sweden's most important political task was to set ambitious domestic climate goals and achieve them, making it a *real* frontrunner and not just a country portrayed as such. This would allow Sweden to present itself as an international example of how climate-related considerations, economic development and welfare could be reconciled. If, as proposed by the Liberal–Conservative government, Sweden bought its reductions overseas, overall emissions would actually increase. If ambitious emissions targets were not possible in Sweden, with its image as an environmental leader, what country would follow suit? (Axelsson, 2007). This way of deconstructing flexible mechanisms was in line with the broader, global critique of ecomodern discourse (Bailey et al., 2011). As noted by leading representatives of the SSNC, the Swedish Church and the Swedish United Nations Association: "To profit from cheap emission reductions in poor countries because we in the rich world do not want to adjust at home, can be rightly perceived as egoistic. Regardless how much we help others, we must also do our own homework" (Axelsson et al., 2008a). In addition they declared that efforts to reduce Swedish emissions – for example by altering the transport system, increasing energy efficiency and changing consumption patterns – eventually had to be implemented anyway, and that it was better to do it early, and gradually lower emissions, than to postpone changes until a future time and be forced to implement them hastily.

The Left Party, the Social Democrats and the Green Party were similarly critical towards the government's reliance on flexible mechanisms. Green Party spokespersons questioned both the wisdom and morality of "shifting the responsibility to someone else, somewhere else". They also wondered which country could reduce its emissions to the necessary levels if Sweden could not (Eriksson, 2007a). In a joint article, the three parties said the use of flexible mechanisms risked becoming "a modern indulgence" if used as a reason for not reducing emissions domestically (Ohly et al., 2008). The use of the religious concept of indulgence amounted to calling the government position a scam. It was also an example of religious metaphors being used in the global climate debate. When this kind of language was even used by actors within the Green Keynesian discourse it signalled the importance of such words in the debate (for the UK see Woods et al., 2012; for the US see Foust and O'Shannon Murphy, 2009). Several representatives of the three opposition parties also interpreted the government's argument for flexible mechanisms as a signal that Sweden intended to "buy" itself free from requirements on emission reductions while making "the poorest people pay the consequences for our emissions" (Westlund et al., 2008; Gabelic and Ygeman, 2008). On Sweden's left-leaning cultural and editorial pages the tone was, at times, even sharper: describing, for example, flexible mechanisms as an expression of an "imperialist climate policy". Reaching climate goals through economic-structural violence amounted to "climate wars" (Lenas, 2009). Editorials published in the Social Democrat oriented *Aftonbladet* in 2008 and 2009 expressed severe criticism of the government's efforts to increase the share of climate-related measures conducted abroad, while protecting domestic industry from energy reduction targets. They accused the Conservative Party of being a "traitor" by boasting of high environmental standards while acting within the EU to increase the proportion of emission reductions it achieved abroad. Withholding cheaper climate action in "developing" countries at the same time as they planned to build new motorways in Sweden was seen as a provocative expression of the Liberal–Conservative government's double standards with regard to climate politics. Opinion pieces in the Social Democrat press exclaimed that "free-riding" should be abandoned and that a Sweden that bought itself "free from environmental responsibility" could never be a model of international climate politics. A rich Europe, and a Sweden unprepared to deal with its own emissions, were perceptions that demoralized the entire international community, and were especially unfortunate given that the UN conference in Copenhagen was imminent (*Aftonbladet*, 2008a, 2008b, 2009a, 2009b).

The double standards in Swedish climate politics criticized by Green Keynesianism actors were also evident in the way that the government delayed the introduction of more stringent emission standards for the industry. At the same time, the government – during EU negotiations – also pushed for a greater share of emissions targets to be accommodated through flexible mechanisms. Environmental organizations, commentators and opposition politicians made much of the discrepancy between the government's claim of being a political pioneer and its actions in EU negotiations. In the latter context, the Liberal–Conservative government and EU representatives from the Conservative, Christian Democrat, Liberal and Centre Parties were perceived increasingly as "reactionaries" and opponents of ambitious goals for protecting the climate. Like Poland and Italy, Sweden was safeguarding the competitiveness of its domestic industry at the expense of progressive climate policy. Critics argued that thanks to favourable conditions in Sweden (the country was sparsely populated and had shifted its energy system from fossil fuels to nuclear power, and to some extent biomass, during the preceding 30 years), the government could foster the pretence of being a world climate leader. Sweden should not accuse Poland of carrying out a "climate hoax" while doing the same at home (Bolund, 2009; Gustafsson and Svensson, 2009; Westlund, 2008; Schlyter, 2009).

The ecological debt of the economically rich world

A central idea in the Green Keynesian discourse was that the economically GDP rich world owed an ecological debt to poor countries. The rich countries' material wealth, according to this idea, had been built on industrialization fuelled by increasing use of fossil energy, which caused environmental degradation. Thus, citizens of these countries caused the greenhouse effect through their carbon emissions, a situation that now risked destroying low-lying countries in the southern hemisphere. It was not fair to move the problem to countries such as India and China, where industrialization was incipient: such a measure was immoral, lacking historical perspective and not based on per capita emission standards. What right did the rich countries have to deny these and other countries the opportunity to increase the material wealth they [the rich countries] themselves had supported? The conclusion reached by leading representatives of the SSNC, the Swedish Church and the Swedish United Nations Association, as well as environmental debaters, was that Swedish climate politics must start from a perspective of global justice. Poor countries, in the short term, need to be allowed to increase their carbon dioxide emissions, while rich countries reduced theirs drastically (Svensson, 2007; Wijkman, 2007b; Larsson, 2007; see also Adger et al., 2003).

It was also important that the rich countries should pay their long-term ecological debt by financing the transfer and implementation of new climate-friendly technologies – especially in respect of energy and transportation – to create prosperity that was sustainable and did not dramatically increase carbon emissions. The overall assessment was that unless the rich world took up this responsibility and paid off its long-term ecological debt, low-income countries would never accept any international agreement on global cuts in greenhouse gas emissions. If international efforts to protect the climate were to have any chance of success, this was an absolute prerequisite for getting countries such as India, China and Brazil to accept international agreements. Countries such as these were at a transformative stage in the process of industrialization and accounted for a large part of the global growth in emissions of greenhouse gases. Climate politics with the potential to succeed therefore had to rest on rich countries' recognition of their long-term ecological debt and environmental justice. Anything else was likely to lay the foundation for a global climate collapse. In 2008, Wijkman summed up the situation:

> The poor countries have every right to development, but must not make the mistakes of the industrialised countries in terms of climate and environment. If they do, the planet will literally collapse under the rapidly increasing pressure on the natural resource base and the atmosphere. An alternative climate-friendly development requires financial and technological support.
>
> (Wijkman, 2008)

Wijkman saw three obstacles for the environmental justice movement. First, rich countries had barely begun to reduce their own greenhouse gas emissions, so why should the poor countries do it? Second, rich countries had done "extremely little" so far in order to facilitate the use of climate-friendly technologies in poorer countries. Added to this, rich countries had "neglected" to offer the support needed by low-income countries that had been hit hard by the effects of climate change. Against this background, he proposed a "Marshall Plan", a global contract of financial assistance to low-income countries to ensure that climate-friendly technologies were transferred and that economic development and limitations on greenhouse gas emissions in these countries were implemented. Without such programmes, Wijkman felt that it would be "politically and morally impossible to fully integrate developing countries into climate change initiatives" (Wijkman, 2008). Similarly, the 59 writers, researchers and journalists who were involved in forming the social movement Climate Action also called for new and more ambitious climate politics from Sweden (Finnveden et al. 2008).

In the same spirit, the four largest environmental organizations – the WWF, the SSNC, Greenpeace and Friends of the Earth – demanded that rich countries should recognize their historical responsibility and respect that low-income countries could "rightly" expect substantial support for climate initiatives. The organizations called on the EU to create a new way of financing "developing" countries' adaptation to climate change, the transition to sustainable energy sources and conservation of the rainforests. They said that the EU must set aside at least 35 billion dollars a year for the purpose of financing climate action in "developing" countries and that this commitment must be in addition to ordinary assistance. They also argued, along with others, that financial support for climate measures should not erode conventional foreign aid (Wejryd et al., 2007). Relatively few politicians in the Green Keynesian discourse raised the global equity issues. One who did was European Commission vice president and Social Democrat, Margot Wallström. She declared that in order for international climate negotiations to bear fruit, the rich countries that caused the most pollution must financially support the climate-protection action implemented in "developing" countries that were at risk of being hit hardest by climate change: "the less polluting countries should win on carbon trading" (Wallström, 2009). Green Party spokespersons shared this view and argued that each country should contribute in proportion to its population's prosperity in terms of per capita income, because it was the rich countries who were predominantly responsible for the emission of greenhouse gases (Wetterstrand, 2009).

All the voices from different organizations that raised the issue of global climate justice emanated from a historical perspective: that the citizens of rich countries had a debt to pay and that a great moral responsibility rested upon them. Without strong financial commitments from rich countries, it would not be politically or morally legitimate to impose emission requirements on low-income countries. On this point there was much dispute with the Industrial Fatalist discourse, the actors of which trusted that flexible mechanisms benefited all parties and provided a cost-effective method for the transmission of investments and technology. Given the extensive demands for rapid, large-scale and effective action to cut global emissions of greenhouse gases, the Green Keynesian discourse required ambitious climate politics and effective changes in the regulations. To trust only in future technological changes, market mechanisms or changes in individual consumption choices was both uncertain and insufficient. Again and again it was mentioned that it was time for politicians to shoulder their responsibilities.

This conclusion was supported by several energy and technology researchers. Christian Azar was among those who repeatedly complained that Sweden, as well as the rest of the world, needed a "stronger climate policy" because the rich countries needed to cut their greenhouse gas emissions by 15 per cent per decade to avoid severe climate change. According to Azar, major climate problems could only be solved by political decisions on laws, prohibitions and economic instruments. It was therefore important that state politicians took responsibility for a change: what was technically possible must also become politically possible (Azar, 2007, 2008). In the same vein, other researchers called on the government to start pushing for progressive climate politics and wondered which other country might take the lead if Sweden, with its almost unique conditions, did not take action. They wondered what the government was waiting for (Berggren et al., 2007).

The reasons given as to why Sweden should be the leader in combating global climate change varied depending on who was speaking. Several environmental organizations, plus editorials in *Expressen*, stated that the citizenry demanded political action. The Swedish Church, the SSNC, the Swedish United Nations Association and other individual environmental commentators argued that global justice and Sweden's ecological debt demanded it. Researchers and individual politicians argued that the country's economic, technological, geographical and demographic conditions allowed and encouraged it. What they all agreed on was the seriousness of the threat and the need for rapid and effective action. It was irresponsible to wait and see what actions other countries took. The Swedish government urgently needed to walk the talk on climate change.

When will the real Sweden stand up?

Representatives of the SSNC, the WWF Climate Campaign, all three opposition parties, the Swedish Church, the Swedish United Nations Association and a long list of individual environmental commentators all declared that Sweden had an obligation to really show that ambitious climate political objectives were feasible. (e.g. Axelsson, 2008a, 2008b; Ekman, 2008; Wetterstrand and Wijkman, 2008). The SSNC concluded: "We need to do more here at home, while at the same time putting more resources into technology transfer to developing countries. We cannot avoid the home-work because only this will show a good example of how it is possible to combine rich welfare with very low greenhouse gas emissions" (Axelsson, 2007).

What was it that the critics thought should be done? The SSNC, the Red Cross, the Swedish Church and the Swedish United Nations Association began by lobbying for substantial reductions in Sweden's greenhouse gases. Emission reductions were neither to be pushed on to future generations or other countries. They demanded a reduction of 40 per cent, compared to 2010 levels, by the year 2020. The government was subjected to extensive criticism for its reluctance to take sufficiently ambitious measures in order to reduce domestic emissions. The SSNC argued repeatedly that such a goal was not only necessary, but also feasible "without major financial sacrifices". In the spring of 2008, the SSNC, the Swedish Church and the Swedish United Nations Association circulated a petition containing this requirement with an explicit call to Sweden's politicians to accept their responsibilities. Meanwhile, Climate Action was formed with the express purpose of putting pressure on politicians to lower Swedish emissions by 4 per cent a year (Westerberg, 2007; Wejryd et al., 2007). The political opposition joined the demand for a 40 per cent domestic reduction by 2020 (Ohly et al., 2008). Second, the Green Keynesian discourse was founded on the knowledge that fundamental changes in the energy and transport systems in Sweden had to be implemented. As noted by Wejryd, western societies "have to undergo a dramatic transition in the forthcoming decades" (Wejryd, 2008). The SSNC, the Swedish Church and the Swedish United Nations Association interpreted this to mean that Sweden urgently needed to begin converting its transport systems from fossil fuels to renewable energy, setting requirements for energy efficiency in homes and industries, and changing consumption patterns in a climate-friendly direction. The Swedish Farmers' Association endorsed similar requirements. In a debate article with the SSNC and Wijkman, the Swedish United Nations Association said that both the government's and the opposition's climate politics were far too defensive. Extensive efforts that included the use of biofuels, wind power and solar energy were opportu-nities for Sweden to increase its renewable energy supply by 70 TWh per year by 2020, which would mean that renewables would constitute 70 per cent of the energy consumed in a year. Along with the Swedish tenants association

for savings and construction (HSB) and the Swedish organization for collaboration between tenant associations (Riksbyggen), the SSNC also campaigned for a climate-related property tax to encourage conversion to
renewable energy sources. At that time, the SSNC aligned itself with a large
number of influential organizations in order to launch concrete proposals
and marshal public opinion in order to convince politicians that the proposed changes to the infrastructure in Sweden were desirable, feasible and
necessary (e.g. Pettersson et al., 2009; Axelsson et al., 2008a).

The demands of the SSNC were similar to those proposed by the Green
Party. Sweden, it said, must undergo a "gigantic" change. Green Party members
declared on several occasions that this transition required investment in
renewable energy, energy efficiency, public transport, high-speed trains and
extensive renovations of apartment buildings. Along with the opposition
parties they declared that it was time to demand a restructuring of Swedish
industry that was oriented in a climate-friendly direction. It would be in the
industry's interest to initiate emission reductions immediately (Wetterstrand
and Svensson Smith, 2008; Gröning, 2008). The Social Democrats also presented similar ideas to those of the Green Party, but chose instead to list
concrete proposals for rebuilding society. The Social Democrats presented
127 proposals for reducing greenhouse gas emissions in Sweden, none of
which would jeopardize employment (Hulthén and Messing, 2007; Karlsson
et al., 2008).

Time and again Green Party spokesperson Karin Svensson Smith accused
the Liberal–Conservative government of increasing car traffic by building
new roads instead of making the transportation system more climate friendly
(i.e. through increased use of public transport). They said the government's
costly and carbon dioxide generating road construction projects were solutions from a bygone era. Subsidizing cars and investing 25 billion SEK to
build the Stockholm bypass, instead of expanding public transport, in a time
of global climate change, was described as an attack on reasonable climate
politics. That the taxpayers subsidized fossil fuels – in the form of tax
deductions for car trips and grants to non-governmental airports, for example –
was called "absurd" (Svensson Smith, 2008). In the light of climate change,
the Green Party's representatives claimed that their proposal was rational
and forward-looking. There were elements of Svensson Smith's argument
that showed a great frustration with the government's reluctance to think in
new ways. She noted that "regardless of how many facts are put on the table,
it seems nearly impossible to get the Liberal–Conservative government to
abandon its stubborn support for private road traffic (Svensson Smith,
2008). The Green Party claimed that traffic was the most important measure,
because Sweden's carbon dioxide traffic emissions were well above the EU
average and had even increased significantly in the last couple of years. In
their view, the reason for this resistance was that the government did not
dare to take measures that conflicted with subsidies for the Swedish automobile industry, in essence subordinating government climate politics to an

outdated technology. Charging for road freight transport was seen by the Liberal government as inhibiting domestic economic growth. Green Party spokespersons called that stance short-sighted and counterproductive (Eriksson, 2007b; Eriksson and Svensson Smith, 2008). This sentiment was shared entirely by the 59 signers of the petition "Act Now!" when Climate Action was created. As one of their three main points they emphasized the development of a transportation system with no carbon footprint. All funding for new highways should immediately be directed towards the expansion of rail transport and "infrastructure and transport planning that is consistently aiming for an expanded and more attractive public transport" (Finnveden et al., 2008). This was a position shared also by both the Social Democratic Party, their women's union and the Left Party as well as editorials and a range of individual debaters (e.g. *Norrländska Socialdemokraten*, 2008; *Aftonbladet*, 2008b, 2008c). However, no one else did it as consistently, persistently and with such polemics as Green Party representatives. They made it into something of a defining issue for the party during the period.

Third, and finally, actors within the Green Keynesian discourse insisted that infrastructure rearrangements should be implemented through government regulation. Mandatory laws and prohibitions should be combined with economic instruments such as taxes and subsidies. This was the only way to quickly achieve significant changes. The SSNC, for example, called for increasing the carbon tax, laws to restrict fuel consumption and distance taxes for heavy traffic (Axelsson, 2007). The Green Party calculated that climate taxes of at least 30 billion SEK over ten years were needed to make energy and transport systems feasible (Eriksson and Valtersson, 2008). *Aftonbladet* writers also advocated new taxes to promote trains and public transport, such as a "hefty air-flight tax", tough building codes and taxes that favoured climate-friendly housing, mandatory climate labelling and climate-friendly procurement in the public sector (*Aftonbladet*, 2007a, 2007b). Professors Berggren, Jacobsson and Laestadius, who had proposed an "EU-tax on carbon dioxide", also supported this position (Berggren et al., 2007). What united all these actors was their conviction in the need for specific mandatory government regulations. Individual responsibility, informed consumption choices and international negotiations helped little, they argued, unless the state implemented changes through taxes, bans, subsidies and investments in extensive infrastructural changes. No other players had enough power to carry out these changes, which is why a lot of responsibility rested on politicians. What were the politicians in power waiting for? Why did they not use the power they had?

Climate change as a unique business opportunity

Innovation professors Berggren, Jacobsson and Laestadius were among those who argued that a "window of opportunity" would be created if the Swedish government decided to take the lead in industrial transformation, a transformation that would be required sooner or later. With a formulation that strongly supported the SSNC and Greenpeace as well as the Green Party's arguments, they stated:

> To return our planet's climate back to equilibrium is our century's greatest challenge. The need for smart, energy-efficient and cost-effective solutions will over a number of decades be nearly infinite in transport, production, materials, heating and energy supply ... Swedish industry has great potential to be among the winners and with the right growth strategy it will belong to those who are at the forefront.
>
> (Berggren et al., 2007)

A prerequisite for these opportunities to be exploited was that government would take a comprehensive approach to energy, industrial, fiscal and environmental policies in order to accelerate the transformation of Sweden. This would also allow the Swedish economy to be "a winner" (Berggren et al., 2007). This sort of argument was not translated into policy before the major financial crisis and the sharp decline in stock prices that arrived in the fall of 2008. Several commentators warned the crisis risked making the whole issue of climate change irrelevant in the same manner that energy and environmental issues were neglected at the beginning of the 1990s (Olsson, 2008; Von Sydow, 2008). When short-term economic and employment needs voiced by Industrial Fatalism actors led to neglecting long-term ecological needs, it became even more important that the Green Keynesian discourse justified ambitious climate action with economic arguments. In late 2008, a number of Social Democrats began to argue that the economic crisis demanded structural changes; in fact, they said, it created a unique opportunity to replace old "dirty" technology and production with climate-friendly investments. Such investments would address the jobs crisis while also transforming transport, energy, manufacturing and construction in a manner that reduced greenhouse emissions. This would allow a Swedish company to develop climate-friendly technologies for export on the world market. Party leader Mona Sahlin announced that Sweden should invest itself out of the economic crisis and "use the untapped potential of green jobs to save both the economy and the climate" (Sahlin and Gabelic, 2009). In the same spirit, European Commission vice president, Margot Wallström, claimed that those who wanted to lower climate policy ambitions because of the recession were on a dangerous road. The economic costs of climate change only increased when measures against it were postponed for longer. This demonstrated the need for an inevitable shift towards climate-friendly production, and creating "new jobs, competitiveness and growth" (Wallström, 2008). Wallström summed up the situation as: "Investing in climate smart growth and green technology not only solves the climate problem and increases the quality of life, it also strengthens our ability to get us out of the economic crisis" (Wallström, 2009). The Social Democrats proposed a classic

Keynesianism approach to politics where economic recession and high unemployment were offset by extensive government stimulus and investment; this time Keynesianism was motivated not only by welfare or equality, but also by long-term environmental concerns. The Social Democrats were not alone in arguing for Green Keynesianism, as shown throughout this chapter; the Green Party's Peter Eriksson criticized the government for its willingness to rescue banks, while saying no to climate action that could create new jobs. He envisioned "green modernization" of Europe's industries and economies to ensure future competitiveness. The economic crisis had revealed an excellent opportunity for investment in renewable energy, energy efficiency, expansion of railways, high-speed rail and other climate-friendly projects. A strong climate politics could constitute "an engine for job creation and eco-driven business throughout Europe", but Eriksson saw no hint of such a politics coming from the Liberal–Conservative government (Eriksson, 2009a). His party colleague Jonas Eriksson feared that the government would pass up on a "golden chance" for the energy system, which could create more than a hundred thousand new jobs. Such politics would "pull Sweden out of the recession" (Eriksson, 2009b). The tone from the Green Party was remarkably similar to those heard from the Social Democrats. The Green Party's participation in the European Green party's election campaign for the European elections in spring 2009 emphasized this further. The joint manifesto, "A New Green Deal for Europeans", that Peter Eriksson and Maria Wetterstrand tried to win support for, assumed that the economic crisis had created a historic opportunity for Europe to become the "world leader" in the production of green goods and services. What was needed was massive government stimulus, a new green deal for Europe, in order to allow for a climate-friendly conversion of energy and transportation systems (Eriksson and Wetterstrand, 2009).

These political party representatives were not alone in advocating Green Keynesianism. Representatives of the World Wildlife Fund, the SSNC, Greenpeace and Friends of the Earth together called on the EU to use taxpayer money to "support a new, green package that at the same time tackles climate crisis and the financial crisis". Let the recession be used as an opportunity for structural rationalization and adjustment to climate-friendly production processes, renewable energy and energy efficiency, they argued (Gustafsson et al., 2009; Bränfeldt, 2009). Wijkman argued that a transitional programme would give the European economy and the job market a much-needed boost. The economic crisis constituted a "unique opportunity" to begin decarbonizing the economy, he said. Unfortunately, the crisis was handled with a conventional growth mind-set. In the future, another type of growth that did not consume its own resources would be necessary, he claimed (Wijkman, 2009; see also Berggren and Laestadius, 2008). In this way, economic arguments could be incorporated into the Green Keynesian discourse and mobilized in defence of moving energy, transport and production systems in a climate-friendly direction. In this context, the principles of a market economy or system were never questioned, only the absence of active state control of the economy consistent with the long-term interest of its citizens. Thus, in all the voices that supported the Green Keynesian discourse there existed a strong belief that a market mechanism supplemented by government control, public investment and subsidies could deal with all the problems and crises, both economic and ecological. It was an approach used by Social Democrats throughout the whole of the twentieth century, in order to manage the downside of a market economy including housing crises, mass unemployment and economic recessions (Anshelm, 1995). It was now argued that green state politics could also tackle the climate crisis without questioning the entire market economy. If handled correctly, market mechanisms could be used by the state to power large-scale climate-friendly conversions. The state, in fact, was the only player who had the requisite economic and political power to initiate such an extensive process. Only when the process achieved a certain momentum could responsibility be transferred to market participants.

Discussion

The Green Keynesian discourse shared many of the assumptions of the Industrial Fatalist discourse, while also criticizing it profoundly. This meant, first and foremost, that the threat of climate change should be understood not as an isolated management problem, but as a symptom of a self-generated crisis in the rich industrialized world's economic system. This crisis could not be met solely with "business as usual": new technologies, reliance on market mechanisms, enlightened consumer choices and international negotiations. Those supporting Green Keynesianism were profoundly critical of industrial capitalism. Fundamental system changes, behavioural changes and fundamental valuation changes were necessary to meet the threat of climate change. Economic models had to be reformed, growth concepts reclassified, ecological considerations internalized, and a gentler approach to nature developed in order to meet global justice demands. Already Hajer (1995) noted that ecological modernization discourse could be interpreted both as institutional learning and technocratic project. Changes of this type could not be left to the market in the Green Keynesian discourse. They required an institutional learning process.

Green Keynesians asked politicians to take a number of specific steps, such as atoning for the rich world's ecological debt to poor countries through comprehensive reductions in carbon emissions in wealthy countries while at the same time providing aid to poor countries, so that they could develop their economies without creating excessive carbon emissions. In Sweden, this required comprehensive changes in energy, transport and production systems to renewable energy, rail-mass transit and energy efficiency, while using taxes and bans to discourage carbon emissions. The Swedish government was said to be hiding behind the myth of Sweden as an ecologically progressive country and the country's relatively small size, combined with the need for international agreements, helped legitimize domestic policy inaction. Actors within the Green Keynesian discourse also emphasized the importance of binding international agreements. But the difficulty of achieving such agreements was used as an argument to accelerate domestic climate adaptation in order to demonstrate its feasibility: Sweden had to implement its own goals before making demands on other countries. Despite its ambitious climate declarations, the Swedish Liberal–Conservative government, like other governments in EU countries, mainly acted to protect its own large-scale industries' short-term economic competitiveness while meeting emission reductions through investments in other countries.

Actors within Green Keynesianism consistently identified Sweden as a country exceptionally well positioned to implement a climate transition, not least because the country had largely phased out coal and oil from its energy system by building nuclear power stations and burning waste and biomass in combination power plants. Therefore, Sweden had a special moral obligation to use this positive starting point to demonstrate the feasibility of radical cuts in emissions and not to use it as grounds for stating that the country had already done all that could reasonably be expected. The case for climate adaptation within the Green Keynesian discourse was not only based on moral and political arguments, but also economic ones. Sweden was said to be able to combat the economic recession through green innovation and Green Keynesianism, which in the long term would provide economic benefits and export earnings, as sooner or later all countries would be forced to deal with fossil-fuel emissions. International leadership in this restructuring was promoted as a business opportunity of major proportions. In the UK the most visible counter-hegemonic discourse was characterized by Rogers-Hayden et al. as an approach that:

> [A]lthough not rejecting the environmental aspects of climate change, offers an alternative framing of climate change as a symptom of unsustainable living. This meaning implies the necessity of refocussing societal consumption, changing the use of recourses (e.g. seriously encouraging the production of energy from renewables amongst other options) and leads 'naturally' to reducing demand for energy. Interestingly, like the energy security discourse, the counter hegemonic discourse does not necessarily exclude limited new build nuclear power.
>
> (Rogers-Hayden et al., 2011)

Although climate change in the Green Keynesian discourse was understood as a sign of a profound institutional crisis within the economic system that prevailed in highly industrialized societies, it also assumed that the crisis could be handled within that system. Given this logic, economic rationality complemented moral or ecological values, but no alternative to the market economy was mentioned. This showed confidence that it was possible to integrate the ecological aspect into the economic calculations and move the market economy in a greener direction. It is clear that this discourse nourished a belief in a fundamental shift of society in a more climate-friendly direction through political decision-making, and that it was Sweden's obligation to show concrete and practical change.

References

"Alliansen fortsätter att blunda", *Aftonbladet* 2/2 2007a.
"De sjunger för en sjuk planet", *Aftonbladet* 7/7 2007b.
"Bara prata om miljön räcker inte, Reinfeldt", *Aftonbladet* 13/12 2007c.
"Stäng smitvägarna från miljöansvaret", *Aftonbladet* 24/1 2008a.
"Smitarna", *Aftonbladet* 19/2 2008b.
"Vi behöver fler gröna alternativ", *Aftonbladet* 17/5 2008c.
"Handla nu!", *Aftonbladet* 18/5 2008d.
"Byteshandeln var i full gång", *Aftonbladet* 13/12 2008e.
"Snacka klimat med Reinfeldt", *Aftonbladet* 11/2 2009a.
"Syna hans klimatbluff", *Aftonbladet* 19/3 2009b.
"Höj ribban", *Aftonbladet* 4/7 2009c.
"Vägen framåt i klimatfrågan", *Dagens Nyheter* 3/12 2006.
"Rött mot grönt i USA", *Dagens Nyheter* 14/5 2007.
"Klimathot AB", *Expressen* 29/4 2008a.
"Öppet mål", *Expressen* 11/5 2008b.
"Kloka råd", *Expressen* 13/12 2008c.
"Klimatfokus i norr", *Göteborgs-Posten* 18/6 2007.
"S prioriterar klimatet", *Norrländska Socialdemokraten* 26/8 2008.
"Efter floden kommer en våg av flyktingar", *Sydsvenska Dagbladet* 3/2 2007.
"Pengar till skänks", *Sydsvenska Dagbladet* 3/5 2009.
"Världen väntar på professor Chu", *Uppsala Nya Tidning* 16/12 2008.
"Trend och övertygelse", *Västerbottens-Kuriren* 13/9 2007.
Adger, W. N., Huq, S., Brown, K., Conway, D. and Hulme, M. (2003). Adaptation to climate change in the developing world. *Progress in development studies*, 3(3), 179–95.
Åkesson, A. and Werner, C. "Möt den gröna framtiden", *Helsingborgs Dagblad* 19/3 2007.
Alizadeh, E. "Klimataktion lanseras i Uppsala", *Uppsala Nya Tidning* 12/9 2008.
Andersson, M. "Svag svensk klimatpolitik", *Borås Tidning* 28/2 2008.
Anshelm, J. (1995), *Socialdemokraterna och miljöfrågan – en studie av framstegstankens paradoxer*, Stockholm: Stehag.
Anshelm, J. (2000). *Mellan frälsning och domedag. Om kärnkraftens politiska idéhistoria i Sverige 1945–99*. Symposium.
Anshelm, J. (2004). *Det vilda, det vackra och det ekologiskt hållbara: om opinionsbildningen i Svenska naturskyddsföreningens tidskrift Sveriges natur 1943–2002*. Print and Media, Umeå universitet.
Anshelm, J. and Hansson, A. (2011). Climate change and the convergence between ENGOs and business: on the loss of utopian energies. *Environmental Values*, 20(1), 75–94.
Asteberg, L. "Reinfeldt kastar sten i glashus", *Göteborgs-Posten* 4/7 2009.
Axelsson, S. "Grönlandsisen smälter bort snabbare än någon trott", *Dagens Nyheter* 1/2 2007.

Axelsson, S., Karlsson, S.-Å and Stigh, K.-O. "Växla till klimatskatt på bostäder", *Svenska Dagbladet* 26/5 2008b.

Axelsson, S., Wejryd, A. and Gabelic, A. "Vi gör gemensam sak för skärpt klimatpolitik", *Göteborgs-Posten* 15/5 2008a.

Azar, C. "Kraftig ökning av koldioxidutsläpp i EU", *Göteborgs-Posten* 2/2 2007.

Azar, C. (2008). *Makten över klimatet.* Stockholm: Albert Bonniers Förlag.

Bailey, I., Gouldson, A. and Newell, P. (2011). Ecological modernisation and the governance of carbon: a critical analysis. *Antipode*, 43(3), 682–703.

Baltscheffsky, S. "Köp av rätter minskar inte utsläppen", *Svenska Dagbladet* 16/5 2007.

Berggren, C. and Laestadius, S. "Gör krispolitiken till hävstång för klimatomställningen", *Tiden* 2008:6, pp. 10–14.

Berggren, C., Jacobsson, S. and Laestadius, S. "En myt att Sverige minskat utsläppen av växthusgaser", *Dagens Nyheter* 7/2 2007.

Bolund, P. "Kärnkraft omväg till hållbarhet", *Uppsala Nya Tidning* 23/12 2007.

Bolund, P. "Beskyll inte Polen för uteblivna klimatpengar", *Svenska Dagbladet* 1/4 2009.

Bränfeldt, L.-E., "En grön Keynes ska rädda världen", *Affärsvärlden* 2009:14, s 20–26, 29.

Daléus, L. "Rädda klimatet utan att skada ekonomin", *Sydsvenska Dagbladet* 23/12 2006.

Domeij, Å. "Regeringen har inga klimatåtgärder", *Uppsala Nya Tidning* 7/2 2007.

Edman, S. "Varan och intet. Den icke-materiella konsumtionen måste öka", *Dagens Nyheter* 9/5 2007a.

Edman, S. "Två meter i timmen", *Dagens Nyheter* 21/11 2007b.

Edman, S. and Sörlin, S. "Har vi gjort det här?", *Dagens Nyheter* 2/7 2008.

Edman, S. and Wijkman, A. "Våga ompröva tillväxttänkandet", *Svenska Dagbladet* 11/1 2007.

Ekman, B. "Klimatet är ingen blockfråga", *Svenska Dagbladet* 17/11 2006.

Ekman, B. "Det stora hotet är människan", *Svenska Dagbladet* 5/2 2007.

Ekman, B. "Stoppa snarast industrins miljöbovar" *Svenska Dagbladet* 4/3 2008.

Ekman, B. et al., "Vår tids största utmaning", *Svenska Dagbladet* 28/6 2007.

Engström, M. "Syna hans klimatbluff", *Aftonbladet* 19/3 2009.

Eriksson, J. "En radikal rödgrön klimatpolitik", *Nerikes Allehanda* 6/4 2009.

Eriksson, P. "Våra myndigheter fegar i klimatpolitiken", *Svenska Dagbladet* 28/6 2007a

Eriksson, P. "Sverige behöver nya stambanor", *Expressen* 22/12 2007b

Eriksson, P. "Sabotage mot energipolitiken", *Västerbottens-Kuriren* 7/2 2009a.

Eriksson, P. "Stark klimatpolitik ger nya jobb", *Sydsvenska Dagbladet* 19/3 2009b.

Eriksson, P. and Bolund, P. "500 förlorade dagar för klimatet", *Östgöta Correspondenten* 31/12 2007.

Eriksson, P. and Özdemir, C. "Kärnkraft – energi för dem som gett upp", *Svenska Dagbladet* 18/12 2008.

Eriksson, P. and Svensson Smith, K. "Ett helt vanvettigt slöseri med skattepengar i Sverige och utomlands", *Västerbottens-Kuriren* 22/1 2008.

Eriksson, P. and Valtersson, M. "Vi river inte upp jobbskatteavdraget", *Dagens Nyheter* 9/9 2008.

Eriksson, P. and Wetterstrand, M. "Ett grönt kontrakt för Europa och framtiden", *Göteborgs-Posten* 27/3 2009.

Finnveden, G. et al. "Handla nu!", *Aftonbladet* 18/5 2008.

Flood, L. "Bolag slipper betala för ökade utsläpp", *Svenska Dagbladet* 29/5 2009.

Foust, C. R. and O'Shannon Murphy, W. (2009). Revealing and reframing apocalyptic tragedy in global warming discourse. *Environmental Communication*, 3(2), 151–67.

Fröberg, J. "Industrin fri att släppa ut mer", *Svenska Dagbladet* 16/5 2007.

Gabelic, A. and Ygeman, A. "Regeringen vill köpa sig fri", *Östgöta Correspondenten* 29/12 2008.

Grenholm, A. "Avliva tillväxtmyten", *Västerbottens-Kuriren* 21/5 2008.

Gröning, L. "Vi måste satsa ordentligt för att möta klimathotet", *Aftonbladet* 18/10 2008.

Gustafsson, L. et al., "Hög tid att agera för ett nytt globalt klimatavtal", *Göteborgs-Posten* 2/3 2009.

Gustafsson, M. and Svensson, E.-B. "Regeringens koldioxidbluff", *Östgöta Correspondenten* 3/6 2009.

Hajer, M. A. (1995). *The Politics of Environmental Discourse: Ecological Modernization and the Policy Process*. Oxford: Clarendon Press.

Holm, J. "Klimathotet, EU och vänsterns roll", *Socialistisk Debatt* 2008:1, p. 116.

Hulthén, S. and Messing, U. "Klimatmärkning en del av morgondagens miljöpolitik", *Göteborgs-Posten* 31/7 2007.

Hultman, Martin (2010), *Full gas mot en (o)hållbar framtid. Förväntningar på bränsleceller och vätgas i relation till svensk energi-och miljöpolitik*, Linköpings Universitet.

Johnsson, J. "Klimatkampen har inte börjat än", *Uppsala Nya Tidning* 14/1 2008.

Karlsson, M. "Klimatrådets tyckande långt ifrån sanningen", *Göteborgs-Posten* 11/9 2007.

Karlsson, S. et al. "Så vill S rädda klimatet", *Östgöta Correspondenten* 29/8 2008.

Krüger, M. "Kärnkraftens onödiga risker", *Östgöta Correspondenten* 26/4 2008.

Kurz, T., Augoustinos, M. and Crabb, S. (2010). Contesting the "national interest" and maintaining "our lifestyle": A discursive analysis of political rhetoric around climate change. *British Journal of Social Psychology*, 49(3), 601–25.

Larsson, N.-A. "Varför tror vi att vi kan fortsätta?", *Göteborgs-Posten* 1/11 2007.

Larsson, P. "Klimatfrågan är historiens största orättvisa", *Vestmanlands Läns Tidning* 16/11 2007.

Laurent, E. (2009). Bleu, Blanc … Green? France and Climate Change. *French Politics, Culture and Society*, 27(2), 142–53.

Lenas, S. "Klimatkrig", *Dagens Nyheter* 11/3 2009.

Levy, D. L. and Spicer, A. (2013). Contested imaginaries and the cultural political economy of climate change. *Organization*, 20(5), 659–78.

Lillemets, A. "Sveriges verkliga utsläpp", *Aftonbladet* 19/3 2009.

Lindstedt, G. "Vi står inför den andra industriella revolutionen", *Veckans Affärer* 30/11 2006.

Lönnaeus, O. "Efter floden kommer en våg av flyktingar", *Sydsvenska Dagbladet* 3/2 2008.

Lundqvist, L. (2004). *Sweden and Ecological Governance: Straddling the Fence*. Manchester: Manchester University Press.

Lyytimäki, J. and Tapio, P. (2009). Climate change as reported in the press of Finland: From screaming headlines to penetrating background noise. *International Journal of Environmental Studies*, 66(6), 723–35.

Malm, R. "Dags att betala på vår eko-skuld", *Götesborgs-Posten* 12/2 2008.

Mol, A. P. and Sonnenfeld, D. A. (eds) (2000). *Ecological Modernisation around the World: Perspectives and Critical Debates*. Environmental Politics, 9(1), 3-14.

Norberg, L.-G. "Marginella förbättringar räcker inte för att skapa en bättre, säkrare värld ", Västerbotten-Kuriren 28/8 2008.

Ohly, L. "Satsa en procent av BNP på klimatet", Göteborgs-Posten 5/6 2007.

Ohly, L. et al. "Aktiv eller radioaktiv klimatpolitik?", Östgöta Correspondenten 29/10 2007.

Ohly, L., Sahlin, M. and Wetterstrand, M. "Vi kräver 40 procent utsläppsminskningar", Dagens Nyheter 15/2 2008.

Olofsson, S-Å. "Uppskovens tid är nu", Helsingborgs Dagblad 21/2 2007.

Olsson, K. "Miljöns fiende nummer ett", Expressen 5/12 2008.

Pekgul, N. "S måste verka för tuffa miljöåtgärder", Göteborgs-Posten 10/2 2008.

Pettersson, L-G., Axelsson, S. and Wijkman, A. "Sveriges klimatmål bara hälften av EU:s", Dagens Nyheter 16/6 2009.

Reusswig, F. (2010). The new climate change discourse: A challenge for environmental sociology. In Environmental Sociology (pp. 39–57). Netherlands: Springer.

Robért, K.-H. "Pest eller kolera?", Aftonbladet 3/3 2007.

Rogers-Hayden, T., Hatton, F. and Lorenzoni, I. (2011). "Energy security" and "climate change": Constructing UK energy discursive realities. Global Environmental Change, 21(1), 134–42.

Rognerud, K. K. "Gamle Volvochefen kräver krafttag för att rädda miljön", Dagens Nyheter 11/2 2008.

Roos, R. "Kina måste med", Dagens Nyheter 9/4 2008.

Rosenberg, G. "Den korta siktens tyranni", Dagens Nyheter 9/1 2007.

Sahlin, M. and Gabelic, A. "Använd klimatkrisen för att lösa jobbkrisen", Östgöta Correspondenten 20/4 2009.

Sampei, Y. and Aoyagi-Usui, M. (2009). Mass-media coverage, its influence on public awareness of climate-change issues, and implications for Japan's national campaign to reduce greenhouse gas emissions. Global Environmental Change, 19(2), 203–12.

Schlyter, C. "Bli inte lurad av moderaterna!", Borås Tidning 1/6 2009.

Sievers, J. "Sveriges klimatframgångar är kanske en myt", Östgöta Correspondenten 12/3 2008.

Sommestad, L. "Regeringen blundar för miljöproblemen", Aftonbladet 4/1 2007a.

Sommestad, L "Tuffa klimatkrav ska gälla för alla företag", Dagens Samhälle 25/10 2007b.

Stern, N. (2006). The Economics of Climate Change. Cambridge: Cambridge University Press.

Sternlycke, H. "Rädda klimatet – investera i järnvägen", Göteborgs-Posten 20/7 2007.

Svegfors, M. and Wåhlstedt, H. "Klimathot kräver helhetsgrepp", Dagens Samhälle 23/8 2007.

Svensson Smith, K. "Alliansen rustar ner tågtrafiken", Borås Tidning 2/10 2008.

Svensson, T. "Klimathotet gör klyftorna större", Aftonbladet 6/4 2007.

Von Sydow, E. "Finanskrisen skymmer klimatkrisen", Sydsvenska Dagbladet 8/10 2008.

Wallström, M. "Lönsamt att ställa hårda miljökrav", Göteborgs-Posten 12/11 2008.

Wallström, M. "U-länder ska vinna på utsläppshandel", Göteborgs-Posten 28/1 2009.

Wallström, M., Harlem Brundtland, G. and Robinson, M. "En klimatpolitik på rättvisans grund", Göteborgs-Posten 12/12 2008.

Wejryd, A. et al., "Ansvarslös senfärdighet i klimatfrågan Reinfeldt", Dagens Nyheter 15/10 2007.

Wejryd, A. "Skyll inte klimatproblemen på länder utanför Sverige", Dagens Nyheter 9/11 2008.

Westerberg, B. "Regeringen måste skärpa sig i klimatfrågan", Göteborgs-Posten 13/4 2007.

Westlund, Å. "2008 ett händelserikt miljöår i EU", Helsingborgs Dagblad 29/5 2008.

Westlund, Å. et al., "Det går att ställa om Sverige", Västerbottens-Kuriren 10/12 2008.

Wetterstrand, M. "Det går att avveckla kärnkraften!", LO-Tidningen 17/4 2008.

Wetterstrand, M. "Jag ger gärna Reinfeldt råd!", Aftonbladet 16/4 2009.

Wetterstrand, M. and Svensson Smith, K. "Klimatfrågan kräver mod av kommunerna", Östgöta-Correspondenten 28/1 2008.

Wetterstrand, M and Wijkman, A. "Regeringens klimatsvek", Dagens Nyheter 4/3 2008.

Wijkman, A. "Inlägg: klimat", Dagens Nyheter 7/2 2007a.

Wijkman, A. "Klimatsäkra biståndet – så kan vi klara fattigdomsmålen", Göteborgs-Posten 23/5 2007b.

Wijkman, A. "En marshallplan för att rädda miljön", Göteborgs-Posten 9/6 2008.

Wijkman, A., "Fattiga länder lämnas i sticket", Svenska Dagbladet 27/3 2009.

Wolodarski, P. "Kärnkraften räddar Sveriges klimatbokslut" Dagens Nyheter 11/1 2008.

Woods, R., Fernández, A. and Coen, S. (2012). The use of religious metaphors by UK newspapers to describe and denigrate climate change. Public Understanding of Science, 21(3), 323–39.

4 The Eco-socialist discourse

Introduction

During the years 2006–9, all parliamentary parties, as well as interest groups, ranging from the Confederation of Swedish Enterprise to the Swedish Church, identified ambitious climate action as a prerequisite for the survival of industrial civilization. Even the Conservative Party, which had almost no history of working on behalf of the environment was obliged to take climate change seriously. Prime Minister Reinfeldt even described climate change as the most important issue facing civilization. Almost everyone seemed to agree on the fact that our industrialized world was in trouble. The comic apocalyptic dimension of the global climate-change debate could have created a moment in time in which an alternative, green eco-socialism could have defined the future. If the world was addicted to oil (to paraphrase US President George W. Bush's declaration in his 2006 State of the Union address) surely the solution was not going to be more of the same, was it?

The Eco-socialist discourse and ideas of sustainable lifestyles were marginalized during the climate-change debate, in Sweden and elsewhere (e.g. Levy and Spicer, 2013; Blühdorn, 2011). If we take a look at these ideas historically, the Eco-socialist discourse in Sweden began around 1972, the year that alternative meetings were held in order to oppose the UN conference in Stockholm. From 1972 until early 1990, an Eco-socialist critique was influential. At the beginning of the 1970s, a number of Swedish public intellectuals, together with an awakening environmental movement, formulated criticisms of economic growth as a measure of prosperity and nuclear power as a panacea for environmental problems (Anshelm, 2000). A vision of another society was developed and practised; these visions, which challenged dominant modern industrial energy and environmental politics, were seriously discussed throughout the 1980s (Larsson, 2004; Wiklund, 2006). The rise of the Green Party in the parliament assembly, new regulations and small-scale renewable energy projects are examples of this change. It was a "no" to large-scale industrial socio-technical solutions and a "yes" to small-scale renewables and decentralization (Bergquist, 1996; Hultman, 2014b). Thus, in early 1990, ecomodern discourses in the forms of Industrial

Fatalism and Green Keynesianism, and their actors, moved to the centre of the energy and environmental debate: and they pushed the Eco-socialist critique to the margins (Hultman, 2010). Until the apocalyptic climate debate began it seemed as if their suggestions were obsolete; they were almost non-existent in the public arena.

In many parts of the world, Sweden is still thought of as a social democratic utopia (McCarthy and Prudham, 2004; Tranter, 2011) despite two decades of neo-liberalism and ecomodernization: similar political situations to those in the UK, the Netherlands and Germany (Hajer, 1995; Jänicke 2008). Sweden might have been imagined as a country where green democratic socialism could blossom because of its previous progressive environmental politics (Barry, 1999; Dryzek et al., 2003; Kronig, 2010), but interestingly this was not the case when the climate-change debate was at its height. Although the consensus pictured an apocalyptic future if the climate issue was not handled, it was not matched by political action; in Sweden the ecomodern discourse still prevailed as part of both Industrial Fatalist and Green Keynesian discourses.

There was a small group of Eco-socialist debaters who tried to make their voices heard in tandem with scientists' apocalyptic framing of climate change. This chapter will describe the Eco-socialist discourse and ask the question: why did it not gain more attention and influence during a period in which capitalist environmental politics was described as a market failure, even by mainstream economists such as Lord Nicholas Stern? This chapter analyses the green socialist argument in the Sweden's public sphere and discusses why these ideas did not flourish in the way they might have been expected to. The green socialists in Sweden were actually no more influential in the public debate than their opposite counterparts, the Climate Sceptics, as we will discuss in the next chapter.

Placing eco-socialism in Sweden

Even though eco-socialism was not prominent on the Swedish political scene during the climate-change debate at the beginning of the twenty-first century, it has a forty-year-long history in the country. From the 1970s onwards, a number of influential environmental commentators took on the consequences of their critique of nuclear power, global warming and the industrialization of rivers. Their conclusion was that the risks of industrialization were not worth taking. These commentators formulated an alternative vision of a low-energy society. This discourse criticized economic growth as a measure of prosperity and argued for small-scale industry, decentralization and renewable energy technologies (Anshelm, 2000).

In opposition to large segments of the political and scientific elite, initiatives such as eco-villages, labelling requirements, and cooperative wind and solar projects were begun during the early 1980s. Existing knowledge about society's impact could now be translated into practical projects and through creating new kinds of communities. Change initiatives were supported by the growing environmental movement that, together with concerned scientists, questioned consumer waste, the notorious smog in Swedish cities, the demise of forests and the number of seal deaths (Linderström, 2001). The early 1980s saw the formation of various environmental organizations, which joined the media debate on environmental issues. They rejected modern industrial projects and favoured a small-scale, renewable and decentralized infrastructure. On the surface this movement appeared to have a similar approach to romantic ideals and conservative currents that had existed since the beginning of industrial modernity. However, there was one major difference: the green wave in the 1980s not only proposed a recycling of old technology and old values, it created a vision of intentional communities based on eco-socialism, thus offering an alternative version of modernity (Oredsson, 2003; Holmberg, 1998). These agents of change did not shut themselves off from society, but created alternative projects amidst the dominant model. Their models and experiments were part of a significant international peak in environmental consciousness in the mid-1980s (Vedung and Klefbom, 2002). This environmental awareness translated into many laws and regulations, but lost momentum in the 1990s in favour of the ecomodern discourse that came to dominate Swedish and international environmental politics from then on (Hultman, 2010).

Green socialism back on the agenda

One of the first internationally recognized signs of green socialist ideas in the wake of climate change came from journalist and researcher George Monbiot who published the book *Heat: How to stop the planet from burning* in 2006. The following year journalist Mark Lynas' book, *Six Degrees*, arrived in bookstores. In the books by Monbiot and Lynas we find a strong critique of market liberalism, capitalism and big business. Both advocated concrete action against greenhouse gases and direct action aimed at pressuring policy-makers to reduce road and air traffic, as well as the use of fossil fuels in the production of electricity and heat. Monbiot's and Lynas' books were both part of, and an inspiration for, a growing movement in Britain to combat climate change. Their books also had a clear impact on the Swedish climate-change debate. The two authors were referenced, reviewed and interviewed in Swedish journals and in Swedish newspapers by Eco-socialists (Malm, 2006; Jönsson, 2007).

In 2007 several writers and political commentators started to question the dominant strands of the climate-change debate and how the mass media reported on it. The media had a tendency to deal with individual consumption patterns and made very little reference to the economic system in line with the dominating Industrial Fatalist discourse. Political commentator Johan Ehrenberg went so far as to claim that there were no climate politics that were worthy of being discussed. All the while, the government continued to make assurances: "It will probably be all right, you'll see", was the overriding tone. The government spoke about climate change as if it were important, but when major and necessary changes in production, transport, housing and lifestyles were called for, those in political power were unwilling to carry out a real transition. Ehrenberg came to similar conclusions, but used more drastic terms in his analysis, in which he called Swedish practices "fake politics" to assure citizens that everything was under control (Ehrenberg, 2007a, 2007b; see also Berggren and Palmaer, 2007). Proposing new climate-friendly technologies provided an excuse for not undertaking active changes and was seen as an expression of industrial civilization's fundamental self-deception, through which technology had become life itself, even at the cost of the collapse of the ecosystem.

These green socialists argued that it was somewhat absurd to discuss changes in individual consumption patterns, when no attention at all was being paid to the capitalist system that demanded increased consumption. Eco-socialists argued that it was vital that this question should be asked: is it possible, in the long run to reconcile capitalism with sustainable development? (Greider, 2007a). In journals such as *Arbetaren*, *Clarté*, *ETC* and *Ordfront Magasin*, a green socialist discourse was developed that focused on the conflict between capitalism's short-term profit motive and the need for long-term sustainable development with immediate climate action. Climate change was understood as the clearest sign of capitalism's inherent self-destructive-ness (Warlenius, 2007; Berggren and Palmaer, 2007; Forsberg, 2007; Borgnäs, 2009).

The central idea for green socialists in Sweden was that the problem of climate change could not be resolved without creating a different economic system. The critique was directed primarily at efforts made by actors to promote the Industrial Fatalist discourse, which articulated climate change as something that could be solved by technological innovation, economic instruments and international negotiations between heads of state. However, the green socialism discourse also included a harsh criticism of a naive Green Keynesian discourse that said it could internalize climate considerations within the dominant economic model, which was based on the hope of lowering greenhouse emissions simultaneously with economic growth. From the perspective of the Eco-socialist discourse, the two dominating discourses shared a common problem – they were based on a belief in, and practice of, industrial capitalism.

The green socialism discourse rested on the assumption that climate change is a productive force that fosters a change in the pathological growth ideology of industrial capitalist society and unjust global exchange relationships. This perspective grew out of a global non-parliamentary movement that, to some extent, affirmed civil disobedience and direct action. The green socialist discourse outlined an alternative society, not just climate-friendly technology. This discourse was supported by a crew of journalists, writers and commentators who were linked to small, independent magazines and newspapers, new climate activist organizations such as Climate Action and Climax Stockholm, environmental organizations, and individual researchers and politicians. This discourse could be found primarily in alternative magazines, in books from alternative publishers and in articles in the cultural pages of major Swedish newspapers. Throughout the entire climate change-debate of 2006–9, the green socialist discourse remained marginal both in terms of the space it took up in the media and the degree to which it was even mentioned in the climate debate. The only time eco-socialism was mentioned was when the actors of the Industrial Fatalist discourse spoke about the need for economic growth and dismissed everything else as representing a return to an age of earthen floors or horse-drawn carriages.

Economic growth as fetish

In the green socialist discourse, climate change emerges as a sign of an insurmountable institutional crisis in global capitalism. The focus of the discourse deals with economic structures and the operational logic of the economic system, not the choices of individuals and lifestyles. Green socialists believe that the dominant approach to common resources is based on collective delusion and increasingly irrational fantasies regarding what economic growth is and the idea that it must be the solution to almost every societal problem.

The most important book in the Swedish Eco-socialist discourse was Andreas Malm's book, *Det är vår bestämda uppfattning att om ingenting görs nu kommer det att vara för sent* [It is our firm belief that if nothing is done now, it will be too late] (Malm, 2007a). This book was widely cited. He summarized and discussed, in a popular scientific way, the different aspects of climate research, winning recognition for his synthesis of the causes and mechanisms of climate change. With the support of studies on science and philosophical assumptions conducted by American climate scientist James Hansen, Malm claimed that the Intergovernmental Panel on Climate Change (IPCC)'s assumptions were overly optimistic, and that climate change actually needed to be accompanied by radical social change. According to him, it was reasonable to assume that huge shifts in climate conditions could occur when certain critical levels were reached; and that it was impossible to predict when the threshold would be exceeded and the entire biosphere would be put into a self-reinforcing state of imbalance.

Malm likens the human situation to a group of passengers on a bus. They are heading to the beach, just as they have so many times before, to enjoy the sun and surf. Gradually, they discover that the bus is not on its way to the beach at all, but is accelerating through an inhospitable landscape towards a ravine. Some passengers make futile attempts to make contact with the driver, but in the end they have to open the doors and throw themselves off the bus, which continues over the edge. The surviving passengers that approach the edge of the ravine can see the bus in flames at the bottom. Some of the passengers were injured, but they have escaped with their lives intact. In Malm's analogy the bus is "our economic system and its processes" which is travelling at top speed towards a biospheric catastrophe. The passengers have no alternative but to act quickly in order to survive. Even though the industrial capitalist system is ill-fated, humanity can still save itself in order to avoid self-inflicted doom: but there is not much time left. It was necessary to implement system change straight away and it had to be disruptive (i.e. outside of the bus), according to Malm (2007a).

Ecomodernization and the mainstream environmental movement: two obstacles to a green socialist utopia

Another important book in the Eco-socialist discourse was *Tillväxtens sista dagar* [The last days of economic growth] (2007), in which Björn Forsberg wrote that growth was a fetish in the sense that it was worshipped by Swedish society. According to Forsberg it had become taboo to question whether economic growth was compatible with profound ecological considerations, even though it was clear that many Swedish environmental objectives would have been achieved decades before had it not been for conflicts with major economic interests. The "blind faith" that the market mechanism was able to solve all kinds of problems had basically turned Swedish environmental politics into harmless administrative babble. According to Forsberg, an almost religious and unconditional submission to the primacy of economic growth in the name of rationality had prevented critical reflection and meaningful political action, among other things, in relation to the increasingly hostile climate crisis. Within the green socialist discourse, allegations reappeared that the growth of contemporary Swedish society was treated and revered as something "sacred" and could never be questioned. As noted by many it had become "blasphemy" not to consume, and even the notion of a scaling back of the economy was "taboo" (Greider, 2007a, 2007b; Larsson, 2007; Schwarz, 2007). As we saw in the second chapter this analysis is actually in line with the approach of actors within the dominating Industrial Fatalist discourse, who claimed that anything other than more economic growth would send society "backwards". In a major article Alf Hornberg, a professor of human ecology, diagnosed contemporary civilization as: "Like the Easter Island stone statues and Mayan temple pyramids, our machine technology has become such an indispensable part of our identity and life purpose that it must be preserved at all costs – even at the price of the ecosystems that ensure our survival" (Hornborg, 2008). In a metaphor similar to that of Malm's bus, Hornborg draws from the history of collapsed empires unable to reduce their dependence on large-scale worship to more suitable dimensions. Richard Warlenius described this condition as a "physical dependence". The rich world had shown that it is incredibly difficult for it to shed its "carbon drug use" (Warlenius, 2007).

All of these voices claimed that there was something unhealthy, compulsive or fundamentalist about the dominance of ecomodern climate politics (i.e. the belief in GDP growth and trust in technology) in the Industrial Fatalist and the Green Keynesian discourses. They all pointed to the urgent need for a paradigm shift – a mental and material alteration. Climate change had finally proved the need for radical social changes, which had to be be based on in-depth reviews of contemporary society's relationship with nature "out there" and nature "inside", value hierarchies, self-understanding, development logic and claims of rationality. More fundamentally, the green socialist discourse maintained that people in industrialized countries were dominated by a mechanistic cosmology in which life was nothing but a struggle for survival and domination. Nature and people were resources to be used efficiently, and the only value to which anyone could aspire was to have more power to satisfy their appetites. Within this system people had become blind to the natural and social destruction brought about by capitalism and rendered incapable of even imagining that there could be a better form of society. The reassessment of growth was considered urgent. The problem was that market liberalism determined what measures were acceptable and realistic, and which were not worthy of consideration (Lundberg, 2006; Borgnäs, 2009). However, the market liberalism ideology was now faced with a problem that it was not able to solve, and its apologists looked increasingly worried, vociferously rejecting any attempt to take the climate issue as a starting point for thinking outside the box (Greider, 2007c; Gustafsson, 2007).

The actors within the green socialist discourse also accused the large Swedish environmental organizations of uncritically accepting and adapting to a neo-liberal ideology that postulated that effective action on climate change was fully compatible with continued economic growth. From an Eco-socialist perspective, the problem was not only the total dominance of liberal perspectives that prevented vital thinking on measures to combat climate change, but also "an environmental movement that repressed the necessary critique of industrial civilization" (Greider, 2007c). A stark example is the Swedish Society for Nature Conservation's sale of carbon emission allowances. Their chairman guaranteed stable economic growth while reducing carbon emissions – in essence, here was one of Sweden's most prominent debaters peddling environmental measures because they were profitable. According to the author and journalist Göran Greider, this was a clear sign that much of the environmental movement had lost its transformative potential (Greider, 2007a). The mainstream environmental movement needed to let go of its consensus thinking and industry-friendly practices.

Forsberg and others spoke of "the established environmental movement's gradual adaptation to the political and economic growth agenda". The environmental movement was said to have evolved from being uncomfortable and challenging, to becoming pliant and loyal in relation to dominant discourses (Forsberg, 2007; Berggren and Palmaer, 2007; Brandell, 2007; Söderberg, 2008). Contemporary environmental movements had given up all ideals of zero growth and downscaling in exchange for practical opportunities to influence politicians and businesses. This pragmatism undoubtedly resulted in increased access to established and dominant forums for political debate in addition to an increased influence on decision-making in parliament and in the business world, and to a greater impact on civic opinion. This change in the environmental movement had been noted in previous research both in Sweden (Hultman, 2010; Anshelm, 2004) and internationally (Spaargaren, 2000; Anshelm and Hansson, 2011); it transformed the environmental movement from being critical of the system to maintaining the system. This provided some environmental benefits, but it also produced problems for climate change and prevented effective action.

A green socialist world is possible

In light of the extensive critique of market liberalism, the eco-socialists demanded a political paradigm shift. The threat of climate collapse necessitated the development of a political system based on the findings of climate scientists and brokered a vision of another world. In most cases though, it remained unclear what this meant in concrete terms. The combination of enthusiasm, resourcefulness, passion and analytical sharpness that permeated the critique of liberal market climate politics dissolved as soon as a positive alternative was articulated. The proposals were usually only hints and vague hopes, perhaps reflecting the actors' weakness and lack of confidence within this discourse. But common to the calls for a different politics was the implication that extensive changes in the social structure were needed because of the climate crisis, and that this was not something that could be achieved through voluntary, individual consumer choices and market solutions. It required powerful public politics and politicians who assumed long-term responsibility for the biosphere, even if it meant interfering in citizens' consumption habits and behaviour (Skansvik, 2008; Grenholm, 2008). Only party politics and societal regulations could save humanity from destruction, which meant there would need to be major limitations on the market economy (Wilhelmson, 2007; Josefsson, 2007; Froster, 2007). What would the relationship between the state, citizens and the market look like in a society that was able to deal with climate change?

Göran Greider was extremely careful to distinguish between a democratically planned economy and the totalitarian economy that had once prevailed in Eastern Europe. The reason that socialism could contribute to addressing climate change, according to him, was that it had become necessary to think in terms of the democratic planning of consumption on a global basis and the regulation of transport to reduce emissions of greenhouse gases (Greider, 2007b; Greider, 2008). In several articles published in 2007, Greider discussed democratic economic planning. In his opinion it had the potential to introduce the idea of equality and allocation issues into the ecological debate with regard to the sustainable use of natural resources, while providing a space both for state instruments and market mechanisms. In Greider's perspective, international climate justice, the downscaling of consumption and the planning of transport systems could only be made possible through democratic green socialism. This did not mean that he believed that market mechanisms were not adequate to address climate problems, but only that they were not sufficient and that the situation could be complicated if they were not restrained by strict regulations (Greider, 2007a, 2007b, 2007c). He summed up the situation in this way: "Transition programs, even utopian [ones], need to be formulated to downshift industrial civilization to ecologically sustainable levels" (Greider, 2008). The transition movement also started in Sweden at this time. Local experiments with eco-villages, organic food and zero-energy housing were included in a network of transitions inspired by the movement in the UK (Bradley and Hedrén, 2014). However, these examples of localization of the economy and transitional projects did not garner that much attention.

Another eco-socialist explained that socialism in a decentralized form represented a possible solution if transport and production systems were reset (Warlenius, 2007). Ola Inghe argued in similar terms in *Clarté*. A successful strategy to address climate change must, in his opinion, rest on substantial state investment in the areas of transport and energy supply. If such a strategy were identified as socialist, which according to Inghe would be a major exaggeration, he had no objection to it (Inghe, 2007). One of his like-minded colleagues, Daniel Brandell, argued that socialism was a humanistic and democratic solution to the climate problem. All citizens should be assigned an equal quota of energy to expend. It followed that the financial scope for consumption should be equal for all. How this transition would go to practice and whether it would be possible to implement it in a democratic way, he never discussed (Brandell, 2007). Characteristic of most descriptions of alternatives was that the green democratic socialists argued about climate political solutions in abstract terms and in a highly generalized manner.

Localizations from below

Some efforts to depict how a radically different climate-friendly society could emerge and what it would look like were made, however. This started from the idea of a "localization" of the economy. As outlined by Forsberg (see above), the contours of a sustainable social system must rest on the principle that all economic activity that impoverishes ecosystems must end and that the economy needs to be adapted to minimize environmental burdens. The consequence of this was that a number of carbon- and energy-intensive phenomena – such as air traffic, the long-distance import of vegetables, and mining – must end. The economy must return to a locally defined context where the power over production and consumption would be held by members of the local society and not by global market forces. This required circular flows, as well as local and small-scale solutions. This did not mean that national or transnational trade would be banned, but that the needs of the local economy would take preference. Forsberg stressed that a localized economy was more realistic and reasonable and that it also had a much longer history; it was also already practiced by the majority of the world's people. The big problem was how the downsizing of a major economy would proceed. Two complementary strategies were needed: reform from the inside of the growth economy and the development of "pockets of alternative economic thinking" that could serve as good examples (Forsberg, 2007). Ehrenberg touched upon similar ideas when he emphasized the changes made by individual citizens with regard to their lifestyles and consumption in the light of a growing awareness of what was needed. He also emphasized citizens' increasingly radical and democratic demands on politicians to use public investment to make changes to energy, transport and production systems that threatened basic living conditions (Ehrenberg, 2007a, 2007b, 2009a, 2009b)

The issue of peak oil combined with climate change and globalization had persuaded significant numbers of people that shortages in supplies of cheap oil were inevitable and that the only realistic response was a comprehensive localization of economies (Heinberg, 2004; Hopkins, 2008). In several respects, the localization and transitional movement offered a radical alternative to globalization (Bailey and Wilson, 2009; North, 2009). At the same time, it continued the long tradition of grass-roots movements and other environmental–social movements that had campaigned against environmentally and socially damaging practices, or sought to challenge the normative base and practices of neo-liberal globalization more deeply – a fight fought today not least by indigenous peoples. The one eco-socialist in Sweden to actually create a picture of this localized future society was David Jonstad who wrote enthusiastically about those who had already started with the downscaling in "Transition Towns". Jonstad sketched a picture of a future Sweden where climate problems were a thing of the past. In this sketch cooperative ownership flourished and no one consumed more than they really needed. No unnecessary trips occurred and the necessary ones were done almost exclusively by public transport that produced no carbon emissions. The goal of the country's economy was no longer growth but the management of resources. In the cities organic food became a part of everyday life, eco-neighbourhoods became a success and carbon rationing became popular (Jonstad, 2009). This was the ecotopia of tomorrow for green democratic socialists in Sweden during the period 2006–9.

The need for carbon dioxide rationing and personal allowances

A very concrete proposal was introduced by green socialists based on Monbiot's ideas on carbon rationing and personal allowances. Their ideas meant that all citizens had equal quotas for carbon emissions and that any purchases that involved the emission of this gas should be charged to a personal account. If the quota was exhausted, a person who felt the need to make a purchase with additional emissions had to buy allowances from people who had not used or did not plan to use their quota. In this way, a market for personal allowances would arise and an economic redistribution would occur while emissions would be reduced due to the common ceiling introduced by state regulation. The ceiling would be reduced each year and included in, for example, the price of air travel (Monbiot, 2006; Warlenius, 2008). The British debate on personal allowances made a deep impression on the Swedish debate. Andreas Malm argued enthusiastically that the reform was both feasible and effective (Malm, 2006). The idea gained favour in the national climate movement, political commentators and even politicians on the green–red side. Personal allowances and carbon rationing were discussed by representatives from different political philosophies and among environmental journalists (Rosenberg, 2008; Steiner, 2008; Ekstrand, 2008; Holm, 2007; Fridolin, 2006). This idea of personal allowances could fit smoothly with another popular idea: carbon markets. The same actors could thus reject carbon markets as a failure and at the same time propose personal allowances which would make an even stricter marketization of emissions and nature inevitable.

Support for rationing during the Second World War was offered as an example: it was possible to get people to rally together and make sacrifices, and to encourage solidarity during a crisis that called for extraordinary measures. Jonstad invoked George Orwell as well as Winston Churchill when he likened the fight against climate change as mobilization for war (Jonstad, 2009). Others referred to the unification of spirit and morality during the Second World War and hinted that nations must now bond in a similar way in the fight against a new external threat of annihilation (Berggren and Palmaer, 2007). However, it was not just citizens who would have to submit to common goals. In Malm's words, it also required "a political mobilization not seen since Hitler was crushed" (Wilhelmson, 2007). This portrayal of climate change was an exception in the debate, but it was brought up by those who saw the antagonism most clearly. It thus framed climate change as a war-like situation. Climate change thereby mutated from a process rooted in everyday human activities to a dangerous "other" that was somewhere out in the world. The nature of the initial activity that causes climate change – human interference – was accordingly concealed through the use of the statement that climate change itself would be dangerous. This was the logic of the apocalypse; it represented an all-encompassing and universal threat. This was especially prominent when climate change was articulated as a global war against an evil competitor. It was both a desperate rhetoric to get the issue on the agenda, and a comic apocalypse because it aimed at getting people to act. In a similar way as in the classic Greek comic drama, the apocalypse is said to be possible to overcome if ordinary people come together and help each other out (Methmann and Rothe, 2012). What was needed was a massive environmental movement that would exert strong pressure on governments to take action against climate change. If governments really focused their resources on building systems to replace fossil fuels, there were technical solutions. A whole new political dynamic was required along with the active involvement of citizens (Malm, 2007a; Josefsson, 2007; Wilhelmson, 2007).

Direct action and civil disobedience

In his book, Malm called for direct action and civil disobedience. Newspapers in the UK reported actions carried out against companies and airports, which were designed to draw attention to activities that harmed the climate, such as air flights (e.g. Rootes, 2011; Saunders, 2008). Reports of action groups in the UK and Sweden were published throughout the news media (Färnbo, 2007a, 2007b; Hallmert and Hindi, 2007). The Eco-socialists claimed that peaceful civil disobedience carried out in the spirit of Mahatma Gandhi and Martin Luther King was necessary to bring about radical changes to established political decision-making (Chamberland et al., 2006). Representatives of the most activist climate group in Sweden, Climax Stockholm, could no longer accept how the Swedish government prioritized corporate profitability over global survival. It called for direct action "against the capital from fossil fuel industry" to "sweep across the country". They claimed to have both science and morality on their side in the struggle for the survival of the biosphere and for an equitable global distribution of responsibility (Hallmert and Hindi, 2007).

Not all within the green socialist discourse preferred extra-parliamentary methods and confrontation. Many preferred appeals and public opinion rallies to demands on decision-making assemblies and institutions. Several Eco-socialists were involved in the formation of Climate Action, which we discussed in the chapter on Green Keynesianism. The strength of Climate Action was that the network was able to unite a broad and diverse group of people, all with different views on social issues, on the need to raise the level of ambition of Swedish climate politics significantly. The network called on the Swedish government to pressure the world's rich countries to reduce their carbon emissions by 50 per cent from 1990 levels, by the year 2020. Although local initiatives to reduce greenhouse gas emissions were important, the climate problem could not be handled without international commitments that were concrete and binding. Although many people that spoke within the discourse doubted strongly that solutions within the framework of a global capitalist economy were possible, and that international negotiations in the UN would result in necessary emission reductions, they chose to participate in Climate Action because of the need to take united action (Finnveden et al., 2008).

Discussion: Green socialism in the time of climate change

From one way of thinking, the Eco-socialist discourse was marginal in Sweden during the years leading up to Copenhagen. On the other hand, the mobilization that occurred in relation to issues such as climate justice actually had a great impact in the overall debate. This mobilization was not to be taken lightly, according to scholar David Featherstone. The articulation of climate-change politics as antagonistic during the years between 2006 and 2009 was a victory for the Eco-socialists, and worth celebrating, according to him (Featherstone, 2013). The pressure put on the Green Keynesian discourse to more or less abandon a technology- and innovation-centred eco-modern discourse and embrace climate justice could not have been done without groups such as Climate Action, who were influenced by eco-socialist ideas. At the same time eco-socialist visions of the future and changes towards a more localized economy were not especially present in the Green Keynesian discourse.

The eco-socialist discourse promoted the image of climate science as an authority which revealed the destructiveness of industrial capitalist society and compelled extensive and immediate changes in basic economic structures, relationships, lifestyles, transport and energy systems, and forms of production in contemporary capitalist society. The impetus for radical social change was said to no longer come from the social sciences, but from the journals such as *Nature* and *Science*, and from some of the world's most trustworthy climate scientists. Hopes were pinned on an alliance between the global scientific elite and local opposition groups with strong commitments to the global environment, similar to that seen in the late 1960s and 1970s. In the 1970s and 1980s, an eco-socialist image of an environmental utopia, an ecotopia, was imagined and practical work was done to bring it to life. In an ecotopia, humans were part of the environment, economic growth was criticized, a decentralized democracy was proposed and small-scale technology drove development (Kumar, 1991; Pepper, 2005). It was a version of utopia that was created in response to an era of criticism of the industrial modern discourse of centralization, large-scale technologies and capitalism (Kumar, 1987). Eco-socialism's historical materialist analysis located the causes of contemporary environmental abuse in the workings of the economic mode of capitalist production, and the institutions and world view that undergirded its functioning. Eco-socialism argued that environmentally unsustainable development was inherent to capitalism, therefore it must be abolished and replaced by democratic socialism (De Geus, 1999). With eco-socialism, it was argued, people could end their alienation from nature and from each other, which was the root cause of environmental degradation. In the wake of the climate-change debate, numerous practical examples, theoretical elaborations and utopian visions were presented as transition paths towards a sustainable future (Bailey and Wilson, 2009; Darley et al., 2006). In Sweden this type of eco-socialist utopian thinking was very rare. In contrast to an apocalyptic and harsh critique of the current economic system, there were very few actors who appeared (or were allowed to appear) on the public scene in Sweden expressing ecotopian, transitional visions.

What was visible in contemporary political debates in Sweden was mostly an anti-utopian utopianism, a conservative utopianism, in which the claim to pragmatism served to repress its utopian character. The consequence of this was the continued possibility of rejecting challenges and alternatives as "utopian" while placing the ideological/utopian claims of one's own position beyond scrutiny. One argument for the importance of utopianism was its inevitability, that is, by legitimizing the process of holistic thinking about the "good" society, it enabled the content of different "utopian" visions to be brought to the table. The green socialists argued critically against the hegemonic capitalistic system in their portrayal of a future ecotopia. Their description of utopia was characterized by the image of a future human community in which conflicts were no longer present. Utopia does not appear bizarre or uninteresting, but attract its readers with scientific terminology, logical necessity and emotions (Manuel and Manuel, 1979). As Bloch argued, utopian visions of the future and concrete actions for a better world underpin the human propensity to long for and imagine another life. Crucially, however, this longing cannot be articulated other than through imagining its fulfilment (Bloch, 2000). If utopia is understood as the expression of the desire for a better way of being, then it is perhaps a secularized version of the spiritual quest to understand who we are, why we are here and how we connect with each other (Harvey, 2000). Reality must include the horizon of future possibilities; utopia as forward dreaming is not esoteric culturally, or a distraction from class struggle, but an unavoidable and indispensable element in shaping the future. Utopia, in this sense, does not require the imaginative construction of whole other worlds. It occurs as an embedded element in a vast range of human practice and culture (Bloch, 2000).

Green socialists in Sweden proclaimed that it would require collective political action and opinion formation to bring about climate-friendly decisions. This process could be extra-parliamentary and consist of occupations and boycotts, but it could also consist of appeals, mass demonstrations and the creation of local pockets of people who were striving towards climate-friendly lifestyles. Closely related was the notion that the discourse included both strong rationalist and romantic images of a climate-friendly society. The rationalist idea, that the way to achieve a climate-friendly society was through massive public investment and government-planned programmes, actually dominated the discourse. Large-scale government action programmes, comparable to the mobilization for war, rationing schemes and reconstruction that took place during the Second World War, were preferable. Side by side with this rationalist idea was the eco-socialist image of a climate-friendly society characterized by localization of the economy, cooperative forms of ownership, decentralization, small-scale self-sufficiency and self-determination.

The ecotopian picture was evoked only a few times in the climate-change debate by the green socialist movement in Sweden, instead of being offered as the concrete possibility of making another world possible and thereby

putting forward ecotopian visions (Frankland et al., 2008). Ecomodern utopias such as an "eco-efficient economy" or a "low-carbon economy" flourished in the Industrial Fatalist and Green Keynesian discourses and as a
result the eco-socialists in Sweden lost their opportunity. They could have
used the occasion to describe the pockets of transitions that were already
occurring internationally (Doherty and Doyle, 2007; Woods, 2007) or in
Sweden (Bradley and Hedrén, 2014). One example that could have been
cited and described was that of the Mondragon collectives in the Basque
region of northern Spain. They started in the 1950s, founded on the principles and inspiration of Robert Owen. They produce goods and services for
the international market such as automobile components, white goods and
food products, and run many other diverse enterprises. They support their
own collectives, servicing these with community banks, education and
training, and producing an independent infrastructure (social security, health
and housing). And there is also a global network of associated cooperatives.
The Mondragon Cooperative Corporation's principles include the subordinate
nature of capital and the appropriation of the surplus for the community
and the workers (Morrison, 1991). Examples of other small-scale alternative
localized forms could also have been presented, such as "rural social enterprises" (Johanisova, 2005). Additionally, there are examples of community
cooperatives that own village shops or small industries such as an apple-juice
manufacturing plant (Imhoff, 1996). Different practices of ethical community
banks (supporting, for instance, community-sponsored farms and farmers
markets that sell directly from the farm to the consumer) and local curren-
cies could also have been described (Aldridge et al., 2001). Or why not talk
about ecopreneurs: transitional agents who base their business on ecological,
holistic values? (Hultman, 2014b.)

Why then is the green socialist movement in Sweden lacking the utopian
energy and eagerness to show concrete positive examples of an ecotopian
nature? We think there are many answers to that question, but two of them
might be more important than the others. First there is Sweden's self-
understanding as an environmental frontrunner, which delimits the possibility
of radical critique in the public sphere. Ever since the UN Conference on
the Human Environment in 1972, Sweden has been thought of as a country
that takes extra care of its environment and has the mind-set that nature
comes first. If it has ever been true, it is certainly not true today, according
to the analysis of environmental goals that Sweden fails to meet, or the rise
of carbon dioxide emissions from a consumption-based society (Lidskog and
Elander, 2012; Hysing, E., 2014).

Second, there is the Swedish self-understanding as a socialist, or at least, a
social democratic country (Boréus, 1997; Ryner, 2004). This idea is also
pervasive because it hinders Swedish citizens to act according to their values.
In the environmental field, citizens in Sweden are aware of the great challenges that climate change poses for society, yet little action is taken and the
Liberal–Conservative government was once again elected in 2010. When all

different political parties claim that they take climate change seriously and work to lower emissions, there is not much room for critical voices.

What is needed in Sweden, and all over the industrialized world, is a socialist commitment to the ecological crisis that combines a critical analysis of the socially and environmentally destructive imperatives of globalized capitalism with a utopian vision of the future, while being presented with the use of concrete examples (Prugh et al., 2000). Such a vision of the future should be self-confident and built upon realistic and proven examples of alternatives to a much greater extent than the green socialists in Sweden have been prepared to consider. Such a vision calls not merely for more of what we have at present but also affirms values for all of humanity, which are only seen in transitional pockets under the present regime. To take the example of "Transition Towns", it is not only necessary to expose and attack the exploitation and destruction of the existing social order: it is necessary to provide a captivating, workable, practical alternative to the consumerism of the affluent to which most people in the world now aspire, and to justify this alternative with examples that are already up and running. Ultimately, the struggle to create an ecological socialist economy will be determined by the ability of its proponents to create a culture superior to that of capitalist societies.

References

Aldridge, T., Tooke, J., Lee, R., Leyshon, A., Thrift, N. and Williams, C. (2001). Recasting work: the example of local exchange trading schemes. *Work, Employment and Society* 15(3), 565–79.

Anshelm, J. (2000). *Mellan frälsning och domedag. Om kärnkraftens politiska idéhistoria i Sverige 1945–99.* Stockholm Symposium.

Anshelm, J. (2004). *Det vilda, det vackra och det ekoloiskt hållbara. Om opinionsbildningen i Svenska Naturskyddsföreningens tidskrift Sveriges Natur 1943–2002,* Institutionen för historiska studier, Umeå Universitet.

Anshelm, J. and Hansson, A. (2011). Climate change and the convergence between ENGOs and business: on the loss of utopian energies. *Environmental Values, 20*(1), 75–94.

Bailey, I. and Wilson, G. A. (2009). Theorising transitional pathways in response to climate change: technocentrism, ecocentrism, and the carbon economy. *Environment and planning. A, 41*(10), 2324.

Barry, J. (1999). *Rethinking Green Politics.* London: Sage Publications.

Berggren, J. and Palmaer, A. "Klimatångest, Om koldioxidens effekt på vår mentala hälsa", *Ordfront magasin* 2007:12.

Bergquist, M. (1996). *En utopi i verkligheten.* Etnologiska Föreningen i Väst-Sverige.

Bloch, E. (2000). *The Spirit of Utopia.* California: Stanford University Press.

Blühdorn, I. (2011). The politics of unsustainability: COP15, post-ecologism, and the ecological paradox. *Organization & Environment, 24*(1), 34–53.

Boréus, K. (1997). The shift to the right: Neo-liberalism in argumentation and language in the Swedish public debate since 1969. *European Journal of Political Research, 31*(3), 257–86.

Borgnäs, K. "För en ekonomi bortom tillväxtjakten", *Tiden* 2009:6, s 16–19.

Bradley, K. and Hedrén, J. (2014). Utopian thought in the making of green futures. In Bradley, K. & Hedrén, J. (eds) *Green Utopianism: Perspectives, politics and micro-practices*. New York: Routledge.

Brandell, D. "Klimathotet: Hur ska vi hinna rädda klotet?", *Röda rummet* 2007:3, 7–11.

Chamberland, A. et al. "Civil olydnad kan rädda klimatet", *Göteborgs-Posten* 14/11 2006.

Darley, J., Room, D. and Rich, C., (2006). *Relocalise Now! Getting Ready for Climate Change and the End of Cheap Oil*. Post Carbon Institute/New Society Publishers.

De Geus, M. (1999). *Ecological Utopias: Envisioning the Sustainable Society*. Utrecht: International.

Doherty, B. and Doyle, T. (2007). *Beyond Borders: Environmental Movements and Transnational Politics*. London: Routledge.

Dryzek, J. S., Downes, D., Hunold, C., Schlosberg, D. and Hernes, H. K. (2003). *Green States and Social Movements: Environmentalism in the United States, United Kingdom, Germany, and Norway*. Oxford University Press.

Ehrenberg, J. "Det är nu vi måste agera", *Dagens ETC* 2007a: 44, 12–15.

Ehrenberg, J. "Vill inte borgare rädda miljön?", *Dagens ETC* 2007b:8, 12–14.

Ehrenberg, J. "Medan klimatet skenar gör politikerna – ingenting", *Dagens ETC* 2007c:49, 12–13.

Ehrenberg, J. "Kan krigsekonomi rädda världen?", *Dagens ETC* 2009a:39, 30–33.

Ehrenberg, J. "Ekonomens våta dröm", *Dagens ETC* 2009b:44, 28–31.

Ekstrand, L. "Smarta val kan löna sig", *Göteborgs-Posten* 18/4 2008.

Färnbo, M. "Nyväckt motstånd mot marknadslösningar", *Arbetaren* 2007a.

Färnbo, M. "Vem kämpar för klimatet?", *Arbetaren* 2007b.

Featherstone, D. (2013). The contested politics of climate change and the crisis of neo-liberalism. *ACME: An International E-Journal for Critical Geographies*, 12(1).

Finnveden, G. et al. "Handla nu!", *Aftonbladet* 18/5 2008.

Forsberg, B. (2007). *Tillväxtens sista dagar*, Stockholm: Ruin.

Frankland, E. G., Lucardie, P. and Rihoux, B. (eds). (2008). *Green parties in transition: the end of grass-roots democracy?* Ashgate Publishing, Ltd.

Fridolin, G. "Inga änglar väntar i framtiden", *Arbetaren* 2006:48, 14–15.

Froster, A. "Mot klimatkaos i första klass", *Arbetaren* 2007:17, 12–13.

Greider, G. "Naturen som marknadsplats", *Dagens Nyheter* 25/4 2007c.

Greider, G. "Sosseklimat", *Dagens Nyheter* 12/2 2007b.

Greider, G. "Varan som varat", *Dagens Nyheter* 9/5 2007a.

Greider, G. "Ökad tillväxt och ökad lycka följs inte längre åt", *Fliluftsliv* 2008:4.

Grenholm, A. "Avliva tillväxtmyten", *Västerbottens-Kuriren* 21/5 2008.

Gustafsson, L. "Liberalt vägskäl", *Expressen* 17/12 2007.

Hajer, M. A. (1995). *The Politics of Environmental Discourse: Ecological modernization and the policy process*. Oxford: Clarendon Press.

Hallmert, A. and Hindi, N. "In med flygplanen i hangarerna", *Arbetaren* 2007:17.

Harvey, D. (2000). *Spaces of Hope*. Edinburgh: Edinburgh University Press.

Heinberg, R., (2004). *Powerdown: Options and Actions for a Post-Carbon World*. Gabriola Island: New Society Publishers.

Holm, J. "Ransonering steg mot klimaträttvisa", *Arbetaren* 28/11 2007.

Holmberg, C. (1998). *Längtan till landet – Civilisationskritik och framtidsvisioner i 1970-talets regionalpolitiska debatt*. Göteborgs universitet, Historiska institutionen. Göteborg.

Hopkins, R., (2008). *The Transition Handbook: From Oil Dependency to Local Resilience.* Dartington: Green Books.

Hornborg, A. "Den vite konsumentens börda", *Dagens Nyheter* 28/1 2008.

Hultman, M. (2010). *Full gas mot en (o)hållbar framtid. Förväntningar på bränsleceller och vätgas i relation till svensk energi-och miljöpolitik.* Linköpings Universitet.

Hultman, M. (2014a). Ecopreneurship within planetary boundaries: Innovative practice, transitional territorialisation's and green-green values. Paper at *Transitional green entrepreneurs: Re-thinking ecopreneurship for the 21st century.* Symposium at Umeå University June 3rd – 5th, 2014.

Hultman, M. (2014b). Transition Delayed. The 1980s Ecotopia of a Decentralized Renewable Energy Systems. In Bradley, K. and Hedrén, J. (eds) *Green Utopianism: Perspectives, Politics and Micro Practices.* London: Routledge.

Hysing, E. (2014). A green star fading? A critical assessment of Swedish environmental policy change. *Environmental Policy and Governance,* 24(4), 262–74.

Imhoff, D. (1996). Community supported agriculture. In Mander, J. and Goldsmith, E. (eds), *The case against the global economy: And for a turn towards the local* (pp. 425–33). San Francisco: Sierra Club Books.

Inghe, O. (2007). "Medan marknaden pumpar på", *Clarté* 3: 10–23.

Johanisova, N. (2005). *Living in the Cracks.* Bideford: Green Books.

Jonstad, D. (2009). *Vår beskärda del. En lösning på klimatkrisen,* Stockholm: Ordfront.

Josefsson, E. "Ekonomin måste ställas om", *Västerbottens-Kuriren* 20/12 2007.

Jänicke, M. (2008). Ecological modernisation: New perspectives. *Journal of Cleaner Production,* 16(5), 557–65.

Jönsson, D. "Grader i helvetet", *Dagens Nyheter* 8/3 2007.

Kronig, J. (2010). *Climate Change: The challenge for social democracy.* London: Policy Network.

Kumar, K. (1987). *Utopia and Anti-Utopia in Modern Times.* Oxford: Basil Blackwell.

Kumar, K. (1991). *Utopianism.* London: Open University Press.

Larsson, J. (2004). *Aiming for Change. Intentional Communities and Ideology in Function.* Örebro: Örebro Studies in Political Science 12.

Larsson, N.-A. "Vi borde vara rädda att flyga", *Göteborgs-Posten* 7/11 2006.

Larsson, N.-A. "Varför tror vi att vi kan fortsätta?", *Göteborgs-Posten* 1/11 2007.

Levy, D. L. and Spicer, A. (2013). Contested imaginaries and the cultural political economy of climate change. *Organization,* 20(5), 659–78.

Lidskog, R. and Elander, I. (2012). Ecological modernization in practice? The case of sustainable development in Sweden. *Journal of Environmental Policy & Planning,* 14(4), 411–27.

Linderström, M. (2001). *Industrimoderniteten och miljöfrågans utmaningar. En analys av LO, SAF, Industriförbundet och miljöpolitiken 1965–2000.* Linköpings Universitet.

Lundberg, B. "Vem bryr sig?", *Borås Tidning* 19/11 2006.

Malm, A. "Klimatets politik", *Dagens Nyheter* 13/11 2006.

Malm, A. (2007a). *Det är vår bestämda uppfattning att om ingenting görs nu kommer det att vara för sent,* Atlas.

Malm, A. "Framtiden är redan här", *Arbetaren* 2007b:51/52, bilaga 16–19.

Malm, A. "Miljömärkta avlatsbrev", *Dagens Nyheter* 17/4 2007c.

Manuel, F. E. and Manuel, F. P. (1979). *Utopian Thought in the Western World.* Cambridge: The Belking Press.

McCarthy, J. and Prudham, S. (2004). Neoliberal nature and the nature of neoliberalism. *Geoforum* 35(3), 275–83.

Methmann, C. and Rothe, D. (2012). Politics for the day after tomorrow: The logic of apocalypse in global climate politics. *Security Dialogue*, 43(4), 323–344.

Monbiot, G. (2006). *Heat: How we can stop the planet burning*. Penguin UK.

Morrison, R. (1991). *We Build the Road We Travel: Mondragon, a Cooperative Social System*. Santa Cruz: New Society Publishers.

North, P. (2009). Eco-localisation as a progressive response to peak oil and climate change – a sympathetic critique. *Geoforum*, 41(4), 585–94.

Oredsson, S (2003). *Svensk oro – offentlig fruktan under 1900-talets senare hälft*. Lund: Nordic Academic Press.

Pepper, D. (2005). "Utopianism and Environmentalism". *Environmental Politics*, 14(1), 3–22.

Prugh, T., Constanza, R. and Daley, H. (2000). *The Local Politics of Global Sustainability*. Washington, DC: Island Press.

Rootes, C., (2011). New issues, new forms of action? Climate change and environmental activism in Britain. In Van Deth J.W. and Maloney, W. (eds) *New Participatory Dimensions in Civil Society: Professionalization and individualized collective action*, pp.46–68. London: Routledge/ECPR.

Rosenberg, Göran. "Jordens ranson", *Dagens Nyheter* 9/1 2008.

Ryner, J. M. (2004). Neo-liberalization of social democracy: the Swedish case. *Comparative European Politics*, 2(1), 97–119.

Saunders, C., (2008). The stop climate chaos coalition: climate change as a development issue. *Third World Quarterly*, 29 (8), 1509–26.

Schwarz, N. "Polarisering", *Expressen* 2/11 2007.

Skansvik, P. "Den omöjliga ekvationen", *Borås Tidning* 4/4 2008.

Söderberg, B. "Ekonomisk tillväxt ett större hot mot klimatet", *Göteborgs-Posten* 19/5 2008.

Spaargaren, G. (2000). Ecological modernization theory and the changes discourse on environment and modernity. In Spaargen, G., Morland, A.P.J. and Buttel, F.H. (eds) *Environment and Global Modernity*, London: Sage.

Steiner, M.-L. "Utsläppsrätter kan rädda miljön", *Helsingborgs Dagblad* 22/2 2008.

Tranter, B. (2011). Political divisions over climate change and environmental issues in Australia. *Environmental Politics*, 20(1), 78–96.

Vedung, E. and Klefbom, E. (2002). *Ozonhålet globalt, nationellt, lokalt*, Stockholm: Liber.

Warlenius, R. "Klimatets politiska ekonomi: klimatet och kapitalet", *Arbetaren* 2007:17.

Warlenius, R. (2008). *Utsläpp och rättvisa*. Stockholm: Cogito.

Wiklund, M. (2006). *I det modernas landskap: historisk orientering och kritiska berättelser om det moderna Sverige mellan 1960 och 1990*. Stockholm: Östlings bokförlag Symposion.

Wilhelmson, M. "Besatt av klimatfrågan", *Dagens Nyheter* 4/11 2007.

Woods, M. (2007). Engaging the global countryside: globalization, hybridity and the reconstitution of rural place. *Progress in Human Geography* 31(4), 485–507.

5   The Climate Sceptic discourse

Introduction

From the autumn of 2006 until 2009, climate change was communicated globally as a matter of apocalyptic dimensions. The dominant Industrial Fatalist discourse and the Green Keynesian discourse accepted climate worries as explained by science while promising that existing institutions, new technology and the economic system would be able to adjust to the challenges ahead. The Industrial Fatalist discourse and Green Keynesianism dominated the public sphere as their Eco-socialist counterpart was marginalized. What the three discourses agreed on was the seriousness of the situation: its presentation as a comic apocalyptic framing was part of all the discourses. Even those known as Climate Sceptics, who we will analyse in this chapter, claimed it was an issue of civilizational dimensions. But they had a completely different view of what this apocalypse looked like.

There was a small group of Climate Sceptics in the public sphere who did not agree with the majority of scientists regarding the anthropogenic cause of climate change, or the need to expedite drastic changes in Western society. This small group, with only one exception, consisted of elderly men with influential positions in academia or large private companies. In this chapter, we discuss how they described themselves as marginalized, banned and oppressed dissidents who felt compelled to speak against a faith-based belief in climate science. This discourse was characterized by strong beliefs in a market society, a great mistrust of government regulation, and a sturdy belief in engineering and rational natural science. With inspiration from gender studies we contend that the Climate Sceptic discourse in Sweden can be understood as being intertwined with a – currently declining – masculinity found in industrial modernity. Another important element in the discourse was the salvation of industrial society, of which the sceptics were a part, from the values of eco-modern practice. In this chapter, we will analyse the Climate Sceptic discourse, who the proponents were and what they argued. By using a gender analysis of Climate Scepticism we move beyond the previous research, which perceived this discourse as solely an ideologically-based outcry against science and politics, and recognize identities, historical structures and emotions.

Denouncing the theory of global warming as a scam or a swindle is not a new phenomenon. In the US, and to some extent in Canada, the link between scepticism on climate science and Conservative think tanks has been revealed in an array of studies. It is well recognized that in order to maintain an illusion of intense controversy, industry lobbies, as well as special interest groups and PR firms, have exploited the US media (e.g. Gelbspan, 2004; Leggett, 2001; Rampton and Stauber, 2001; Lahsen, 2005; Austin and Phoenix, 2005; Knight and Greenberg, 2011). The number of Climate Sceptics is also greater in the US than in any other country (Demeritt, 2001; Lahsen, 2005) and rather than humankind being responsible for global warming, these sceptics argue that climate change is all part of the Earth's natural cycle and that arguments to the contrary amount to a conspiracy on the part of the scientific community to gain funding for their research projects. Jacques et al. (2008) conclude that this type of scepticism is the tactic of an elite-driven movement designed to combat environmentalism. The successful use of this tactic has contributed to the weakening of the US commitment to environmental protection. This line of reasoning is also often accompanied by disdain for scientific peer review (Dunlap and McCright, 2010). Sceptics also blame the media for regularly and unjustifiably exaggerating the climate threat, frequently aided by credulous or opportunistic politicians and the media. It is also commonly claimed that climate-change research is akin to a religious faith (Lawson, 2008). In previous research about Climate Sceptics we found that there is also the claim that climate change is nothing to worry about because it might actually have substantial benefits (McCright and Dunlap, 2003; Gelbspan, 2004; O'Neil and Boykoff, 2012). Furthermore, it is said by the sceptics that insofar as global warming does present a threat, mitigating or regulatory action will actually do more harm than good (McCright and Dunlap, 2003). Many of these studies link the US public's lower sense of urgency to the relatively low priority on the national agenda (Leiserowitz, 2005) and suggest that sceptical news coverage may be an important factor in this. One of the most recent published research in the field, by Painter and Ashe, is a cross-country study showing how news coverage of scepticism is mostly limited to the US and the UK, but occurs much less often in Brazil, China, France and India. Additionally, the types of sceptics who question whether global temperatures are increasing are almost exclusively found in US and UK newspapers (Painter and Ashe, 2012). Aaron McCright and Riley Dunlap identify the Conservative movement as a central obstacle to US proposals concerning human-induced climate change, and examine how a small group of "dissident" or "contrarian" scientists lent crucial scientific credentials and authority to Conservative think tanks (McCright and Dunlap, 2003). Carvalho (2007) found that US sceptics have also featured prominently in higher-quality British media, in which they have shown support of a neo-liberal agenda. In research based on Gallup surveys in the US, McCright and Dunlap have found a correlation between self-reported understanding of global warming and climate change denial among Conservative white males, reflecting that climate change denial is a form of identity-protective cognition (McCright and Dunlap, 2011).

Previous research on Climate Scepticism in the US (and to some extent in the UK and Canada) provides a good picture of who the sceptics are and what they claim. Research either tends to focus on quantitative analysis of data sets containing press articles written by journalists or is based on public surveys (e.g. Boykoff, 2011; Dunlap, 2013). Very few studies of mediated climate change address articulated arguments in a detailed and focused manner. Antilla (2005) only assesses coverage of specific claims made by Climate Sceptics with regard to climate science. Grundmann's (2007) work on American and German media is confined to a profile of proponents and opponents of climate change. Jacques et al. (2008) target book publishing, where sceptics have a smaller audience. In this chapter, we make a qualitative, close study of Climate Scepticism in Sweden and relate this to findings all over the globe.

In recent years, gender-related research in environmental studies has become increasingly important. Looking through the lens of gender has revealed different perspectives and has demonstrated the need for inter-disciplinary analysis, which includes research on identity, bodily inter-connectedness and nature-cultures (Alaimo 2010). Gender analysis has, for example, dealt with how women are affected by climate change and how mothers engage in environmental activism (Neumayer and Plümper 2007; Culley and Angelique 2003). There has been less interest in studying how different types of masculinity influence environmental issues. This lacuna is surprising since one of the first studies in which the concept "hegemonic masculinity" was used dealt with men and transitional masculinity in environmental social movements (Connell 1990). Since we are dealing with a quite homogeneous group of elderly men, we analyse their discourse with the help of gender studies.

A group of elderly men with successful careers in academia or industry

In Sweden there was almost total agreement among scientists and politicians that the greenhouse effect was real and that we needed to take action against it. Even though they proposed different solutions, the dominating Industrial Fatalist discourse and Green Keynesianism took concerns about the climate seriously. Climate sceptics disagreed. Primarily, this discourse was created by Liberal–Conservative think tanks and by a group of elderly men with successful careers in academia or the corporate world, with only one female exception. The Climate Sceptics had very little association with parliamentary politics or the environmental movement, but they did have connections with the Royal Swedish Academy of Engineering Sciences (IVA) and similar associations where representatives of business and scientific and technological research met (e.g. for Canada, see Knight and Greenberg, 2011).

The release of Al Gore's film and Nicholas Stern's report in autumn 2006 aroused great interest globally, giving rise to strong reactions among those who remained sceptical as to whether anthropogenic warming was taking place. Industry-related think tanks such as Timbro, Captus and Eudoxa described this new climate focus and the troublesome climate science results as "speculative alarmism", while physical chemist Peter Stilbs claimed that it was "disgusting" (Carlbom, 2006). According to the Climate Sceptics, the fact that it had become warmer was nothing more than an indication that a new phase had started in a natural temperature cycle. Two periods in the previous millennium were cited: first, in the Middle Ages it was possible to grow grapes in southern Sweden, as this was a warmer period in Earth's history; and second, during the Little Ice Age a few hundred years later, Karl X Gustav's army was able to march on the ice across the Great Belt, a strait that divided Denmark and Sweden. According to the Climate Sceptics, both these periods were indications of how natural cycles in the temperature on Earth influenced the weather. The argument was that climate change would happen again and again and was not caused by humans (e.g. Bränfeldt 2006).

After Gore, Stern, the IPCC report, and the general enlightenment in Sweden, the burning of fossil fuels for transport, food production, heating and other activities became intertwined with societal discussions. Towards the end of 2006 and during 2007, newspaper editorials in the Liberal and Social Democratic press even wrote that the Climate Sceptics could keep on doing what they were doing, for no respectable contemporary society would take them seriously. They could hold their seminars and write their blogs, but their number, it was said, was declining steadily (Ekdal, 2006; Avellan, 2007). An editorial in the Liberal press proclaimed that, in conjunction with the Nobel peace Prizes awarded to Al Gore and the IPCC, it was now impossible to deny the threat of climate change (*Expressen*, 2007). When George Monbiot showed in his book, *Heat* (2006), that Climate Sceptics in the US were largely funded by ExxonMobil and other oil companies, the information was used to discredit the sceptics (Lindstedt, 2006). In 2007, the Climate Sceptic discourse did not have a place in the Swedish public debate. But this was about to change.

In early June 2008, Per-Olof Eriksson, former director of Volvo and former president of the steel and large-scale industrial component company Sandvik, wrote an article in *Dagens Industri* in which he declared his doubts that carbon emissions affected the climate. He explained that the Earth's average temperature had risen due to natural variations. Eriksson said that many in the business world and academia shared his opinion but dared not admit it publicly for fear of reprisals (2008). Eriksson was supported by the chairman of the international forestry and pulp company, SCA, Sverker Martin-Löf, who claimed that there was no real evidence that mankind had created climate change. He also expressed his sympathy for the Bush regime's decision not to sign the Kyoto Protocol. The problem of global warming was exaggerated, he argued (Karlsson, 2008).

At the end of June 2008, the Stockholm Initiative was formed. This new network, in which Per-Olof Eriksson became active, stated as its mission: "to critically examine the issue of climate change and highlight its political and economic consequences". It consisted mainly of older men who were, or had been, active in academia or the corporate world (e.g. Ahlgren et al., 2008a; Fagerström, 2009). In the summer of 2008, the major Swedish newspapers *Svenska Dagbladet*, *Expressen*, *Aftonbladet* and *Dagens Industri*, having been influenced by the Stockholm Initiative, opened their opinion pages to Climate Sceptics. At the same time, public radio produced a series of reports where Climate Sceptics had their say. This happened directly after formation of the new network, demonstrating the influence of these actors in the debate.

The greenhouse effect does not exist

The starting point for the Climate Sceptic discourse was that the greenhouse effect did not exist, other than in the minds of certain scientists and politicians. In any case, no scientist could prove the hypothesis that elevated carbon dioxide levels led to a rise in the average temperature of the Earth. The period of extreme weather events, melting glaciers and polar ice caps was reported to be the result of natural variations. Some actors within the Climate Sceptic discourse, such as Professor Fred Goldberg, argued that the greenhouse effect was "deeply flawed"; others, such as Lars Bern, the former CEO of one of the largest engineering consultancies in Sweden, Ångpanneföreningen, and a board member of the second largest daily newspaper in Sweden, *Svenska Dagbladet*, said he did not think it explained the Earth's rising average temperatures (Goldberg, 2008; Bern, 2008a). Against this background, representatives of the Stockholm Initiative claimed that this hypothesis would soon "end up on the rubbish heap of bad science". Members of the initiative went a step further and claimed that it was the result of a "scam", which a large portion of the world's politicians had allowed themselves to be deceived by, courtesy of Al Gore and his advisor James Hansen (Ahlgren et al., 2008a).

A recurring example, which was said to prove the mendacity behind both Gore's film, and the falsity of the IPCC's warnings, was a model called the "hockey stick", designed by American geologist Michael Mann. The model demonstrated that the temperature of the Earth had been stable for 900 years and only began to increase during the 1900s, rising dramatically after 1975. According to Mann, the tip of the stick could only be explained by rapidly increasing levels of atmospheric, anthropocentrically-produced carbon dioxide. For the Climate Sceptics, Mann's model came to represent evidence that the greenhouse hypothesis was based on false grounds: it rested simply on a "lie" that was maintained through "manipulation" (Pettersson, 2006; Synnemar, 2008; Hjelmstedt, 2008).

Climate science claimed to be politics with other means

Within the discourse constructed by Climate Sceptics, the IPCC was depicted as a political body whose reports were politics camouflaged as science.
Ingemar Nordin, philosophy of science professor and member of the
Stockholm Initiative, said the selection and review of the scientific material
was consistent with what politicians would recommend. Nordin claimed that
politics had a formative influence over basic scientific research, and that
scientists who submitted to political censorship and produced politically
acceptable truths were awarded funding (Nordin, 2008). IPCC reports therefore were regarded as purely tautological, as products of an essentially
political body that operated under a "supposedly scientific flag". Members
of the Stockholm Initiative claimed that a hundred "politically appointed
scientists" were faking the supposed scientific "evidence" of atmospheric
warming (e.g. Ahlgren et al., 2008a, 2008b). These kinds of arguments were
based largely on insinuation and the suspicions of individuals and organizations: no effort was made to substantiate the allegations. Regarding the
IPCC's scientific modelling, Climate Sceptics were, however, more likely to
engage in a substantive discussion.

From the autumn of 2008 onwards, the data models undergirding IPCC
scenarios for future changes in the Earth's temperature and climate were the
vital elements in this discourse. The Stockholm Initiative claimed the models
were designed without a basis in fact or science that would allow them to be
verified. Since the models could not be examined, they could not form the
basis of scientific evidence (Bern, 2008a, 2008b). New satellite measurements
were also said to indicate that climate models were based on completely
erroneous data and invalid conditions (Ahlgren et al., 2008a, 2008b). Such
claims have been widely recognized as part of Climate Scepticism around the
globe. Complaints included a lack of integrity with regard to computer
modelling and satellite data, or that natural and solar variability were over-
whelmingly responsible for the temperature fluctuations. The "medieval
warming period" was also cited, given that could not be attributed to
industrial CO_2 (Oldfield, 2005; Dessler and Parson, 2006).

Representatives of the Stockholm Initiative declared repeatedly that
forecasting models used by the IPCC were "speculative" (Fagerström et al.,
2009; Stockholmsinitiativet, 2009). Two influential economics professors,
Marian Radetzki and Nils Lundgren, went further, claiming that the IPCC
deliberately constructed their models "from an alarmist perspective" with
feedback mechanisms to give the impression that significant and serious
climate change was taking place. The two economists also pointed out that
this was not the first time that computer simulations were designed to
demonstrate that contemporary society was on a collision course with disaster. It also happened in the 1970s when Club of Rome models predicted
that the planet's resources would soon be exhausted. According to the

economists these models were totally misleading, and were another reason to cast doubt on IPCC climate projections (Radetzki and Lundgren, 2009).

A green fatwā scares honest scientists

The message that disagreement within the scientific community was far greater than politicians and journalists were prepared to acknowledge was closely linked to the charges that the IPCC was manipulating data. Philosophy of science professor Ingemar Nordin argued that Gro Harlem Brundtland and Al Gore had been fundamentally wrong when they claimed that the debate in the scientific community about the causes of rising temperatures was over. He argued the "strictly scientific" issue was by no means based on consensus. He said that the reverse was true and that "a significant minority" of climate scientists in the world were sceptical of the theory that mankind caused variations in the climate (Nordin, 2008). On several occasions during 2008, the Stockholm Initiative and their allies even argued that "a large proportion" of the world's climate scientists were sceptical of the greenhouse hypothesis, and in support of this, appeals and petitions signed by international researchers were highlighted as evidence. However, references to scientific studies or published scientific articles were rare, and the identities of the scientists who signed the petitions were unclear. It was stated at various times that "many", "thousands", and anywhere from 3,100 to 32,000 anonymous researchers of unknown disciplinary affiliation and academic status had objected to the IPCC's report (Goldberg, 2008; Pettersson, 2008; Fagerström and Thauerskiöld, 2008; Synnemar, 2008; Fagerström, 2009; Bern and Thauerskiöld, 2009). According to sceptics, the "eco-fundamentalists" of the environmental movement were to blame for this situation (e.g. for the UK, see Woods et al., 2012).

The former executive editor of the major Swedish newspaper *Dagens Nyheter*, Hans Bergström, insisted that there were "serious researchers" who questioned the greenhouse hypothesis, while representatives from the think tank Captus explained that even at "prestigious" Swedish universities, many scientists were sceptical, in contrast to "alarmist professors" such as Erland Källen and Christian Azar (Petterson, 2006; Bergström, 2009). Interestingly, however, hardly any of these respectable scientists were named. They were mostly faceless, never appearing in public to declare their positions, with one exception. At Newsmill, the Swedish internet debate page with a reputation for publishing controversial views, fifteen Swedish professors, all men, proclaimed themselves as Climate Sceptics (Einarsson et al., 2008). Of these professors many were already members of the Stockholm Initiative. Among the natural and social scientists that supported the Stockholm Initiative, there were none who had any specific expertise in the field of climatic change. There were physicists, chemists, mathematicians, geographers, oceanographers and economists, but no meteorologists, geologists, glaciologists or ecologists.

To explain this omission they claimed that dissenting voices from the appropriate disciplines had been silenced. This type of argument, which has been analysed in previous research, is advanced to activate a kind of balancing norm in mainstream media and put pressure on journalists to present both sides of an issue (Boykoff and Boykoff, 2004). Because of the influence of the Climate Sceptics and their access to the media, they were able to create a situation in which major media outlets portrayed climate science as an almost evenly divided debate between sceptics and believers.

A common claim was that dissident researchers were threatened by nothing less than a "green fatwá", which forced them to adapt (Bergström, 2009). The economist Radetzki used himself as an example and claimed he could say things that younger researchers did not dare to say, because his academic career was not in jeopardy (Schück, 2009). A further explanation was given by the think tank Captus, which argued that journalists and politicians singled out Climate Sceptics as "deniers", similar to "Holocaust deniers", in their efforts to silence dissenting voices. In their opinion, the Climate Sceptics should instead be understood as in a similar situation to Galileo, who once had to renounce his beliefs in order not to fall out of favour with political and religious regimes (Pettersson, 2008a, 2008b). Lars Bern and Maggie Thauerskiöld stated in the preface to their book *Chill-out* (2009) that they could not thank the many researchers who had assisted them because they might miss out on funding and career opportunities owing to the conformism within "the political and bureaucratic establishment". Internationally renowned Danish political scientist and economist Bjørn Lomborg even compared the persecution of dissidents to the McCarthy era in the United States during the 1950s (Lomborg, 2009). The alleged oppression that actors in the Climate Scepticism discourse endured made them fearless truth-tellers who took great risks when they questioned the dominant climate scenario. They claimed to defy a "green fatwá" and thereby presented themselves as heroic crusaders fighting fundamentalist religious beliefs (Radetzki and Lundgren, 2009).

Some kind of invisible power behind it all

A recurring argument in this discourse was that researchers associated with the IPCC, Al Gore and the UN – along with their Swedish allies, the archbishop, the prime minister, the whole government, the leaders of the parliamentary opposition parties and the Swedish climate researchers – were spreading scientifically unsubstantiated visions of horror. Uncertain forecasts were said to be the basis for alarmism designed to intimidate citizens into submitting to a political agenda connected to dramatic and transformative social change. Alternative views were ignored in the media, as was the message from the Climate Sceptics. "Doomsday prophets", it was said, were given free space to speak, prompting representatives of the Stockholm Initiative to accuse the main Liberal newspaper, *Dagens Nyheter*, of "climate hysteria", saying that its science editorial reporting read like the children's magazine "Donald Duck" (Fagerström, 2008). Climate Sceptics maintained that media climate reporting was, in effect, "brainwashing". Representatives of the Stockholm Initiative claimed that the media had created a veritable "mass psychosis"; others spoke of "tunnel vision" (Ahlgren et al., 2008a; Hjelmstedt, 2008). They offered a variety of explanations to explain why climate science had gained so much ground and had become so appealing to scientists, journalists, politicians, government agencies, citizens and environmental organizations. The internationally renowned Climate Sceptic, Bjørn Lomborg, who sought an explanation as to how this situation arose, found that it was a result of researchers and journalists being "engaged in greenhouse activism" (Lomborg, 2007).

Those who shaped the Climate Sceptic discourse were challenged to explain the established climate scenario's almost limitless popularity among influential states, organizations, and among scientists and politicians world-wide. If climate change was based only on speculative predictions, conjecture, myths, lies and fear, how then did the idea of rapid, radical and necessary climate action become so generally accepted? From a Climate Sceptic's point of view, explanations for this could only be found in underlying causes. What these causes had in common was that they were never easily displayed or they could never be disclosed.

One reason given was that politicians in different countries could strengthen their positions through disaster scenarios and regulations in order to extend their influence over the market and citizens. Using regulations they could control more and more aspects of social life. Politicians and politics were much more important in a society that was facing a global threat and, in the opinion of the Climate Sceptics, this situation provided them with a strong incentive to unite behind the climate story. Another theory linked climate strategy to market-hostile forces who viewed the situation as an opportunity to nationalize large parts of society. Some Climate Sceptics suspected that the so-called climate hysteria was a way of improving the state's finances through increases in tax revenues. Carbon taxes were a new "gold mine" for politicians "to cash in on". According to these theories, the central government, rather than the environment, was the source of "climate alarmism" (Nordenskiöld and Ottosson, 2008; Karlsson, 2008). Some Climate Sceptics also found explanations for the hold that climate politics had over the minds of people and society in psychological terms. The greenhouse effect was claimed to play on the guilt that many people in the rich world bore as a result of the environmental degradation that rapid post-war indus-trialization had produced. Sceptics argued that climate politics offered a kind of collective penance, which had a strong appeal to politicians and environmental organizations, journalists and citizens. It was also put forward that these psychological foundations were likely to include a deep human longing for suffering and privation (Hortlund, 2006).

Climate-ism

Religion was the favoured explanation for the dominance of the greenhouse effect. All over the globe Climate Sceptics projected religious beliefs onto climate science and politicians (Woods et al., 2012). Climate research had been taken over by "climate-ism", a new religion in a secular society. Representatives from the Stockholm Initiative and their allies declared that the political structure had evolved into an "eco-fundamentalist" belief, where myths and metaphysical notions of doomsday, downfall, and the last days became more important than scientific facts. "Climate-ism", according to the Climate Sceptics, had become a state religion. Marian Raditzki and Nils Lundgren accused politicians, scientists and journalists of issuing a "green fatwā" that forced citizens to submit to a "religious truth" based solely on beliefs (Radetzki and Lundgren, 2009). Other sceptics said that IPCC reports were treated as "gospel songs", while Al Gore was looked upon as being "the Pope". Words and phrases such as "prophets", "priests", "fundamentalists", "saviour", "inquisitors", "preach", "spread the gospel", "prophecies" and "penance" were used frequently (e.g. Pettersson, 2008; Bern and Thauerskiöld, 2009; Höglund, 2007, Hortlund, 2006). The abundant use of these metaphors created the impression that man-made threats to the climate were profoundly irrational and taken from a pre-modern world view (Fagerström and Thauerskiöld, 2008). This use of religious metaphors was well in line with Climate Scepticism in the UK (Woods et al., 2012; Boykoff, 2011), the US (Foust and O'Shannon Murphy, 2009) and Canada (Knight and Greenberg, 2011).

The underlying and sometimes explicit meaning of the sceptic rhetoric was that it was time for citizens to free themselves from religious oppression, to use their own common sense and to stand up to authorities. The idea of religious delusions was so common in the discourse that it can be considered a constitutive discursive element, a significant metaphor. It portrayed actors, such as the Swedish Liberal–Conservative government, Al Gore and the UN climate panel, as religious authorities and preachers. Conspiracy theory coloured speculative allegations against a heterogeneous and nebulous group of actors; the enemy motif, pejorative metaphors and the lack of reasoning on the part of the Climate Sceptics did not seem to gain them support. To counter disaster scenarios associated with the threat of climate change, Climate Sceptics articulated alternative images of disasters that they branded as more real, serious and urgent. These scenarios were no less dramatic or doom-drenched. To that extent, their discourse was no less alarmist than the discourses that they argued against.

The death of the industrial market economy

Climate Sceptics agreed that ambitious climate policies threatened to "pull the carpet from under modern industrial society" (Nordin, 2008). They argued that mass unemployment and loss of wealth would force industry to relocate. In the Climate Sceptic discourse there was no room for the notion that ambitious climate measures could be compatible with economic growth. Instead, the sceptics argued that climate stabilization required a radical change in the economic system. Representatives of the Stockholm Initiative as well as several influential Swedish business leaders testified that Swedish industries, especially those that were electricity-intensive, had already been damaged by climate propaganda and that rootless climate politics risked seriously deepening the global economic recession (e.g. Ahlgren et al., 2008a).

Perhaps the sceptics' biggest warning about the consequences of climate-change policies rested heavily on their strong belief in free-market solutions. The Stockholm Initiative claimed that the Conservative prime minister, the minister for the environment and their allies were preparing a communist planned economy, while other sceptics warned of an "undemocratic revolution" (Ahlgren et al., 2008b; Fagerström and Thauerskiöld, 2008). The person who articulated this concern most clearly was the former editor-in-chief of Sweden's major newspaper *Dagens Nyheter*. Bergström articulated a thought that was often suggested, or was implicit, in the Climate Sceptic discourse:

> There is also recognition of the political interests that try to plan gigantic decisions in the name of saving the world. Radicals of various types, trading and market-haters, all those that for ideological reasons feel they know exactly how the world should be organized according to their plan – they will now get information that strengthens their case [...] The open society has its flaws. But the alternative has usually led to grandiose follies at the expense of human freedom, dignity and livelihood. Therefore, there are still a few of us who look with some scepticism at the climate-change motivated enthusiasm for decisions about a new world order.
>
> (Bergström, 2009)

Scholars Christina R. Foust and William O' Shannon Murphy found two types of apocalyptic framing in the climate-change debate: tragic and comic. Earlier on we analysed how the Industrial Fatalist, Green Keynesian and Eco-socialist discourses were drenched in a comic apocalyptic scenario, one in which the ending of anthropogenic global warming created a comic challenge in which people could learn, grow and adapt; the comic version was open-ended. Furthermore, comic variations often presented the apocalyptic telos in a non-totalizing way, again with the effect of amplifying human agency (Foust and O'Shannon Murphy, 2009). Climate Sceptics, by contrast, evoked a tragic apocalypse in which the fear of totalitarian rule and disastrous ideas was bound to happen under a new climate regime. A number of discursive features constituted this tragic discourse: verbs which expressed the certainty of catastrophic effects; a lack of perspective or shortening of time from beginning to telos; and a significant number of religious metaphors and analogies that equated climate-change politics with apocalyptic outcomes. Each feature precludes human agency or frames climate politics as a matter of fate. Within the tragic variation of apocalypse, climate-change politics was viewed as the demise of humanity.

Everyone in the Industrial Fatalist and the Green Keynesian discourses, from the Conservative prime minister to the archbishop, was accused of being part of this destructive movement. This led Climate Sceptics to the conclusion that the most reasonable interpretation of the precautionary principle was that humanity should strive to adapt to climate variability rather than act to influence global temperatures.

A white man's burden?

A common warning in the Climate Sceptic discourse concerned world hunger. Bjørn Lomborg warned early on that costly measures to fight climate change would challenge efforts to combat AIDS, malaria, malnutrition and global trade, which threatened to lead to tragedy in poor parts of the world. Implicit in the argument was that an ethnocentric prioritization of rich countries' problems diminished the importance of the acute crisis in poor countries and that it was not possible to deal with the problems simultaneously. Lomborg declared that warnings of a disaster did not help the world, and so he warned of another disaster (Lomborg, 2007). In this regard, he attracted many followers. He maintained, for example, that money invested in marginal emission reductions in Sweden could have been used to save the lives of millions of people in other parts of the world: this inserted morally irresponsible priorities into Swedish climate politics. Representatives of the Stockholm Initiative further argued that Swedish climate politics meant that world hunger worsened and that human lives were being sacrificed. Climate-motivated investments in biofuel production in poor countries threatened to replace food production and the demand for global cuts in carbon emissions risked preventing these countries' industrial development: both of which would contribute to increased poverty and hunger. The Stockholm Initiative stated that: "Millions of people are starving, lack access to clean water and are suffering from contagious diseases. Ill-conceived political "climate action" has hardly any effect on the climate. However, it can dramatically worsen current problems" (Stockholmsinitiativet, 2009; Thörnqvist, 2007; Munkhammar, 2008; Bern, 2008a). Another ominous scenario described by Climate Sceptics was that "many obvious environmental problems" such as overfishing of the oceans, deforestation of the rainforests and water pollution could not be managed if all resources were grouped together to cut carbon emissions. Stockholm Initiative representatives asked why extensive international efforts would be made to fix "imaginary" environmental problems while there were "real" issues that needed to be tackled straight away (e.g. Eriksson, 2008). This way of thinking was commonly found within a modern industrial society and, in fact, had been a pillar of energy and environmental politics, especially with regard to nuclear energy. This rhetoric demonstrates a typical patriarchal approach in which men, particularly with engineering and/or science backgrounds, claim to have the knowledge to care for an ill-educated working class and for developing nations (Anshelm 2010).

Discussion

There is no such thing as local Climate Scepticism since all actors in this discourse borrow from each other. A limited, homogeneous and elite group of elderly men and three Conservative think tanks articulated Climate Scepticism in the Swedish public sphere. They had successful careers in academia or industry behind them and they had strong beliefs in a free-market society. They deeply distrusted government regulation. A few voices repeatedly made the same allegations. They described themselves as marginalized, banned and oppressed dissidents who felt compelled to speak up against a faith-based belief in climate science. They made a populist appeal to citizen mistrust of the state and the establishment by using labels such as "the elite" or "the fancy people", which created an image that climate policymakers were an exclusive group who had no contact with the general population and were completely alien to ordinary people's everyday lives. In this way, Climate Sceptics tried to create a conflict between the people and the decision-makers: between the concrete, short-term and individual everyday problems and long-term, abstract and global issues. This characteristic of global climate change is found in previous research all over the globe (Dunlap and McCright, 2010; Leiserowitz, 2005; Rampton and Stauber, 2001; Knight and Greenberg, 2011; Whitmarsh, 2011; Dunlap, 2013).

The most important and characteristic feature of the Climate Sceptic discourse was that it completely dismissed the existence of anthropogenic climate change. Doubt was directed consistently in one direction only, which explains why it could be understood as an expression of an ideologically-based "denial" rather than scepticism. The approach to established science adopted by Climate Sceptic discourse was complicated. They showed a strong and positivistic belief in scientific experiments and facts, which they mobilized to support their own position. It was common that the authority of their arguments was strengthened by references to titles in a variety of academic disciplines. In relation to climate science, however, they adopted a constructivist position. Climate science statements were said to be the product of negotiations and a mixture of science and politics in an illegitimate association so intimate that the two elements could no longer be distinguished from each other. Or, rather, climate science was portrayed as having been formed by political decisions. In light of this conviction, statements about climate science were treated with very harsh criticism. Climate research methods, models and forecasts were scrutinized and rejected in favour of alternatives, which largely rested on knowledge produced outside specialized scientific contexts, for example in newspaper articles, in books, on blogs and at gatherings of dissenters. Climate Sceptics exhibited a very high degree of confidence in the scientific system of knowledge production, except when it came to climate: in that field alone, science was seen as politicized and perverted. They communicated their scepticism using religious metaphors. According to the Climate Sceptics, having faith in science was unwarranted, even dangerous, whereas, obviously, having faith in their own sceptical endeavours had to go unquestioned. To take the analysis a bit further, the Climate Sceptics accused climate scientists and politicians of being eco-terrorists who were driven by religious fervour to destroy civilization. Such accusations have a long history. Environmentalism had been accused of being a secular religion for quite a while and this was now being transferred onto climate scientists and science itself. Sceptics attempted to undermine the existing consensus by using religious terms and metaphors. This portrayed scientists as priests, clerics, acolytes, fundamentalists and so on: and it encouraged a position of social inertia, political inaction and even gridlock, which maintained public confusion about climate change and contributed to a crisis in the climate debate. It was possible to conclude that, "religious metaphor provides a means of undermining anthropogenic climate change without actually having to engage with the validity and reliability of evidence" (Woods et al., 2012).

At the same time the Climate Sceptics proclaimed their own apocalypse. They painted a picture of how climate policies that changed the world economic system could mean that world hunger would worsen and human lives would be sacrificed. In their apocalypse, food production was threatened, oceans were overfished, rainforests were cut down and water pollution worsened. Welfare states and a new economic and social poverty among working classes would be a fact if the conclusions drawn by climate science and the resulting politics were put into place, according to the Climate Sceptics. This strategy of replacing one apocalyptic scenario with another was also found in the UK, the US and Canada (Woods et al., 2012; Foust and O'Shannon Murphy, 2009; Knight and Greenberg, 2011).

Faith-based religious rhetoric had a long tradition among industrial engineers and scientists – as the debate over nuclear power demonstrated (Anshelm 2010). In the debate on global climate change these metaphors and wordings seem to be used by every discourse, but primarily by Conservative Climate Sceptics (e.g. for the UK, see Woods et al., 2012). The environmental historian Carolyn Merchant identified a kind of mechanistic and objectifying masculinity that accuses others of religious fervour at the same time as using faith as a basis for embracing modern industrial society. Following the Enlightenment, a separation between man/woman and culture/nature was created, which led to the dichotomy of men/culture as rulers over women/nature. Merchant identified an important change in the organic metaphors of nature which had been dominant until the Enlightenment in Europe and which were subsequently replaced by mechanical metaphors; eventually nature was regarded as dead and therefore open to industrialization. This shift coincided with the rise of industrial-scale operators who viewed nature as a resource: for example, in mining, hydropower and forestry. This separation created a mechanical and economic characterization of nature that helped push society towards industrialization, mechanism and capitalism (Merchant 1994). This industrial-modern masculinity was an important factor in creating energy and environmental politics in industrial society (Hultman 2013), and it was a masculinity that men and women within the environmental movement in the 1970s and 1980s needed to challenge as they tried to create another world view (Connell 1990).

Looking back at the history of energy and environment politics in Sweden, as well as globally, we see that in the 1980s, a clear antagonism existed between an ecological and an industrial-modern world view. These two positions were forced off the scene in the early 1990s and an ecomodern discourse began to dominate politics (Hultman and Yaras, 2012; Hajer, 1995). This change meant that economic growth, technology, market solutions and environmentally friendly consumption came to the forefront and the focus shifted towards emission control. These were values shared both by Liberal–Conservatives and Social Democrats regarding climate change and dominated the debate in Sweden from 2006 to 2009. This ecomodern discourse prescribed that economic growth was needed to support any transition of energy and environmental policies towards a sustainable future. At the beginning of the 1990s, a related shift occurred in hegemonic masculinity from a masculinity of industrial modernity to ecomodern masculinity, in which toughness, determination and hardness were mixed with appropriate moments of compassion and care. The ecomodern masculine character demonstrated care and responsibility towards the environment while, at the same time, promoting economic growth and technological expansion. Ecomodern masculinity, as configured, for example, by Arnold Schwarzenegger, demonstrated an in-depth recognition of environmental problems, especially climate change, while supporting policies and technologies such as hydrogen and fuel cells dependent on fossil fuels that conserved the structures of climate-destroying systems (Hultman 2013).

With the conclusions drawn by climate science and the demand for global CO_2 to be lowered, industrial-modern society was again thoroughly challenged: at least Climate Sceptics thought so, a stand that they actually shared with the Eco-socialist discourse even though their position on the actions needed was at the opposite end of the spectrum. As we discussed in a previous chapter, climate change science was regarded by Eco-socialists as a production force. Taken seriously, it explained that industrial societies needed to be thoroughly changed. Climate Sceptics also understood the situation in this way: that taking climate change seriously would mean an overhaul of modern industrial society, thereby laying bare a historical antagonism between industrial modern and ecological discourses. They assumed that Liberals and Social Democrats did not understand the consequences of scientific findings relating to climate – that the industrialists and engineers currently shaping modern Swedish society would have to change. Since the Climate Sceptics in Sweden were part of the industrialist core and were intertwined with its values and practices, their argumentation therefore evoked dystopia and catastrophe in contrast to Eco-socialists who foresaw the coming need for localization of the economies, small-scale technology and renewable energy. Climate Sceptics, for their part, predicted a society without welfare, without economic growth and on the road to stagnation if climate science was accepted as real. Climate Sceptics were defending an industrial society in which they had invested their whole lives. They utilized their weighty professional experience and titles to strengthen the trustworthiness of this position. Industrial practices had long been influenced by a form of masculinity whose hegemony is today reduced in favour of an ecomodern strategy in which environmental problems such as climate change are handled with a slightly revised industrial modernity, but not an overhaul. For Climate Sceptics, ecomodern ideas were also troublesome because the discourse opened a debate on climate change as a societal issue needing to be addressed by industry, politicians and the public, even though in practice it maintained "business as usual".

In their arguments, the Climate Sceptics defend the rationality and positivistic scientific values that characterize their life's work. Their rationality of domination over nature, instrumentality, economic growth and linearity has been hegemonic in the modern era (Merchant, 1980; Connel, 1990). When we comprehend how progress is intrinsically connected to rationality and positivistic scientific values for Climate Sceptics, it is possible to understand how climate science was seen as an obstacle to maintaining the Swedish welfare system, the development of poor countries and solving global environmental issues. Only through continuing subsidized modernization and economic growth through industrialization of natural resources – that is, what the Climate Sceptics had done their whole lives – could the world's problem be solved. When understood in this manner, ambitious climate politics and international agreements on far-reaching CO_2 limits were threats to civilization equal in severity to the threats posed by climate change. This is where Climate Sceptics used patriarchal arguments and purported to defend the well-being of future generations, poor people and endangered species. They had made industrialization possible and they claimed that they were the ones capable of solving today's global problems.

Even though the actors proclaiming the Climate Sceptic discourse had high status and influence, in Sweden they completely lacked support among parliamentary parties, environmental organizations and daily press editorials – at least, this was not visible before 2010. Neither were they supported by the public sector. Even the most liberal market political parties' representatives distanced themselves from the Climate Sceptics: at least publicly. The only organizations that harnessed similar views were the IVA and the

Conservative think tanks Timbro, Captus and Eudoxa. This may seem odd, given that Climate Scepticism was so strongly focused on defending established social structures and values against forceful and far-reaching change. The requirement for community conservation should not be seen as controversial, and it is hardly the case. But, the accusations made against the UN climate panel, the overwhelming majority of the world's climate scientists and scientific journals, manifest a form of extremism. When these are also accompanied by condemnations of international climate negotiations, the discourse seems even odder.

Through their critique of climate science and politics, it seemed that Climate Sceptics would like to stay at top of society. They argued to reinstall a modern industrial structure that overrode ecomodern politics. However, the Climate Sceptics cannot be dismissed as irrational or ignorant; we need to understand that they were also claiming to save our civilization, based on their world view as influenced by modern industrial rationality, the framework within which they had worked for their whole lives. Understanding Climate Sceptics in terms of a threat to their masculinity may therefore broaden the debate regarding environmental politics and gender policies. The central argumentation of the Climate Sceptic discourse is that prosperity, well-being, progress, "the good life" and employment would be lost as a result of climate politics. It was understood as being at risk because of an elite who betrayed ordinary people; and these social elites could not understand ordinary people's situations and did not care about them either, the Climate Sceptics argued. They evoked the old industrial-modern patriarchal and caring ethics of working for the benefit of the whole population in a common project. This was central in the Swedish Climate Sceptic discourse, an aspect that scholars across the globe have only just begun to highlight and deconstruct when researching this phenomena (e.g. Knight and Greenberg, 2011; Dunlap, 2013). Only future research on global climate change can show if this is something unique to Sweden, owing to its particular historical setting, or if this is something that is prevalent worldwide but had not been recognized earlier.

References

"Ett lysande val", *Expressen* 13/10 2007.
Ahlgren, G. et al. "Kasta inte pengar på klimatbluffen", *Expressen* 27/6 2008a.
Ahlgren, G. et al. "Oseriöst klimatbluffande", *Expressen* 2/7 2008b.
Alaimo, S. (2010). *Bodily Natures: Science, Environment and the Material*. Bloomington: Indiana University Press.
Anshelm, J. (2010). Among demons and wizards: The nuclear energy discourse in Sweden and the re-enchantment of the world. *Bulletin of Science, Technology and Society* 30(1),43–53.
Antilla, L. (2005). Climate of scepticism: US newspaper coverage of the science of climate change. *Global Environmental Change* 15, 338–52.

Austin, A. and Phoenix, L. (2005). The neoconservative assault on the earth: The environmental imperialism of the Bush administration. *Capitalism Nature Socialism*, 16(2), 25–44.

Avellan, H. "Årets ord: klimatförändring" *Sydsvenska Dagbladet* 30/12 2006.

Bergström, H. "Den gröna fatwan", *Dagens Nyheter* 10/7 2009.

Bern, L. and Thauerskiöld, M. (2009). *Chill-out. Sanningen om klimatbubblan.* Stockholm: Kalla Kulor.

Bern, L. "Växthushypotesen gör oss fattiga", *Svenska Dagbladet* 18/11 2008a.

Bern, L. "Attityden är intolerant", *Svenska Dagbladet* 26/11 2008b.

Boykoff, M. T. (2011).*Who Speaks for the Climate? Making Sense of Media Reporting on Climate Change.* Cambridge University Press.

Boykoff, M. and Boykoff, J. (2004). Balance as bias: global warming and the US prestige press. *Global Environmental Change* 14(2), 125–36.

Bränfeldt, L.-E. "Klimathotet – En överhettad fråga?", *Affärsvärlden* 2006:47, s 20–26; 29–31.

Carlbom, T. "Skeptikerna rasar", *Veckans affärer* 2006:48, s 74–76; 78.

Carvalho, A. (2007). Ideological cultures and media discourses on scientific knowledge: re-reading news on climate change. *Public Understanding of Science*, 16(2), 223–43.

Connell, Robert W. 1990. A whole new world. Remaking masculinity in the Context of the Environmental Movement, *Gender and Society* 4, 452–78.

Culley, M. R. and Angelique, H. L. (2003). Women's gendered experiences as long-term Three Mile Island activists. *Gender and Society* 17(3), 445–61.

Demeritt, D. (2001). The construction of global warming and the politics of science. *Annals of the Association of American Geographers*, 91(2), 307–37.

Dessler, A. and Parson, E. (2006). *The Science and Politics of Global Climate Change: A Guide to the Debate.* Cambridge University Press.

Dunlap, R. and McCright, A. (2010). Climate change denial: sources, actors and strategies. In Lever-Tracy, C. (ed.) *Routledge Handbook of Climate Change and Society*, pp.240–59. Routledge: London.

Dunlap, R. (2013), Climate change skepticism and denial: An introduction. *American. Behavioral Scientist* 57(6): 691–98.

Einarsson, G., Franzén L. G., Gee D., Holmberg K., Jönsson B., Kaijser S., Karlén W., Liljenzin J.-O., Norin T., Nydén M., Petersson G., Ribbing C. G., Stigebrandt A., Stilbs P., Ulfvarson A., Walin G., Andersson T., Gustafsson S. G., Einarsson O. Hellström, T. "20 toppforskare i unikt upprop: koldioxiden påverkar inte klimatet", *Newsmill*, 17/12 2008.

Ekdal, N. "I det långa loppet är vi alla föda", *Dagens Nyheter* 19/11 2006.

Eriksson, P.-O. "Jorden går inte under av utsläpp och uppvärmning", *Dagens Industri* 4/6 2008.

Fagerström, J. "Mediernas magplask", *Aftonbladet* 28/9 2008.

Fagerström, J. "Inget dramatiskt med temperaturen", *Aftonbladet* 28/7 2009.

Fagerström, J. et al. "Vetenskapen är inte enig om klimatlarmen", *Västerbottens-Kuriren* 12/3 2009.

Fagerström, J. and Thauerskiöld, M. "USA:s fattiga tvingas betala ett högt pris för Obamas klimatgloria", *Expressen* 6/11 2008.

Foust, C. R. and O'Shannon Murphy, W. (2009). Revealing and reframing apocalyptic tragedy in global warming discourse. *Environmental Communication*, 3(2), 151–67.

Gelbspan, R. (2004). *Boiling Point: How Politicians, Big Oil and Coal, Journalists, and Activists have Fueled the Climate Crisis – and What We Can Do to Avert Disaster*. New York: Basic Books.

Goldberg, F. "Klimatförändring i medieklimatet?", *Aftonbladet* 21/7 2008.

Grundmann, R. (2007). Climate change and knowledge politics. *Environmental Politics*, 16(3), 414–32.

Hajer, M. A. (1995). *The Politics of Environmental Discourse: Ecological Modernization and the Policy Process*. Oxford: Clarendon Press.

Hjelmstedt, L. "Kolla alla fakta – inte bara dem Al Gore för fram", *Borås Tidning* 25/6 2008.

Höglund, E. "Klimatfrågan har blivit en ny religion", *Borås Tidning* 11/12 2007.

Hortlund, Lage: "Domedagsprofeterna breder ut sig", *Norrländska Socialdemokraten* 20/11 2006.

Hultman, M. (2013). The making of an environmental hero: A history of ecomodern masculinity, fuel cells and Arnold Schwarzenegger. *Environmental Humanities*, 2, 83–103.

Hultman, M. and Yaras, A. (2012). The socio-technological history of hydrogen and fuel cells in Sweden 1978–2005: Mapping the innovation trajectory. *International Journal of Hydrogen Energy* 37(17), 12043–53.

Jacques, P., Dunlap, R. and Freeman, M. (2008). The organization of denial: conservative think tanks and environmental skepticism. *Environmental Politics* 17, 349–85.

Karlsson, L.-I. "Larmen om klimathot är inte övertygande" (intervju med Sverker Martin-Löf), *Dagens Nyheter* 14/6 2008.

Knight, G. and Greenberg, J. (2011). Talk of the enemy: adversarial framing and climate change discourse. *Social Movement Studies*, 10(4), 323–40.

Lahsen, M. (2005). Technocracy, democracy, and US climate politics: the need for demarcations. *Science, Technology and Human Values* 30(1), 137–69.

Leggett, J. (2001). *The Carbon War: Global Warming and the End of the Oil Era*. London: Routledge.

Leiserowitz, A. (2005). American risk perceptions: is climate change dangerous? *Risk Analysis* 25, 1433–42.

Lindstedt, G. "Vi står inför den andra industriella revolutionen", *Veckans Affärer* 2006.

Lomborg, B. "Varningar för katastrof hjälper inte världen", *Dagens Nyheter* 13/2 2007.

Lomborg, B. "Stäng inte dörren för klimatdebatten", *Sydsvenska Dagbladet* 28/7 2009.

McCright, A. and Dunlap, R. E. (2003). Defeating Kyoto: The Conservative Movement's Impact on U.S. Climate Change Policy. *Social Problems*, 50(3), 348–73.

McCright, A. M. and Dunlap, R. E. (2010). Anti-reflexivity: The American conservative movement's success in undermining climate science and policy. *Theory, Culture and Society*, 27(2–3); 100–133.

McCright, A. and Dunlap, R. E. (2011). Cool dudes: The denial of climate change among conservative white males in the United States. *Global Environmental Change*, 21(4), 1163–72.

Merchant, C. (1980). *The Death of Naure: Women, Ecology and the Scientific Revolution*. New York: Harper and Row.

Monbiot, G. (2006). *Heat: How we can stop the planet burning*. Penguin UK.

Munkhammar, J. "Bra klimat för särintressen", *Aftonbladet* 5/7 2008.

Neumayer, E. and Plümper, T. (2007). The gendered nature of natural disasters: The impact of catastrophic events on the gender gap in life expectancy, 1981–2002. *Annals of the American Association of Geographers*, 97(3), 551–66.

Nordenskiöld, T. and Ottosson, M. "De tar ton om klimatet", *Dagens Industri* 5/6 2008.

Nordin, I. "Klimatdebatten – en röra", *Östgöta Correspondenten* 9/6 2008.

O'Neill, S. and Boykoff, M. (2012). The role of new media in engaging the public with climate change. In Whitmarsh, L., Lorenzoni, I. and O'Neill, S. (Eds.). (2012). *Engaging the public with climate change: Behaviour change and communication.* London: Routledge 233–51.

Oldfield, F. (2005). *Environmental Change: Key Issues and Alternative Approaches.* Cambridge University Press.

Oreskes, N. and Conway, E. (2010). *Merchants of Doubt: How a Handful of Scientists Obscured the Truth on Issues from Tobacco Smoke to Global Warming.* New York: Bloomsbury Press.

Painter, J. and Ashe, T. (2012). Cross-national comparison of the presence of climate scepticism in the print media in six countries, 2007–10. *Environmental Research Letters*, 7(4).

Pettersson, J. "Bluff om klimatet", *Aftonbladet* 20/8 2006.

Pettersson, J. "Världens största bluff", *Borås Tidning* 6/7 2008a.

Pettersson, J. "Klimatrapporter är inte heliga", *Borås Tidning* 20/7 2008b.

Radetzki, M. and Lundgren, N. "En grön fatwa har utfärdats", *Ekonomisk debatt* 2009:5, s 58–61.

Rampton, S. and Stauber, J. (2001). *Trust Us, We're Experts! How Industry Manipulates Science and Gambles with Your Future.* New York: Tarcher/Putnam.

Schück, J. "Klimatlarmet sågas av tunga ekonomer", *Dagens Nyheter* 23/6 2009.

Stockholmsinitiativet. "Människor orsakar inte uppvärmningen", *Göteborgs-Posten* 19/4 2009.

Synnemar, K.-E. "Miljarder satsas på en ovetenskaplig hypotes", *Byggnadsindustrin* 2008:32, s 19–20. 18/11 2008.

Thörnqvist, L. "Klimat efter Marx", *Sydsvenska Dagbladet* 27/10 2007.

Whitmarsh, L. (2011). Scepticism and uncertainty about climate change: dimensions, determinants and change over time. *Global Environmental Change*, 21(2), 690–700.

Woods, R., Fernández, A. and Coen, S. (2012). The use of religious metaphors by UK newspapers to describe and denigrate climate change. *Public Understanding of Science*, 21(3), 323–39.

6 The UN conference in Copenhagen and beyond

Introduction

The global climate debate came to be associated with a particular date and place as 2009 approached. The whole world seemed to be focusing on a special event that would set standards and rules for the coming years of environmental politics. All kinds of actors, including politicians, NGOs and multinational companies prepared to make their mark in the political field at Copenhagen in December 2009. Virtually all statements related to climate politics that were made around the world, as well as in Sweden, during the second half of 2009 were, in one way or another, connected to the UN conference in Copenhagen (COP15, December 7–18). Sweden was not unique; the whole world was intensely engaged in the climate-change debate leading up to the meeting (Boykoff, 2011; Schmidt et al., 2013). Even though anthropogenic climate change had been on the political agenda before, never had there been so unambiguous a consensus for the need of a transition towards a sustainable society based on the most authoritative science available and put forward by an international body of the highest standing. The near collapse of the international financial system in 2008 and the economic recession only reinforced the message that profound unsustainability was the heart of the industrialized world's established socio-economic order, and not only in the ecological sense (Blühdorn, 2011). In 2008, Barack Obama, who had in part campaigned on the need to address climate change, won the US presidential election along with a large majority of Democrats in both houses of the US Congress. Later on in June 2009, the US House of Representatives passed the first major piece of climate change legislation in American history. As international leaders fully endorsed the IPCC's recommendations and kept reiterating that climate change was the most urgent and severe threat confronting humanity, huge expectations were building up that the United Nations Framework Convention on Climate Change, Fifteenth session of the Conference of the Parties (UNFCCC COP15), otherwise known as the climate summit in Copenhagen, would deliver a genuine breakthrough for a truly sustainable global political framework (Blühdorn, 2011). In 2009, the momentum towards a post-carbon economy seemed strong, as the ecomodern discourse – part of both the Industrial Fatalist discourse and the Green Keynesian discourse – gained popularity. The US was actually leaning towards a federal cap-and-trade system and the new Obama administration was even supportive of the forthcoming Copenhagen climate negotiations. The last bastions of corporate opposition to carbon controls were weakening. Levy and Spicer write, "in October 2009, Nike and Apple defected from the US Chamber of Commerce in a high-profile protest over the climate stance, and a group of multinational companies including Coca Cola, GE, Microsoft, Cisco and DuPont came out in support of a binding emissions cap, stating a preference for predictable policy" (2013).

The conference itself was portrayed as a sort of culmination of the climate discussion presented to the public in the autumn of 2006. At this time, all the good intentions from the UN conference in Bali in 2007 were supposed to be translated into a legally binding agreement following on from Kyoto 1997, which would apply to all 193 countries in the UN. Many of the actors, even from the Industrial Fatalist discourse, talked about a now-or-never moment. There was an urgent need for a new protocol that took all the research presented by the IPCC seriously and envisioned a future with transitioned energy, food and transport systems. All types of actors created high expectations that a crucial step would be taken in Copenhagen. This rested to a large extent on politicians who supported climate scientists' demands for immediate action. It was simply imperative that the conference should become a milestone in climate negotiations and the history of climate politics. At the time, Sweden was president of the EU, which partly hosted the conference. This helped to create special interest in negotiations within Sweden. But this interest was not as unified as it may have seemed at first glance. Our investigation of Sweden's many positions clarifies the different discourses: because the stakes were so high they were very clear-cut. Those who gave expression to – and created – expectations were not only representatives of the Liberal–Conservative government and the Liberal press and editors, but also the parliamentary opposition, the Swedish Church, environmental organizations, international solidarity groups, the climate movement and associations of various kinds. Their expectations of what the negotiations would lead to and perceptions of how they should be conducted differed significantly. The four climate discourses that we discussed in previous chapters were now concentrating fully on the negotiations prior to and in Copenhagen.

The Copenhagen meeting was important for all the discourses in different ways. A diverse range of actors converged upon Copenhagen to participate in the COP15 Summit. They included international elected politicians; negotiators; lobbyists; multinational companies; European autonomist groups and direct action networks such as Camp for Climate Action, the Climate Justice Now (CJN)! Network; grass-roots social movements from the global South exemplified by the presence of members of Via Campesina, the small farmer and peasant network; a range of NGOs from around the world (e.g. Focus on the Global South, Climate Action network); trade unions; politicians; journalists; and concerned individuals. As the week's events unfolded, five different venues in Copenhagen were utilized. First, there was the closed area for states and officially sanctioned lobbying organizations (such as NGOs), which met at the city's main convention centre, the Bella Center. This space brought together those inside and outside the centre in creative and tense ways. Second, there was the area for corporate and business interests who wanted to present climate change as an opportunity to create new and large-scale technology, and science- and market-based solutions to the problems, "Hopenhagen". The third area was an alternative climate summit, the Klimaforum, which took place in a large sports centre in the city centre. This became the place for a range of voices who were critical of the official UN process, and a camp for individuals, grass-roots movements and NGOs from around the world. The fourth area covered several autonomous sites that had been established across the city to house the influx of activists and protesters from across Europe and beyond. These areas provided free communal sleeping spaces, kitchens, information points, Indymedia centres, convergence spaces, and legal information and support spaces, including Christiania. The streets of Copenhagen provided the fifth area, which became the epicentre of numerous demonstrations, scuffles, stand-offs with the police, preventative arrests, street theatre, exhibitions, interventions and stunts. It is worth noting that there was a significant amount of movement, blurring and exchange between these spaces. NGOs, journalists and friendly politicians who predominantly attended the Bella Center, for example, talked and held workshops at the Klimaforum (Chatterton et al., 2013). All of what happened in Copenhagen reflected back into the different discourses. In this chapter we will analyse how the four discourses came into dialogue with and conflicted with each other before, during and after this unprecedented global climate change event.

The Industrial Fatalist discourse and the EU rationalist negotiation logic

The Industrial Fatalist discourse dominated in Sweden before, during and after Copenhagen. We have discussed how the actors practised this discourse. Here we review this practice once again, this time in relation to other discourses at Copenhagen.

An ambitious climate agreement and the two-degree target

From July until the beginning of December 2009, the emphasis was on possible outcomes of the Copenhagen negotiations. Actors in the Industrial Fatalist discourse articulated that the highest priority should be a global, comprehensive and ambitious climate agreement. In particular, Environment Minister Andreas Carlgren repeated until the day before the UN conference that there was no alternative to a broad and comprehensive climate agreement. In his view, climate change was portrayed largely as a technical and economic issue that could be addressed by political negotiations at the highest international level. The focus was on a consistent supply of technology and capital and questions about who should pay and how climate-friendly technologies would spread. The Industrial Fatalist discourse never included questions about the relationship of industrial civilization to nature, ecosystem sustainability or the need for structural changes in our industrial modern society. As the UN meeting approached, the emphasis on the willingness to pay and the how development would proceed became stronger (Reinfeldt and Barroso, 2009; Carlgren, 2009a, 2009b). The central argument in the Industrial Fatalist discourse was that if an international agreement on a rational allocation of emission reductions could be achieved, the climate problem would be brought under control and the climate crisis resolved. The discourse was firmly rooted in a belief in the international planning process and the rationality of the negotiation order. Climate scientists had laid out the necessary steps. Now it was up to politicians to produce a joint solution that demonstrated mankind's ability to manage self-generated ecological risks.

As a benchmark for the many ambitions in Copenhagen, the IPCC declared that the Earth's temperature increase should not exceed 2 degrees Celsius, in order to avoid dramatic climate change. From that it followed that global greenhouse gas emissions must be reduced by 50 per cent, compared to 1990 levels, by 2050. In the Industrial Fatalist discourse these figures were treated as objective reference points (Knaggård, 2014). An international climate protocol in which all UN countries pledged to work to ensure that the limit was not exceeded was both necessary and satisfying. The Industrial Fatalist discourse authorized politics that would hit as close to the target as possible. An unreflective attitude or a profound trust in the IPCC assessments permeated the Industrial Fatalist discourse and set the limits of what "ambitious" climate politics might look like. Certain climate researchers' calculations were established as the only fixed point in a world where everything else was subject to negotiation.

The EU as catalyst

Prime Minister Fredrik Reinfeldt, Minister for the Environment Andreas Carlgren and other representatives of the Swedish Liberal–Conservative government constituted the most prominent and acclaimed interpreters of Industrial Fatalism in the autumn of 2009. They repeatedly emphasized the importance of the EU's leading role in climate negotiations. The EU countries could show the way for the rest of the world by creating "a sustainable economy based on renewable resources" without the need for any changes in society:. "Limiting economic growth is not a possible road out of the climate crisis" (Carlgren and Västerteg, 2009). Added to this were expectations that the EU states were leading the world into a new era by voluntarily committing to limit greenhouse gases within member countries while providing financial and technical assistance to developing countries. It was the EU's skilful political leadership that supported the premise that it would be possible to "stitch together a deal in Copenhagen", proclaimed a joint opinion article from Reinfeldt and Barosso (2009).The internationally renowned negotiator Carl Bildt, now working as a foreign minister in the Liberal–Conservative government, and others, promised that the EU had made "an alliance in Copenhagen" (Bildt et al., 2009). It was claimed that only countries within the European Union had adopted laws related to climate change and had institutions that were technically ready to take on the new legal requirements. Reinfeldt summed up his view of the EU's role: "During the Swedish Presidency, we continue to show leadership and unity on key issues such as financing, technology transfer, adaptation, and an effective and efficient management of financial resources" [...] "now the USA and China must follow the EU" (Reinfeldt, 2009a). This understanding of the EU as a catalyst for the transformation of global climate politics linked to a specific logic that had been developed for the conference in Copenhagen, which viewed negotiation as an effective means of achieving an international climate agreement. Reinfeldt and Carlgren declared that the EU would use its promise to increase cuts in greenhouse gas emissions from 20 per cent to 30 per cent by 2020, compared with 1990, to "pressure" other major emitting countries to increase their commitments substantially. Carlgren described this promise as the "lever" by which deadlocks in negotiations could be broken and other countries in the rich world would be persuaded to follow (Carlgren, 2009c, 2009d). At times this commitment was expressed as an ultimatum. The Swedish representatives of the EU threatened that Europe could not realize its potential unless countries like the US and China expressed their willingness to make more substantial commitments. Carlgren argued for example that the EU had waited "long enough" for the United States, and that any agreement in Copenhagen would not be signed unless the US raised its offer significantly (*Sydsvenska Dagbladet*, 2009a). Even Reinfeldt declared that it was time to "get out of the trenches", since only a few months were left until the crucial event (Pehrsson, 2009). Under Reinfeldt the EU had contributed their "fair share" while other countries were not doing anything. He stated, "We can only reach an ambitious agreement in Copenhagen if all parties contribute to the process". Therefore, other developed countries had to show the same leadership, undertake similarly ambitious emission reductions, present proposals on financing and intensify their work. Developing countries, especially the more advanced, also had to present clear commitments that reflected their responsibilities and capabilities (Reinfeldt, 2009a).

The Swedish environment minister insisted right up to the starting day of the conference in Copenhagen that the EU negotiating strategy would be successful, that it had already begun to "bear fruit" and all that was needed was to "tie things up in Copenhagen" (Carlgren, 2009a, 2009b, 2009c).

Reinfeldt maintained after the conference, despite disappointment that an ambitious deal failed to materialize, that their negotiating strategy was correct and that the EU's intention was to continue "pushing others to take more responsibility" (Reinfeldt, 2009c).

Climate poker

The Industrial Fatalist discourse shared by most EU leaders created a storyline that the EU was the only power that could save the world from climate catastrophe. Through the EU's bargaining methods and special role in the negotiations, its leaders accepted this great responsibility. The image created was that the EU had voluntarily shouldered this difficult role, but that its efforts were unappreciated. According to this narrative, it was entirely possible to recalibrate the relationship between industrial civilization and the atmosphere, provided that adequate technical, legal, administrative and economic fine-tuning was done in accordance with the EU-specified guidelines. Climate scientists had calculated that large emissions cuts were required, which were the same cuts agreed to by EU countries, and the EU had outlined how these could be achieved. Now, the world's nations had to act accordingly, which, according to the rhetoric from actors within the Industrial Fatalist discourse, would be in the interests of people all over the world. The problem was, according to this storyline, that few countries outside the EU were prepared to make any significant commitments or voluntarily take responsibility for the situation. Europe referred metaphorically to its efforts to push other countries that were substantial emitters to raise their bids, as if in a game of "global climate poker". This metaphor implied that the pot included money and technological innovation, but never the global climate or ecosystems. It was a game between heads of state with government budgets at their disposal; the objective was to get all those involved to provide "reasonable" efforts. "Reasonable" was understood to mean that the rich industrialized countries, which produced the vast majority of greenhouse gas emissions, had a particular responsibility to address their own emissions using carbon dioxide markets, while funding emission reductions in low-income countries. But the rich countries would also require 'devcloping' countries with rapidly growing economies and emissions, such as China and India, to commit to limiting their future emissions. Although the fast-growing developing countries were not historically part of the problem, the Industrial Fatalist discourse required them to be part of the solution. Otherwise, all efforts would be in vain (e.g. Reinfeldt and Barosso, 2009; Bildt et al., 2009).

Reinfeldt, Carlgren's and other Swedish government representatives' accounts of the Copenhagen hearings and the EU's exemplary role was also described in Swedish editorials using a similar approach. The negotiations that ministers described were reproduced without question in both editorial comments and reports on the procedings. The journalists repeatedly used poker and card-game metaphors in headlines such as: "EU wants higher bids at the game board", "Put the money on the table, Carlgren", "Last round in the poker game", and "The most influential players have now made their bids" (e.g. *Dagens Nyheter*, 2009; *Östgöta-Correspondenten*, 2009; *Helsingborgs Dagblad*, 2009; *Sydsvenska Dagbladet*, 2009e). It was overall a very powerful metaphor portraying climate politics as a game, and introducing politicians and bureaucrats as players who were in the game to win a victory (e.g. *Östgöta-Correspondenten*, 2009). Political reporters and lead writers described a bargaining game in which players waited, invited, raised stakes or preyed upon each other, each holding their own cards close to their chest. In this supposedly global game the EU played the constructive role while the US and China were the most parsimonious. The Industrial Fatalist discourse dominated Swedish daily newspapers' editorial pages and political reportage about the conference in Copenhagen.

An eco-efficient green economy

According to the Industrial Fatalist discourse, balance and trust between India, China, the US and every European country could only be created if economic growth was guaranteed despite climate measures. Industrial Fatalism actors believed that as soon as one party had to curb economic growth because of climatic issues, favourable conditions for reaching an agreement in Copenhagen would be totally undermined. This could not be allowed to happen. This is why the task to suspend the contradiction between national growth and emission reductions was a top priority in the Industrial Fatalist discourse. Reinfeldt and Barosso argued that an agreement in Copenhagen would lead to climate-friendly investments, lay the foundation for a "green economy" and drive growth over the next 20 to 30 years. Those who took advantage of this growth opportunity would belong to the future "winners" (Reinfeldt and Barosso, 2009). The Swedish environment minister described how the transition to an "eco-efficient economy" at an early stage would give European countries a competitive advantage and turn them into "winners" vis-à-vis the rest of the world. Other countries would be more or less forced to follow the example of European countries. "A switch to an eco-efficient economy before the rest of the world can give Europe significant competitive advantages. Strengthening competitiveness and growth can be achieved simultaneously with a sustainable energy supply, efficient use of resources and the achievement of our climate and environmental goals" (Carlgren and Västerteg, 2009).

Europe would thus show the world how future economic growth prospects looked, and through its economic success would persuade other countries to adapt their economies in a profitable and climate-friendly direction. Similarly, Carl Bildt and five other European foreign ministers expressed views that a transition to economies with low carbon emissions was a prerequisite for sustainable global growth, and that Europe had a special responsibility to take the lead in this process (Bildt et al., 2009). In this context, Sweden was described as the very incarnation of "an eco-efficient economy". Carlgren pointed out that Sweden could be "an international model for ... the major emitting countries such as the US, China, India and Brazil", as it was the country which had developed climate-friendly techno-logical solutions that were now in demand worldwide (Carlgren, 2009a, 2009c). In the Industrial Fatalist discourse, Sweden was living proof that the climate problem could be solved within the framework of the existing world order, and that this world order was actually a prerequisite for Swedish success (and thereby for all other countries, according to this argument). The major concern was that the US, China, India and Brazil were not heeding European blandishments and were reluctant to make any long-term binding commitments; this led to concerns that any agreement at all would be signed in Copenhagen (e.g. Reinfeldt 2009a). The analysis of Sweden as a frontrunner with an eco-efficient economy demonstrated that in the Liberal–Conservative government vision it was not about changing existing institutions, behaviour or power relations. Instead, development was merely extrapolated from the present to the future, with some technological fixes added.

Concrete methods for emission reductions

Against this background, actors within the Industrial Fatalist discourse identi-fied practical ways to reduce emissions that damaged the climate. These were consistently of a financial or large-scale technical nature. The Swedish prime minister, Reinfeldt, stressed that an important way to meet emissions targets and involve more developing countries and the United States was to create a market for global emissions trading. With a global price on emissions, market mechanisms would achieve far more than planning. Moreover, capital to fund climate measures and reductions in developing countries could be generated through the global carbon market, according to Reinfeldt (Brors, 2009; Reinfeldt, 2009a). Representatives from the think tank Fores shared Reinfeldt's opinion, stressing that neither the US, China nor India showed any intention of adopting legislation to limit emissions, which is why a leg-ally binding agreement in Copenhagen seemed distant. What was needed was a concrete process; the best way to kick start such a process was "to create a global market that put the right price on carbon" (Ådahl and Johansson, 2009). This required, in their view, the harmonization of US and European models for emissions trading, minimization of the free allocation of allowances, flexible mechanisms that all parties agreed on, and the estab-lishment of an independent body for continuous monitoring of the system. The common characteristic of these voices in the Industrial Fatalist discourse was that they put more hope in market mechanisms than the political pro-cess. Reinfeldt stressed that it was imperative that the flexible mechanisms developed for climate-friendly technologies could be transferred to developing countries, so that they would not have to repeat the mistakes of rich coun-tries. Wealthy countries could then pursue their climate commitments by buying "cheap" emission reductions (Reinfeldt and Barosso, 2009; Ådahl and Johansson, 2009).

The reluctance of the US, China and India, and the G77 countries' obstruction of the UN process

As the month of December approached, Industrial Fatalist criticism of the US, China and India grew because it was understood that these countries were hindering or even preventing the emergence of an ambitious and binding climate deal in Copenhagen. Reinfeldt stated repeatedly that the leaders of the US, China and India had to make clearer commitments and present concrete goals in order to avoid a deadlock in the negotiations. This did not happen. The unwillingness to establish a legally binding agreement, which Reinfeldt said he had encountered already in exploratory talks with representatives of the major emitting countries, led him to downplay expectations for the conference. For Reinfeldt, Carlgren and their supporters, this reluctance overshadowed hopes for an ambitious agreement that would guarantee that the Earth's temperature did not increase by more than 2 degrees Celsius (Pehrsson, 2009; Törnvall, 2009, Reinfeldt, 2009b; Magnusson, 2009).

Once the conference was underway, for a few days it was clear that the EU's negotiating strategy was not as successful as hoped. Negotiations inside the Bella Center stalled. The cause identified within the Industrial Fatalist discourse was that obstructions were being created by the G77 countries, a coalition of 130 countries that included all low-income countries as well as China, India, Brazil and other oil producers. These countries, which had been almost absent in the Industrial Fatalist discourse before the Copenhagen meeting as a result of environmental justice issues, called for extending the Kyoto Protocol. They accused the EU of wanting to destroy the only ratified and legally binding agreement on emissions. They wanted to continue the Kyoto agreement, while the EU wanted a completely new agreement with commitments from the US and G77 countries.

An important factor was that the G77 countries had signed the Kyoto Protocol, but were not obliged to implement the measures to reduce greenhouse gases that 50 industrialized countries had already agreed to because of historical issues regarding climate justice. Andreas Carlgren now accused G77 of setting up "a number of obstacles" to the negotiating process. However, several political Liberal–Conservative commentators used words such as "blocked", "kidnapped", "sabotaged" or "defected" with regard to this aspect of the talks. Actors within the Industrial Fatalist discourse identified the Sudanese president as a protagonist in this context; he was labelled as "militant" (e.g. Karlsson, 2009a, 2009b; Kjöller, 2009; Baltscheffsky, 2009). Carlgren argued that the G77 was deeply divided and that they were engaged in procedures to obstruct the meeting. An editorial writer for *Dagens Nyheter*, Hanne Kjöller, stated that the G77 countries' actions were an expression of "aid reflexes and victim mentality". She thought that Sudan and the "tail of the G77 countries" did not want a new climate protocol, but rather an extension of the Kyoto Protocol in which "developing countries did not take responsibility". Therefore, they took the climate negotiators as "hostages" and threatened to scuttle negotiations unless they got their way. The editorial suggested that these countries did not regard themselves as objects to be compensated for past injustices but as nations responsible for the future. She stated that it demonstrated the inappropriateness of compensation for corrupt regimes, and a similar view was held by Hans Bergström in the Climate Sceptic discourse. The conclusion was, according to the editorial, that the G77 obstruction constituted a threat to our common climate (Kjöller, 2009). Other Liberal newspapers editorials echoed these ideas and accused G77 countries of halting negotiations (*Sydsvenska Dagbladet*, 2009). When Fredrik Reinfeldt explained the failure of the new protocol, he also blamed the G77 countries. As he understood it, many countries in the G77 group did not want to stick to discussing a new climate protocol; they were raising questions about global resource allocation. According to Reinfeldt, these environmental justice claims did not help the chances of reaching a binding climate treaty. "However, climate change is not going to wait around for us to agree a single accord that will resolve its issues, combat world poverty and achieve global justice" (Reinfeldt, 2009c).

None of the voices from the Industrial Fatalist discourse used the term "climate justice". They assumed that the issue of the unequal distribution of resources and climate commitments should be discussed separately. EU actors defended themselves consistently even after the conference collapsed. They claimed that there were other countries – particularly the G77, but also China, the oil producing countries and the United States – that blocked the process by either mixing in extraneous issues or opposing a legally binding climate commitment. These were the editorial headlines: "Those are described as guilty", "UN fiasco", "Earth is without leadership" and "China missed historical chance" (e.g. Fröberg, 2009; *Dagens Nyheter*, 2009; *Uppsala Nya Tidning*, 2009; *Borås Tidning*, 2009). The disappointment with Copenhagen led many who had shaped the Industrial Fatalist discourse to question the UN process. Representatives from the think tank Fores argued even before the negotiations ended that the Copenhagen conference demonstrated that it was highly uncertain whether climate change could ever be resolved within the UN framework. They suggested instead a more elitist negotiation that excluded presidents who were "mostly preoccupied with lecturing on imperialism [...] perhaps it's just as well that those who have the main responsibility for the problems take the hearings somewhere else" (Ådahl and Johansson, 2009). *Dagens Nyheter* shared that opinion and questioned the rationale of "giving the right to attend to delegates who only use the meeting to peddle their hatred against Western imperialism". The conclusion was that countries who engaged in "sabotage" should be excluded from future climate negotiations (Kjöller, 2009). Prime Minister Reinfeldt also hinted that it might be necessary to make changes in the process and practices for the next UN conference in Mexico. In particular, he pointed to the problem of the G77 countries and the absurdity of treating this group as a collective in future negotiations, given the vastly different conditions and positions of member countries (Reinfeldt, 2009c). Common to all of these statements was that the G77 countries constituted the greatest obstacle to a climate agreement. Meaningful negotiations required a bargaining process in which these countries would not be able to short-circuit talks. From this point of view, it was no longer the United States or China that constituted the main obstacles to a global climate agreement, but a heterogeneous group of 130 more-or-less per capita poor countries with very low anthropogenic emissions destroying the climate.

Actors described the G77 countries and particularly the Sudanese president as irrational, obstructive, and ultimately destructive. No one in the Industrial Fatalist discourse examined the basis of the G77 countries' behaviour or whether their criticism of the EU's refusal to extend the Kyoto Protocol was reasonable or rational. Some statements by the Industrial Fatalists sounded neo-colonial: G77 countries were portrayed as an unreasonable, loud and ignorant group that started conflicts over irrelevant matters such as meeting times and speech order; they should be excluded from negotiations, even if the consequences of climate affected them. With a patriarchal tone, the Industrial Fatalist discourse suggested that the G77 simply did not understand the situation; they needed to be protected from themselves, and the world from them.

Climate change almost becomes a non-issue after Copenhagen

The meeting in Copenhagen and the pressure created by research findings forced all actors to articulate climate change as an important question, and frame it with urgency. The global event that put the issue of climate change on the agenda could not be brushed under the rug: but that was exactly what happened after negotiators failed to sign a new protocol. Leading politicians began to downplay climate change (Schmidt et al., 2013). In Sweden this happened very fast. A review of articles from the leading Swedish newspaper during the UN conference in Durban, December 2011, shows that the tone of the climate debate had shifted radically during the two years after Copenhagen. One editorial noted that expectations were very low before the Durban summit and that the fact that the UN process survived at all was positive. Statements that hope for a binding global climate agreement were not "completely out of the question" were now stressed as a half-victory (*Dagens Nyheter*, 2011). What *Dagens Nyheter* described in 2009 as a fundamental fiasco was now described as encouraging. Their editorial shift illustrated that climate change was no longer articulated as critical for global survival in the long term, or important in Sweden's environmental debate in the near-term future.

Only two years after Copenhagen, climate change was once again only one environmental issue among several. Climate change was no longer an issue that would impact on civilization. A clear indication of this is that a search in the database Retriever using the keywords "climate" and "Reinfeldt" matched 505 newspaper articles between September and November 2009, but only 38 during the same months of 2011 (Axelsson, 2012). Several environmental debaters testified in late 2011 about the same phenomenon. Environment Minister Lena Ek pointed out that the climate issue had "fallen out of favour" significantly in the public debate (Ek, 2011). Johan Rockström affirmed that climate change no longer figured prominently in the media and among world politicians. Recognition of the climate threat had become marginalized, as reflected in the dull negotiations in Durban (Rockström and Szombatfalvy, 2011). Stefan Edman explained that the media "silence" was the result of journalists being tired of crisis talk and a "hangover" after the failed Copenhagen summit. Svante Axelsson claimed that the prime minister "completely abdicated" on the issue (Brundin Danielsson, 2011).

Five years after Copenhagen those articulating an Industrial Fatalist discourse were still in power in Sweden. In 2010, the Liberal–Conservative government secured another four years in office. On the issue of climate, the Liberal–Conservative government still claimed that they had acted with urgency. But five years later, there had not been any legislative, regulatory, tax- or subsidy-related change that demonstrated the leadership to manage one of mankind's greatest decisions. In recent years, environmental problems have instead been described in the same breath as growth, innovation and competitiveness (Lidskog and Elander, 2012). The conflict between environment and resource consumption is still claimed to be false by the Industrial Fatalist discourse, in other words, "we can have our cake and eat it too", is the emphasis. This sublime allure can be seen today in such peculiarities as the Swedish Transport Administration creating a traffic plan for the next ten years without regard for the carbon emission forecasts relating to increased car traffic (Trafikverket, 2013).

What had happened? Instead of functioning as a frontrunner, the Liberal–Conservative government placed the climate issue in the hands of the Swedish state enquiry system, just as nuclear power was studied after the referendum against nuclear power in the 1980s. Two investigative initiatives were begun: a prestigious project called "The Future Commission", and the visionary "Roadmap 2050", in which Sweden would become "a country without any carbon dioxide net emissions in 2050" (Swedish Government homepage: Roadmap 2050, 2014). The Future Commission is an example of the supposedly radical approach to and recognition of environmental problems that are fundamental to society. However, under the surface it shows a preference for the Industrial Fatalist discourse: it does not change the structure of society at all. Among others, the Commission members included Stockholm Resilience Centre leader Johan Rockström, which guaranteed that environmental issues would be analysed seriously. But the final report was heavily criticized by, among others, Rockström himself, because the Liberal–Conservative government's proposals did not match the scientific evidence. A similar change happened with the work on Roadmap 2050: despite early ambitions, work on the project was put on hold in 2014 by the government, which was totally in line with the Liberal–Conservative Industrial Fatalism approach during the climate debate. It seemed that the issue needed further study (Kommittédirektiv 2014). The emphasis was increasingly on presenting Sweden as an environmentally friendly country, where citizens were already decreasing their global ecological footprint (Hysing, 2014). The supposed apocalypse that would force Sweden to become a frontrunner was transformed into what Methmann and Rothe called the "war against nothing", which is a crucial point for understanding the logic of Industrial Fatalism and how it combines apocalyptic framing with conservative action (Methmann and Rothe, 2012).

The Green Keynesian discourse and the defence of the Kyoto Protocol principles

As Copenhagen began, the Green Keynesian discourse was mainly articulated as a critique against the Industrial Fatalist discourse. However, the actors did adjust their positions in a few areas. First of all, they no longer talked much about how climate change could be understood as a market opportunity; instead, profound changes in behaviours and lifestyles were foreseen. Second, climate justice issues became more important since many actors were engaged in the network Climate Action. Finally, social movements all over the world were recognized as change agents.

The resignation of Reinfeldt and the low targets for the EU

In preparation for Copenhagen, the Green Keynesian discourse's critique of the Industrial Fatalist discourse set the tone for virtually all important aspects of the climate-change debate. To begin with, the actors articulating this discourse had very different notions of what was at stake. From September onwards, leading representatives of Greenpeace, the WWF and the Green Party declared that "ecological and social collapse" threatened unless an ambitious and binding climate change agreement was signed and put into effect. They claimed that the ecosystems supporting civilization were in acute danger. The world's heads of state now had an opportunity to "save the world", but also risked ruining the existence of large populations. The stakes involved the future of entire continents (e.g. Krüger, 2009. Björk et al., 2009; Edman, 2009; Matsson, 2009). At the end of 2009, the Green Keynesian discourse focused on how the negotiating mandates were managed, the values and perceptions of nature that formed the basis for the transformation process, the methods for prioritizing emission cuts and the methods of burden sharing imposed.

Prime Minister Reinfeldt was criticized as early as July 2009, when he announced it would become almost impossible to reach a binding agreement on climate change in December. Representatives of the parliamentary opposition claimed that he should put pressure on major emitting countries, instead of expressing resignation that risked undermining confidence in the process (e.g. *Aftonbladet*, 2009; Lönnaeus, 2009; Wetterstrand, 2009). Criticism of this kind became more frequent as December neared. Leading representatives of the SSNC and the WWF argued that Reinfeldt's efforts to "play down expectations" meant that the opportunity to seriously address international climate change was at risk. The focus on what could not be achieved rather than on what was possible was viewed as devastating for climate negotiations (Axelsson and Gustavsson, 2009; Berglund, 2009). Green Party spokesperson Maria Wetterstrand thought that the prime minister's position jeopardized the entire climate summit, and hinted that his pessimism was a tactic. If the summit failed, nobody would blame it on a lack of competence on the part of Sweden, in its role as EU president (Wetterstrand, 2009).

Within the framework of the Green Keynesian discourse, the EU's conference objectives were also criticized. Time and again it was argued that rich countries had to bring about an acceptable climate agreement and act in accordance with the two-degree target. This would require a commitment to reduce greenhouse gases by up to 40 per cent, compared with 1990 levels, by 2020. The EU and the Swedish government's discussion of a 20 or 30 per cent reduction was totally inadequate. The SSNC, the WWF, Friends of the Earth, Latin American groups, Diakonia (a faith-based Swedish development organization that works with 400 local partner organizations in 30 countries), Swedish opposition parties and other solidarity groups endorsed this claim. This demand exceeded by far what rich countries were willing to do, but it was in line with what the IPCC's climate scientists judged as absolutely necessary. It was time for rich countries to take responsibility for climate change in Copenhagen. Anything short of that commitment was unacceptable, unjust and shameful (e.g. Johansson et al., 2009a, 2009b; Axelsson and Lindberg, 2009; Ahlefelt, 2009). Climate scientist Johan Rockström and EU parliament member Anders Wijkman said that the EU's climate goals were unscientific and dangerous. The IPPC had already demonstrated in 2007 that emissions in the rich countries should be reduced by 50 per cent by 2020, and 100 per cent by 2050, in order to meet the two-degree target. To pretend otherwise was to play a deceptive game. The gap between scientific necessity and political feasibility had to be reduced dramatically in Copenhagen, but the EU unfortunately set the bar too low with their politically motivated assumptions that emission reductions of only 20–30 per cent were adequate (Rockström and McGlade, 2009; Rockström and Wijkman, 2009). The SSNC, the WWF and Climate Action expressed the issue in similar terms. The target which the EU formulated was rated as totally inadequate for meeting the two-degree target; in fact, a temperature increase of 2 degrees

Celsius would endanger the existence of particularly vulnerable countries and cause local ecosystem collapses. The goals were alarmingly close to ecosystem thresholds and climate catastrophe (Malméus, 2009).

EU's wrongful negotiation game

Criticism of the EU's low emission goals merged with a blistering showdown with regard to the Union's negotiating tactics ahead of the Copenhagen Conference by actors from the Green Keynesian discourse. The EU claimed to be putting pressure on other countries to cut emissions by 30 per cent in Europe, in exchange for other countries following suit. But environmental organizations like the SSNC and the World Wildlife Fund, and several international solidarity and human rights organizations declared that EU tactics "sabotaged" the possibility of an ambitious climate agreement. The EU's economic and tactical negotiation game threatened to convey and legitimize the position that it was possible to engage in climate change negotiations using game theory in which various players awaited each other's bidding. The EU's action reinforced a negotiation logic in which the actors involved waited to see each other's moves, and everyone wanted to make the last move. According to Green Party spokespersons, Swedish EU representatives, including Reinfeldt and Carlgren, spent far too much time trying to persuade other countries to match EU commitments, and too little time on ambitious emissions targets that were not conditional and practically possible. EU emissions target were so low, in fact, that they were insufficient to meet even the two-degree target (Wetterstrand, 2009). To pay his part of the "bill", but no more was not the same as leadership. The card game metaphor that Carlgren and Reinfeldt used was outdated and had no validity in terms of the climate threat. By its logic, all stakeholders would be losers. With climate change, the Green Keynesians argued, there were either only winners or only losers. The game theory approach was entirely unproductive (e.g. Axelsson and Lindberg, 2009; Caballos and Losman, 2009; Eliasson, 2009). Someone had to take the lead. If the EU was serious about its claim to leadership, this was the time to show it (Morgan, 2009; Nordin, 2009).

Climate justice – a prerequisite for a fair climate protocol

The EU's reluctance to accept their historic environmental debt to developing countries was identified within the Green Keynesian discourse as deeply problematic. Environmental and solidarity organizations criticized the EU for using 2005 as the base year for calculating every country's share of carbon emissions; the rich countries' material well-being had been built on the atmosphere's ability to buffer the exhausted levels of carbon dioxide for more than a century. The EU's insistence that developing countries should help pay for climate action was a deep injustice since the damage caused to the climate had supported the development of rich countries. One form of mitigation included "compensation" to be paid by countries whose ecological footprint had contributed to the problem. Unless the rich countries took responsibility for resolving the crisis by committing to drastically reducing their carbon footprint and fully financing actions needed in developing countries, prospects for a climate agreement were dim. As president of the EU, Sweden had to accept this dual obligation. Commentators said that the EU was "penny-pinching", and that it was "time for climate justice right now" (e.g. *Expressen*, 2009; *Aftonbladet*, 2009). Rockström and Wijkman stated that ethics as well as self-interest favoured this position (Rockström and Wijkman, 2009).

The introduction of the term "climate justice" and the formation of the network Climate Action influenced the climate debate in important ways. The concept emerged and developed during a broad constellation of events that took place well before Copenhagen. The British researchers Chatterton, Featherstone, and Routledge tracked how the term was first used in a 1999 report following the COP6 Climate Change negotiations. The concept achieved formal status in the Bali Principles of Climate Justice 2002; in the Durban Declaration on Carbon Trading 2004; through the formation of the Climate Justice Now! (CJN) network during the COP14 negotiations in 2007; and through the creation of the "Climate Justice Action" (CJA) network, which was formed as an organizing platform prior to Copenhagen. The ideas embedded in climate justice were central to the discussions at the Klimaforum and direct action mobilizations during COP15. Climate justice was also advanced through the World People's Conference on Climate Change in Bolivia in 2010, and mobilizations during the COP16 in Cancun, Mexico and the COP17 in Durban, South Africa (Chatterton et al., 2013). Climate justice refers to principles of democratic accountability and participation, ecological sustainability and social justice, and their combined ability to find solutions to climate change. The notion focuses on the interrelationships between social injustice, ecological destruction and economic domination perpetrated by the underlying logic of growth capitalism (see Martinez-Alier, 2003). Building on Climate Justice Now! declarations in 2007 and 2008, climate justice principles articulated at the Klimaforum's declaration in Copenhagen included a couple of important principles: leave fossil fuels in the ground; reassert the control of peoples and communities over production; re-localize food production; massively reduce overconsumption, particularly in the global North; respect the rights of indigenous and forest peoples; and recognize the ecological and climate debt owed to the people in the global South by the global North, a recognition that includes reparations (Chatterton et al., 2013).

The focus of the Green Keynesian discourse was thus not the reluctance of the US and China to negotiate, but the legitimate demands of developing countries and the G77 countries for climate justice and fair burden sharing. Rich countries, shamefully, were unwilling or unable to satisfy this demand. "Africa was paying for the emission party of industrialized countries" (Machel et al. 2009). According to representatives of the Swedish Church and other groups, the Industrial Fatalist discourse attempted to shift much of the responsibility for dealing with the crisis onto developing countries (Esmailian, 2009). As Svante Axelsson of the SSNC and Lasse Gustavsson, the Secretary General of WWF Sweden, noted in a joint article: "It is provocative when Reinfeldt in the media claims that India with around one tonne per capita emissions is not entitled to increased emissions. It borders [on] cynicism and further undermines the trust between North and South which [is] already lacking" (Axelsson and Gustavsson, 2009). Given this belief, several voices within the Green Keynesian discourse claimed that the EU, in its eagerness to get US support for a climate agreement, had been far too reluctant to listen to developing countries or the G77 representatives and all too willing to abandon the Kyoto Protocol. This meant a new agreement was unlikely to be signed in Copenhagen. The most reasonable tactic now was to create a parallel process that would extend the Kyoto Protocol and develop an entirely new agreement that included all countries. However the EU chose an encounter with the developing countries only, setting the stage for conflicts and complicated negotiations in Copenhagen. Representatives of the Swedish Church, Diakonia, the SSNC, the WWF, Friends of the Earth, and several international justice organizations declared that they shared the developing countries' outrage over the EU's actions (Landinez Wetterstrand and Vennström, 2009). Svante Axelsson and Lasse Gustavsson said that the EU was essentially abandoning a binding agreement with developed countries to reduce their emissions. They argued that the Copenhagen conference should negotiate a second commitment period under the Kyoto Protocol with comprehensive support for climate action in developing countries. As agreed in Bali, these were two separate contracts. When the EU gave up the Kyoto process it meant that the Union's ability to form coalitions with G77 countries was thwarted. The reluctance of the US to sign the Kyoto Protocol and recognize the legitimate demands of developing countries guided the preparations for Copenhagen. Thus, economic competition between the US and China governed global negotiations on the Earth's future. According to Axelsson and Gustavsson, the EU should have defended the Kyoto process and, together with the G77 countries, put pressure on the United States. The rest of the countries of the world could not let climate change accelerate because the US Senate refused to see the distributional aspects of the climate issue. Unfortunately there was, according to the analysis within the Green Keynesian discourse, no indication that the EU was prepared to reorient itself at this point (Axelsson and Gustavsson, 2009; see also Lindquist, 2009). The solidarity organization Forum Syd added that the EU's willingness to "bend over for the US", jeopardized the entire Copenhagen summit because "developing countries had on several occasions made it clear that they would not accept a deal in Copenhagen in which the Kyoto Protocol principles were deleted" (Axelsson-Nycander and Ekelund, 2009).

Spokespersons for Friends of the Earth and several groups dealing with international environmental justice issues shared these views. They declared that the demand from developing countries that historical emissions of greenhouse gases be taken into account in the climate negotiations was reasonable, almost self-evident (Johansson et al., 2009b). Even the Green Party took a similar standpoint, arguing that the distributive principles that formed the basis of the Kyoto Protocol must be included in a new climate agreement (Caballos and Losman, 2009). Archbishop Anders Wejryd pointed out in turn that the EU position was incompatible with the UNFCCC, and was actually "against the fundamental principles of climate justice". The Church's newspaper *Kyrkans Tidning* reported "an anger and frustration that is shared by almost all aid organizations, churches and others in the so-called civil society" (Ahlefelt, 2009). The Swedish Church, the SSNC and Climate Action labelled as "very provocative" the EU's decision to allocate EUR 22–50 billion to support climate action in developing countries despite a UN estimate that it would take 500 billion dollars (Holmbäck, 2009). Niklas Hellström, a climate expert at the SSNC was indignant that the EU, despite its failure to recognize developing countries was pushing the blame for the negotiation failure onto those countries (Esmailian, 2009).

Much of the Green Keynesian discourse maintained that the EU's intention to abandon the Kyoto Protocol – which meant rich countries' failure to even live up to their commitments under the Protocol – plus their demands that developing countries accept binding emission obligations, radically complicated the possibilities for a global climate agreement. In their assessment, the EU was denying the right of developing countries to prosper as countries with high per capita incomes had by exploiting fossil fuels. Additionally, the EU was not prepared to limit its own emissions nor fully admit its obligation to pay for the necessary climate action. This was reported by those who shaped the Green Keynesian discourse to justify the refusal of these countries to sign a binding agreement in Copenhagen (e.g. Westlund, 2009; Krüger and Strömberg, 2009). Climate Action spokesperson Mikael Malméus declared that developing countries had good reason to abandon negotiations (Holmbäck, 2009). This insight was evident well before the summit. In July 2009, Social Democrats Wallström, Brundtland and Robinson, said the following:

Few analysts who are familiar with the UN negotiations believe that developing countries will make any decisive engagement before the industrial countries have made clear their approach to emissions reductions, access to technology and financing. Reducing the gap between North's and South's attitudes to climate change and development needs is a prerequisite for an agreement to be concluded in Copenhagen.

(Wallström et al., 2009)

Foreign aid becoming a flexible mechanism

Green Keynesianism actors said it was bad enough that developing countries were proposing to fund a large part of their own climate adaptation. But when it became clear that the EU intended to fund its limited adaptation aid from the regular aid budget, humanitarian and environmental organizations, and Swedish parliamentary parties, took umbrage. In effect, developing countries would have to fund their own climate action with funds earmarked for reducing poverty and maternal and child mortality. The fact that Sweden's Liberal–Conservative government was willing to transfer billions to climate aid and let the world's poor pay for the consequences of Swedish emissions aroused considerable resentment from the World Wildlife Fund, Greenpeace, Forum Syd as well as the Left Party, the Green Party, Social Democrats and Christian Democratic women's organization. Sweden, which traditionally had relatively ambitious aid targets, now risked creating an example for other countries to emulate through its "double moral" actions, something consistently characterized as sinister and unjust. Martina Krüger from Greenpeace and Ylva Strömberg from Action Aid warned that the Swedish Liberal–Conservative government's "double bookkeeping" was part of an "ugly game" and could lead other rich countries to follow suit. They found that no "developing nation" had any reason whatsoever to sign a new climate agreement that rested on such a premise (Krüger and Strömberg, 2009). To blunt this effort, these organizations formulated, along with like-minded people, a requirement that no climate measures could be financed with regular assistance funds, and declared that climate justice could never be served by this kind of manipulation, which would lead to "poor women paying the cost of climate change" (Ohly et al., 2009; Fälth et al., 2009). Closely linked to this criticism were Sweden's efforts within the EU to increase the share of emissions cuts to be accommodated through flexible mechanisms, by financing emission reductions abroad, preferably in developing countries. Representatives of the SSNC, WWF and Friends of the Earth, the Social Democrats and the Green Party opposed these efforts. They argued that a prerequisite for developing countries to sign a climate agreement was that rich countries show a willingness to make substantial reductions "at home". The rich countries still needed to provide comprehensive support to the developing world, but if this support meant a lower limit in rich countries, the strategy would undermine their "credibility" (Westlund, 2009; Bengtsson, 2009). Some complained that the Swedish government was guilty of a significant double standard by financing activities in developing countries that brought Sweden opportunities to build new highways, such as the Stockholm Bypass. They argued that this conduct damaged the Swedish representatives' opportunities to foster confidence in Copenhagen:

> The Liberal–Conservative government ruthlessly go to Copenhagen with their climate flag flying – but without reflecting upon our common

responsibility for building a society here and now. We can talk as much as anything about climate emissions, but if we do not walk the talk, and only buy ourselves free from our own emission reductions through action in developing countries, there is nothing to be proud of.

(Svensson Smith and Edman: 2009)

The need to change the culture of consumption

On the whole, the Green Keynesian discourse questioned the Liberal–Conservative government's focus on market-led solutions that made it possible to escape emission reductions at home. This focus, which mirrored the EU's conditional bidding on emissions cuts, was a "signal" that it was possible to "negotiate with the climate" (Holmbäck, 2009). Rockström, Wijkman and Wetterstrand, among others, found such hidden messages objectionable and potentially devastating. Let the common starting point for negotiations be the opposite, they argued (e.g. Rockström and Wijkman, 2009; Wetterstrand, 2009). This was also advocated by representatives of Friends of the Earth, Climate Action, the SSNC, the WWF, international solidarity organizations, the Left Party and the Green Party. Social movements in the global South stressed the importance of tackling the unsustainable level of consumption in rich countries. This opened up the question of whether global consumption and a shift towards more sustainable consumption patterns should be raised in Copenhagen. Without significant changes in lifestyle and behaviour patterns in rich countries, international emission reductions would be ineffective; any "consumption space" that reductions created would soon be eaten up by increases in consumption. Long-term, sustainable climate action therefore required a politics approach that held back consumption growth in rich countries, along with a collective awareness among these countries' citizens that their culture of consumption actually posed a threat to global survival. Representatives from Climate Action pointed out that the responsibility for addressing climate change neither should nor could be turned over to politicians in Copenhagen. However, the problem certainly could not be solved simply by individual citizens changing their lifestyle: it required more extensive lifestyle changes. It is important to note that what was being recommended was not the idea of individual consumption choices – as encouraged by the Industrial Fatalist discourse – without structural and collective patterns of sustainable consumption globally. In the Green Keynesian discourse climate change was not a matter of individual morality, but needed to be handled in accordance with an idea of a shared responsibility. Profound societal changes that could only be implemented with civic support were essential (Malméus et al., 2009).

According to Friends of the Earth, issues relating to rich countries' consumer culture should not be ignored in Copenhagen in the manner which had long been the case in UN negotiations (Johansson et al., 2009a). The major transition from industrialized systems of production and consumption, as

Rockström and Wijkman emphasized, would require getting a grip on the emissions from our "cars, meat and houses"; it also required a substantial impairment of economic growth. According to the two debaters this presupposed a "miracle" in Copenhagen, because it was precisely on this issue that the most influential actors – the EU, the US and China – had the greatest difficulty compromising (Rockström and Wijkman, 2009; see also Falk, 2009; Borgström-Hansson, 2009; Lillemets and Schlaug, 2009). Claims that ambitious climate action could be undertaken without affecting domestic economic growth and material prosperity, a view that had been prominently expressed by the actors speaking in the Green Keynesian discourse, ceased almost entirely as Copenhagen approached. The talk about Green Keynesianism or green growth that was prevalent from 2006 to 2008 made way in November and December 2009 for ideas about global economic and ecological compensation. The necessary and inevitable economic growth in developing countries was now said to require that rich countries restrain their economic growth and reduce their ecological footprints. Optimization growth in all the world's countries appeared to be increasingly difficult to reconcile with the need for immediate and powerful cuts in global emissions of greenhouse gases. In terms of this point it seemed that the Green Keynesian discourse was substantially affected by the argument of the G77 countries and the people's movements in developing countries, which took it closer to the Eco-socialist discourse.

Causes of the failure in Copenhagen

One month before the conference, Axelsson and Gustavsson complained that the EU, by abandoning the three-year negotiations on the continuation of the Kyoto Protocol because of the unwillingness of United States to sign up, virtually negated the possibility of achieving an ambitious climate protocol in Copenhagen. By ignoring the G77 countries' readiness to extend the Kyoto Protocol and negotiate a parallel agreement, and instead focusing on a single agreement in which all countries were expected to make significant commitments, the EU created an almost insurmountable contradiction between the rich and poor countries. This was the baggage that country representatives carried to Copenhagen (Axelsson and Gustavsson, 2009).

Towards the end of the Copenhagen negotiations, with Reinfeldt as the EU's chief spokes person, Axelsson noted that the process ended "at an impasse" simply as a result of the EU investing in a completely new agreement (Halldin, 2009; Henriksson, 2009). Maria Wetterstrand, spokesperson of the Green Party, and Jan Eliasson, the former foreign minister for the Social Democrats, presented a similar analysis. Wetterstrand argued that a negotiation tactic in which the big players constantly compared their aspirations with others and questioned those of the EU, the US and China, created adverse conditions in which the goal became to limit commitments as much as possible. The EU claimed that the negotiation dynamics made it impossible for any of the rich countries to control the process. Eliasson noted that the EU's hopes of playing a catalytic role were dashed, partly because of the narrow national approaches of the US and China, and partly because of the EU's "antiquated" negotiation game. Eliasson added that the "subordinate role" played by the countries with the lowest per capita incomes prior to the conference had been detrimental to the process. Despite the knowledge that the G77 countries wanted the Kyoto Protocol tightened up, rather than creating a new non-binding declaration, the EU chose to completely ignore that fact; the result was extensive conflicts between rich and poor countries (Eliasson, 2009; Wetterstrand, 2009). Green Party member Carl Schlyter, who declared that the "Climate fiasco is a crime against humanity", added that leaders from rich countries possessed both the necessary resources and knowledge to act, but chose not to. He blamed leaders of these countries for the collapse of a climate deal (Schlyter, 2009). This sentiment was shared entirely by Diakonia. Diakonia General Secretary, Bo Forsberg, claimed it was the rich countries' unwillingness "to accept their historic responsibility" and commit to making substantial emission reductions that put developing countries in a position where they were not willing, or even able to offer more extensive commitments. With reference to the climate convention chairman, Yvo de Boer, Forsberg argued that large developing countries such as India and China had made commitments to reduce their emissions by 28 per cent, a level that was more ambitious than commitments from developed countries. Forsberg's conclusion was that climate negotiations in the future should not be organized as if rich countries had the "right to dictate the terms of what is to be negotiated and what to come up with". Sweden, as president of the EU, and Denmark, which chaired the climate conference, blamed the failure on unfair negotiating stances. For Forsberg, the "democratization" of the UN process, a process made necessary by the fact that some G77 countries would not go along with what was proposed, provided a foundation for changes needed in the terms of future negotiations (Forsberg, 2009a, 2009b).

Actors within the Green Keynesian discourse thus identified the EU, and to some extent the United States, as the main culprits in Copenhagen's failure. The G77 countries' behaviour was described as reasonable or logical, and almost inevitable, given the underlying logic of the international negotiation scheme as well as the environmental debt. The contrast to the Industrial Fatalist explanation of the collapse could hardly have been sharper.

After Copenhagen: mobilization from below and changing the economic system

Copenhagen was a massive disappointment for actors articulating the Green Keynesian discourse. The failure to sign a new protocol was described by Greenpeace and the World Wildlife Fund as a "death sentence" for millions of people, while the Green Party's Carl Schlyter regarded the failure as a "crime against humanity" (Holm, 2009; Schlyter, 2009). The polemical tone and the harsh words reflected disappointment with the conference, but also testified to an outrage with the inability to produce a contract that was in proportion to the threat posed by climate change. This led some to place their hopes in the global justice movement and a firmly revised economic system.

Even before the Copenhagen conference, representatives from Climate Action, the Swedish Church and Diakonia observed that negotiations increasingly appeared to be headed for a stalemate. Hopes for real change were based on civic mobilization and popular protests before Copenhagen. As argued by Archbishop Anders Wejryd, for example, it was unlikely that politicians would not be influenced by the popular demonstration that took place in Copenhagen on December 12, which gathered some 100,000 people from all over the world: "The hope was in a strong mobilization of citizens" (Ahlefelt, 2009a). When it became clear that the demonstration had not had the desired effect and that the conference would not lead to any ambitious climate deal, environmental organizations and international justice organizations maintained that popular protests nevertheless conveyed hope for the future even if politicians failed. The WWF General Secretary in Sweden, Lasse Gustavsson, explained, for example, that numerous initiatives at the local level were an encouraging and significant counter-force to what had taken place in the Bella Center (Johansson and Wallberg, 2009). Wetterstrand added that social movements and NGOs had been assigned too little influence in Copenhagen and it was necessary that new initiatives be taken "from below". She said it was vital that the positive power from social movements seen in Copenhagen should be perpetuated and deepened (Wetterstrand, 2009). This sentiment was very close to the evaluation made by Bo Forsberg, who promised that Diakonia, together with like-minded organizations around the world, would continue to exert pressure on political leaders to assume moral responsibility and act accordingly. At the next year's climate negotiations, all those who were part of the "global popular movement [would] continue to fight for climate justice" (Forsberg, 2009). Mikael Malméus, spokesperson for Climate Action, added that citizens' voices were missing in the negotiations, although constructive proposals were put forward by developing countries. This idea was strengthened by the members of environmental and social movements who demonstrated outside the Bella Center. In light of this, he thought it was essential that the climate movement should continue mobilizing citizens to "force a transition" (Malméus, 2009).

Bankrupting nature and the need for another economic system

A few years after Copenhagen, two of the most prominent actors in the Green Keynesian discourse articulated their ideas in a slightly different manner. Wijkman and Rockström, in a clear and straightforward book, proclaimed that Industrial Fatalists as well as those promoting green growth were in deep denial about the magnitude of the global environmental challenges and resource constraints facing the world. In their book *Bankrupting Nature* (2013), Wijkman and Rockström tackle major issues facing global society such as resource depletion and population growth, and makes a strong plea for a radical rethink of approaches to economic stability and sustainable development. As humanity continues to live beyond its means, a series of bubbles will make the credit crises of 2008–10 seem like minor irritations. Wijkman and Rockström write that winners and losers are inevitable. If governments do not get serious about climate change, losers will include investors and businesses that have failed to hedge against fossil fuels and fund substitutes. If governments continue to delay sensible policies and natural systems reach dangerous tipping points, millions more can expect to suffer from violent weather, severe food or water shortages, loss of homes and communities in disruption.

Wijkman and Rockström insist their book is about sustainability. Targets for their criticism are industries that fail to aim for efficiency, media that focus on personality more than message, economists who refuse to recognize the costs of eroding natural resources, politicians who avoid long-term planning or policymaking, and entire societies that waste limited resources without considering sustainability. Their message is that climate has no boundaries, but our planet has: and there is no decoupling from the responsibility. In line with the Eco-socialist discourse, Wijkman and Rockström argue, that few scientists convey the full scope of the challenge that lies ahead. Destabilization of any one of the Earth's nine biophysical processes – stratospheric ozone depletion, acidification of the oceans, loss of biodiversity, pollutant concentration, aerosol concentration, climate instability, the nitrogen-phosphate nutrient cycle, and freshwater resources – could speed up the destabilization of the other processes. The writers note that the many benefits of eco-systems are never reflected in traditional economic models. Wijkman and Rockström point clearly to the fact that today's citizens are reducing the capacity to create prosperity for future generations. In their book they clearly discourage quick fixes, such as geoengineering, which could have unforeseen consequences. Measures that aim at both drastic growth and curbing growth could lead to inequality and conflict. Instead, they suggest regulations, taxes, subsidies and tariffs, while also mentioning that the world already possesses the technology to reduce energy consumption to one-fifth of the present level. Adequate institutional forms are also needed (Wijkman and Rockström, 2013).

These reactions reflect the changes of solutions in the Green Keynesian discourse becoming closer to the Eco-socialist discourse. On the one hand, there were high expectations that the UN process could lead to an agreement on emissions that far surpassed that which any single nation offered, or which Fredrik Reinfeldt and Andreas Carlgren considered it possible to achieve. On the other hand, the Green Keynesian discourse took a very critical stance and expressed strong doubts regarding the political will to push the negotiations to include the production and consumption systems that were perceived as inevitable. The discourse also heavily emphasized social movements, non-parliamentary organizations and civil protests as important to putting bottom-up pressure on politicians, which suggested a belief in the UN negotiation process. The UN was the only body that possessed the legitimacy required to forge an international climate agreement that was legally binding. Any other way was impossible, which explained why the criticism of Copenhagen was directed at individual nations and the EU's actions but never at negotiations conducted under the auspices of the UN. It was the rich countries' attitude that had to change, not the negotiating procedure, although many voices stressed that NGOs should be integrated into the process.

The Eco-socialist discourse and the real value of climate meetings

As discussed earlier, the Eco-socialist discourse was marginalized during the climate-change debate and was not part of the dominant discussion (e.g. Levy and Spicer, 2013). But climate justice rose in stature because it was articulated as a concept that connected democratic accountability and participation, ecological sustainability and social justice, and their combined ability to provide solutions to climate change. Social movement researcher David Featherstone has illustrated – similarly to the way that we do in this book – how matters of justice were thrust into the centre of climate politics and that mobilizations before and during the Copenhagen meeting signified the alignment of political forces that "constructed climate change politics in antagonistic ways" (Featherstone, 2013).

Within the Eco-socialist discourse, the Copenhagen conference showed us a picture of a civilization that was in the process of destroying itself and at the same time totally unable to do anything about it; Copenhagen was the last chance to stop the bus, as Malm put it. Although recent research had demonstrated that high concentrations of greenhouse gases would lead to ecosystem collapse, politicians had not generally shown any confidence that an effective and binding climate agreement was within the bounds of possibility. Although the idea was to "secure the conditions of life on this planet" and save low-lying countries such as Bangladesh, the only suggestions offered by rich countries were essentially "a suicide pact". The Eco-socialists accused Reinfeldt and the EU of "playing roulette with the survival of our civilisation". They posed this question: What were the underlying causes of this neglect? (Jonstad, 2009a; Åberg, 2009; Löfgren, 2009).

Economic GDP-growth ideology is incompatible with a serious climate agreement

Ultimately, the Eco-socialists understood the climate crisis as a crisis of capitalism, an economy that required constant expansion not to fail, resulting inevitably in massive social convulsions. Eco-socialists reported that the incessant quest for economic growth, or "growth fetishism", undermined and counteracted any climate action politics. David Jonstad noted that it was the "hunt for economic GDP growth" that drove the consumption of fossil fuels and that only when this was abandoned would opportunities arise to build global agreement on emissions cuts. Growth would lead to increased emissions since 85 per cent of global energy conversions were made with fossil fuels. He was not impressed by politics that assumed the possibility of decoupling economic growth from carbon emission growth, which was merely an expression of industrial modern logic that proclaimed that nature would always be defeated by increasingly sophisticated technology. Any margin that could be created using new and more efficient technologies would be quickly eaten up by economic growth, and consumption of services was found often to be as resource-consuming as commodity consumption. The big problem, according to him, was that virtually the entire human race had become dependent on economic growth, which was why the Copenhagen negotiations were based on maintaining GDP growth; therefore, all of the solutions to these issues had to be consistent with growth targets that were deemed inevitable. The dilemma seemed unsolvable, but Jonstad saw it as unavoidable that sooner or later the ecological consequences of the current thinking on GDP would force a re-examination of "the social logic of the consumption society", of the global distribution of resources, and of ideas about what "the good life" actually meant (Jonstad, 2009a, 2009b).

That the world's political leaders, as well as the major environmental organizations, chose to avoid talking about these issues created, in Jonstad's view, a gap between what was scientifically necessary and what was politically possible. This gap was widening at a terrifying pace and, at its worst, could make large parts of the Earth uninhabitable in less than a lifetime. Two scientific studies published in *Nature* clarified what the Copenhagen negotiations were about, claimed Jonstad. With the current emission-release rate, the remaining capacity for emissions would be consumed within twelve years. This meant that the percentage reductions in carbon emissions proposed by the EU, which would be the basis for climate negotiations, were totally inadequate and that any country that wanted to see a "serious climate agreement" had to ask itself whether it was prepared to negotiate on economic growth and on citizens' consumption patterns (Jonstad, 2009a, 2009b). Against this backdrop Jonstad stood behind Climate Action's campaign "Emergency Stop". Everyone who participated in the campaign promised that until December 18th, when the Copenhagen conference ended, they would not consume more than citizens who lived on welfare. The purpose of this was to demonstrate to policymakers that significant consumption reductions were necessary in order to bring down carbon emissions to acceptable levels, and that there were citizens who were willing to do this. The campaign was, in his opinion at least, an attempt to challenge the dominant Industrial Fatalism and Green Keynesianism practices of not walking the talk. Yet the SSNC and other environmental organizations, he declared, would not touch such a campaign "with a bargepole" (Jonstad, 2009a, 2009b).

Jonstad was not the only one to describe the problems of the Copenhagen conference in this way. Leif Ericsson, Head of Human Rights Day, said that today's young people would become poor if contemporary material consumption was not reduced significantly and comprehensive efforts were not undertaken to tackle climate change. Furthermore, he said that there was no technology in the world that would be able to maintain the current "unsustainable consumer society". What was needed was a "cultural revolution" and a new poverty ideal such as "voluntary simplicity" to avert civilization's course towards catastrophe (Ericsson, 2009). Kajsa Borgnäs, chairman of the Social Democratic Students of Sweden, painted the image of consumer society as a volcano whose eruption in the form of a climate disaster was coming ever closer. The most important issue, from her perspective, was how a society "beyond the economic growth race" could be designed. If that question could be answered the answer could also lead to significant changes in the economic system. If not, climate change would ultimately ruin all the conditions for prosperity. Like Jonstad and Ericsson, she saw no simple technical solution to the climate problem. Even with the global spread of the best technology possible, global warming could only be delayed by a few decades if the capitalistic model of economic growth were maintained. To switch to a new, sustainable and redistributive economy was of course a great and difficult task, but an acceptable alternative was not available. However, if efforts were not made in this direction, the Copenhagen negotiations would be hopeless (Borgnäs, 2009).

Kajsa Borgnäs received support from the social anthropologist Richard Rehnbergh, who was involved in Climax and the Climate Campaign. In the shadow of the failed climate agreement, it had become necessary for industries in rich countries to cease the escalating production of consumer goods, and to develop climate-friendly solutions and renewable energy (Rehnbergh, 2009). The journalist Lars Åberg added that negotiations in Copenhagen were basically about a consumerism that used "energy at all levels, to all ends"; given this, he asked himself if the capitalist economy's inability or refusal to replace fossil fuels with renewable energy sources indicated a system-specific self-destruction, which could easily give rise to hopelessness and alienation. His conclusion was that the Copenhagen conference was one in a series of opportunities to "face the consumerism lifestyle" and that the climate movement was the inspiration to do so (Åberg, 2009). Others in the Eco-socialist discourse criticized the EU's unbridled economic growth policies, resource waste and unilateral focus on promoting the consumption of goods. The resulting increase in carbon dioxide emissions was completely incompatible with the Union's claim to uphold a progressive position in international climate negotiations (e.g. Larsson, 2009; Ljungbeck, 2009). Common to all these voices was the position that climate negotiations in Copenhagen contained no opportunities to curb climate change unless the necessity of fundamental systemic changes was recognized; a comprehensive transformation of the global economic order had to begin. GDP growth was not consistent with active climate action. In a series of UN conferences, "business as usual" in the form of the Industrial Fatalist discourse had demonstrated the inability to achieve any emission reductions. Time was running out and doubts about the UN process had accelerated. Within the Eco-socialist discourse this highlighted the importance of the global climate movement as the only power that provided hope for change.

The start of a new global climate movement

In connection with the Copenhagen conference, 200–300 lateral seminars were arranged and one exhibition hall in the Bella Center was set aside for interest groups to engage in lobbying (Nordström, 2009). On December 12, about 100,000 people marched in a demonstration organized by a broad coalition of environmental and climate organizations, peace movements, trade unions and Christian groups. More than 350 organizations signed a joint petition which contained the demand that politicians in decision-making positions bring about "a binding climate agreement that is both fair and efficient [and] minimizes dangerous climate change" (Söderin, 2009).

An alternative venue, Klimaforum 09, was created by small and independent organizations and a climate meeting for the grass-root social movements in Christiania. These forums came to be of great importance for those who articulated Eco-socialist arguments (Holmbäck, 2009). Attendees included non-parliamentary groups from representatives of the rainforest Indians and farmers' cooperatives from Latin America to large environmental organizations that had been established in the rich world and newly formed climate networks: all of whom gathered at the alternative conferences to pressure politicians. The Eco-socialist discourse characterized this as the birth of a new global climate movement, which joined environmental groups and social justice organizations and which proposed: "It is our turn now". The power and the will of this bottom-up movement was directed against the political incapacity of the UN negotiators inside the Bella Center (Eriksson and Ölander, 2009; e.g. Featherstone, 2013).

System change, not climate change

Actors within the Eco-socialist discourse were divided on how to pressure politicians. Although few people held any hope that the negotiations would result in an agreement that was even close to what was required to halt climate change, many continued to support the UN process. Despite all its shortcomings, according to representatives from Climate Action and Friends of the Earth, the UN was still the only democratically sanctioned and legitimate international political process that could remodel the world's energy, transport and production systems in a matter of decades. The global capitalist system was certainly a fundamental problem, but if anything could be changed, it would have to emerge from the UN process. If the politicians failed, as they were going to, it was easier to replace them than the global economic system given the short time that was available (e.g. Eriksson and Ölander, 2009).

Other Eco-socialists argued that far too much attention and credence was attached to the UN process. Author and social critic Naomi Klein, who opened the conference on the alternative climate summit at Klimaforum 09, declared that UN negotiations could never lead to any climate measures that could be implemented within a reasonable time, because capitalism does not promote altruism and an agreement within the UN framework would always rest on market conditions. For Klein and other Eco-socialists, capitalist profitability and long-term climate responsibility were simply incompatible. Fundamental changes in the global economic system were needed for long-term survival. These non-parliamentary organizations were banned from the conference itself, and the Klimaforum 09 was surrounded by a massive police operation, which was interpreted within the discourse as a sign of the rich countries' reluctance to familiarize themselves with the new movement's demands. One of the most anti-capitalist associations, Climate Justice Action, which had local branches in Sweden and Denmark, went so far as to pronounce the death of the UN process. The UN had failed 15 times to agree on effective climate action; meanwhile, carbon emissions continued to increase. This showed that it was not possible to solve the climate crisis on capitalism's terms, prompting the conclusion that a new world economic order had become ecologically and socially necessary. It followed that the organizations that were gathered under the message "system change, not climate change" advocated civil disobedience and direct action in order to speed up system change. The goal was to move the issue of climate change from the closed and paralysed UN negotiations to the alternative forum created by the global climate movement, thereby creating new conditions for achieving equitable and effective climate action (Malmberg, 2009; Holmbäck, 2009; Myre, 2009). Although Eco-socialists disagreed about the best method, there was an almost total consensus that the movement's initiative was crucial to the future existence of life on Earth. It was this alternative movement, and not the UN, that raised hopes that it was possible to escape climate disaster.

A promising outcry from poor and vulnerable people

It was not just the development of the climate movement that created hope for the Eco-socialists, but also the actions of the G77 countries. When they angrily suspended their participation in Copenhagen and put pressure on rich countries, this highlighted action of the kind that everyone knew was absolutely necessary (Malm, 2009). Alexander Berthelsen declared that the most important accomplishment during the climate summit was that the G77 countries, with support from the 100,000 demonstrators on the streets and the moral awareness of rich countries' historical guilt, questioned the UN process. Contrary to the editorial position of *Dagens Nyheter* and others within the Industrial Fatalist discourse, it was that action that showed the poorest countries as an "influential political entity within the United Nations" (Berthelsen, 2009). In one striking example of the perception gap, the Industrial Fatalist discourse described the Sudanese president as a dogmatic representative of a dictatorial regime, whereas the Eco-socialist discourse said he had delivered a fair critique of the rich countries' scandalous inability to live up to the demands of the IPCC and avoid climate catastrophe. It was emphasized how, in his speech to NGOs, he rejected the EU's position by stating: "Two degrees means certain death for Africa" (Björkström, 2009). Within this discourse, representatives from Sudan and Venezuela were seen as rebelling against their former colonial powers and disobedience was not interpreted as an irrelevant lecture on imperialism, but as an expression of the legitimate demand for rich countries to take responsibility for the climate problem they had created – an act of climate justice (Löfgren, 2009). In light of such an understanding of the G77 countries' actions during the UN conference, and the overwhelming dedication that social movements from the South demonstrated at Klimaforum 09, representatives of Friends of the Earth declared that the climate conference laid the foundation for an alliance between governments and social movements in the global South, and a broad environmental and solidarity movement in the global North. This alliance was an opportunity to revitalize international politics and establish an alternative to the negotiation logic that the EU brought to an end in Copenhagen (e.g. Eriksson and Ölander, 2009).

Eco-socialism after Copenhagen

After the closing ceremony in the Bella Center, the author and journalist Mikael Löfgren pointed out that "another world had become necessary", but that it was questionable whether it was "politically possible" (Löfgren, 2009). Prominent journalist Nils Aage Larsson said the great value of the Copenhagen climate summit was that it brought together and united climate activists from all parts of the world. As for UN negotiations, he held little hope (Larsson, 2009). Neither did Andreas Malm who claimed that these negotiations were conducted in "sleepwalking mode", meaning that all participants were fully aware that the rich countries would do their utmost to minimize their commitments. The contrast between what was going on inside the UN conference rooms and out on Copenhagen's streets was striking, and he concluded: "Although the UN negotiation process has fallen into a coma, still something new was born in Copenhagen: a global climate movement. Its task is to ensure that the fossil economy is brought to an end in the coming years. No movement has ever been more important" (Malm, 2009).

Nature and Youth Sweden (Fältbiologerna), part of the young environmental movement, strongly agreed with this analysis. It was actually "better with no agreement than a fake one" that would overshadow the one positive outcome of the Copenhagen meeting: the birth of a global climate move‑ ment (Berthelsen, 2009; Kihlberg, 2009; Holmin, 2009). Through events in Copenhagen, this movement had been given both common political ground to stand on and an ecologically and socially important political task. All the actors that gathered outside the Bella Center, despite their differences, formed a "global wave of social movements" which constituted a promise that there was a way out of the climate crisis (Holmbäck, 2009). The Eco‑ socialist discourse concluded that any hope for building a society that did not face severe climate‑change would have to come from the extra‑parliamentary movement that brought together non‑profit civic organizations from around the world and channelled their commitment to a fair global shift towards zero‑carbon economies. In this movement the threat of climate change was connected to issues concerning the separation of powers and democracy; the uneven distribution of resources; consumerist self‑destructiveness and the unwillingness of rich countries to tackle real and profound changes (e.g. Bergdahl, 2009; Söderin, 2009). Alexander Berthelsen, for example, expressed hope that in Copenhagen climate activists had come to realize how impor‑ tant it was to demand systemic change rather than suffer climate change (Berthelsen, 2009). After taking part in a demonstration with Climate Justice Action, Axelsson concluded that "polite" demonstrations were inadequate and stressed the importance of confrontational actions, such as the one in which activists inside the Bella Center chanted, "system change, not climate change" in an attempt to break through the wall that had been built around the UN conference (Axelsson, 2009).

The hoped‑for new and significant global social movement to combat cli‑ mate change has not been seen so far. Even though ideas of climate justice have been combined with new knowledge regarding "de‑growth", the debate and the action almost completely diminished in the years after Copenhagen (Martinez‑Alier, 2012). It might have been a great opportunity for Eco‑ socialists to flourish, but apart from bringing the climate justice issue to the debate, it did not happen this time.

Climate Scepticism and the false premise of UN negotiations

If the three previous discourses consistently assumed that the Copenhagen climate summit rested on a sound scientific basis (i.e. the IPCC research reports), the Climate Sceptics claimed that the negotiations were completely devoid of credible scientific knowledge.

No valid science base

One of the most influential Climate Sceptics, Hans Bergström, a former editor‑in‑chief of *Dagens Nyheter*, made fun of that fact that the world's political leaders, including the right‑wing Swedish Prime Minister Fredrik

Reinfeldt, claimed to possess the scientific expertise to compute the average global temperature forty years on from Copenhagen. The fact that they organized a conference for the United Nations in order to adopt measures that would lead to an increase in the temperature by exactly 2 degrees Celsius above pre-industrial levels was, in his eyes, almost absurd. The joke about the politician who had so much faith in his own power that he could "decide the weather" was ironic, but anything but funny. For Bergström it was deeply problematic that a comprehensive global plan for energy, transport and production systems would be built on this "utopia" (Bergström, 2009a). Bergström was far from alone in expressing concerns of this nature. Several representatives of the Climate Sceptic lobby group Stockholm Initiative called it a mass psychosis (e.g. Ahlgren et al., 2009). One of them, science philosopher Ingemar Nordin, added that it was "downright dangerous" if the IPCC's climate predictions formed the basis for decision-making in Copenhagen. A big problem for him was that all UN nations had become dependent on the IPCC. If they had done their own independent evaluations of climate research they would have discovered what was clear to Climate Sceptics: that is, that there was not a "valid scientific basis for the Copenhagen meeting" (Nordin, 2009). The sceptics also opposed the agenda on climate politics that the EU was establishing. Other representatives of the Stockholm Initiative came to similar conclusions. Lars Bern thought that virtually all politicians, regardless of ideology and national origin, appeared to be ready to decide on major international social change as a result of information that was solely "based on fraudulent UN documentation", while Göran Ahlgren and others declared that the very purpose of the Copenhagen conference, to limit the global temperature rise below 2 degrees Celsius, rested on "an illusion without a sound scientific basis" (Bern, 2009; Ahlgren et al., 2009).

What the Climate Sceptics in general, and the Stockholm Initiative representatives in particular, argued was that the politicians at Copenhagen had allowed themselves to be deceived by the UN's climate panel. Through successful propaganda, IPCC scenarios had become truths. This could lead to an extremely costly climate agreement based on a total misrepresentation of information and the mistaken conviction that it had become an ecological necessity. They argued that the Copenhagen summit should not be held, let alone lead to a legal agreement that could subject the global economy to severe stresses with serious social crises as a result.

UN-planned economic politics and its implications

The task of Climate Scepticism, as the Stockholm Initiative interpreted it, was not only to critically examine the state of climate science but also look at its political and economic implications. Thus, both the UN process and the whole idea of global climate politics being under the auspices of the UN were questioned. Hans Bergström claimed that the UN's "detailed economic planning" was neither desirable nor feasible. The Copenhagen conference, from his perspective, was deeply dysfunctional and should have been abandoned altogether. Bergström thought that new energy technology should be allowed to develop without UN-planned economic regulation and in a free market where "the main innovation system and the most dynamic economy could achieve what a slow and corrupt UN is not able to". Bergström expressed sympathy for the US Senate's aversion to handing power over to a corrupt and inefficient UN bureaucracy in order to create legally binding and economically costly climate agreements. He found the US stance more than justified and interpreted it as a result of the country's constitutional tradition, where scrutiny of the exercising of power and the levying of political responsibility constituted key elements (Bergström, 2009a, 2009b). The Stockholm Initiative's general secretary also pointed out that a global agreement to control energy sources, as with any planned economic intervention, would destroy both the global economy and the environment. Measures aimed at large-scale reduction of carbon emissions were therefore not only meaningless and harmful, but also would "only cost money" (Ahlgren, 2009). This harmfulness was stressed by oceanographer Gösta Walin who also was involved in the Stockholm Initiative, and economist Pär Krause who argued that the "drastic climate policy" being focused on presupposed a "counterproductive planned economy" (Walin and Krause, 2009). Bern and Thauersköld even argued that the UN as an organization, had found in the climate issue an ideal justification, in the wake of the Cold War, for extending supranational governance and imposing a planned economy (Bern and Thauersköld, 2009).

The Climate Sceptics also raised warnings that a climate agreement would have unacceptable and unjust impacts on developing countries. Walin and Krause claimed, for example, that action to stop the use of fossil fuels in these countries would "strangle their development" and keep them in social deprivation and economic poverty forever. They argued that emission reductions to limit global warming were likely to mean a human disaster in the form of lost economic growth and lost opportunities for greater prosperity where it was needed most (Walin and Krause, 2009). Marian Radetzki and Nils Lundgren shared this position, arguing that no financial commitments should be forced on developing countries. On top of this they warned that an ambitious climate agreement would lead to a trade war, in which the introduction of taxes would hit poor countries particularly hard (Lundgren and Radetzki, 2009a). Trade sanctions that would force these countries into a global climate regime were immoral, according to the two economists, since free international trade constituted a precondition for the elimination of hunger and economic poverty. Therefore, the chaos in the world economy, which was predicted to be the inevitable consequence of a comprehensive international climate agreement, would primarily affect those who were already suffering the most. Against this background sceptics claimed: "We do not have enough scientific evidence to take risks with the world economy that a high price for carbon emissions brings to the world" (Lundgren and Radetzki, 2009b).

Like the representatives of the Green Keynesianism and Eco-socialist discourses, the Climate Sceptics alleged that the UN's climate politics were likely to be at the expense of developing countries. The big difference was that Climate Sceptics claimed that free trade and market mechanisms benefited Swedish economic interests, whereas the Green Keynesianism and Eco-socialist discourses assumed that the unequal exchange of world markets was a fundamental reason for the unfair global distribution of resources. It followed that they drew fundamentally different conclusions on the need for political regulation of the market. Climate Sceptics maintained that politically motivated interference in the functioning of the market was counterproductive and risky for developing countries.

Hidden motives and predictions of the UN fiasco

Within the Climate Sceptic discourse, a number of other reasons to question the climate summit were aired. At times, these were expressed in polemical suspicions of hidden political motives. Hans Bergström said he had tried to understand what the EU intended to achieve at the UN negotiations. His conclusion was that the Union's climate documents were so vague that they could be likened to speaking in tongues. He suspected the hidden aim of the EU's politics was to transfer considerable amounts of money from Europe's working class to the UN, so that it could pay climate aid to "dictators in Africa". Why the EU would have such intentions or why it was just the working class that would pay was not obvious in Bergström's arguments (Bergström, 2009b). However, it illustrates the readiness within the Climate Sceptic discourse to try to find other motives, often described as "dubious" and "illegitimate", behind climate declarations. Another example of this was offered by Ingemar Nordin on the day the UN conference began. He explained that the EU's action in Copenhagen was dictated by efforts to expand its political power over the market and over citizens (Sievers, 2009). The search for such motifs was not compatible with the recurrent and central assertion within the Climate Sceptic discourse that world leaders had allowed themselves to be led or deceived by the UN climate panel. The contradiction was obvious and another expression of the Climate Sceptics' efforts to criticize the climate change conference, whose meaningfulness they questioned and whose consequences they decried.

When the climate conference approached, the Climate Sceptics predicted failure. Lundgren and Radetzki envisioned "a decoratively packaged fiasco in Copenhagen", while Bergström stated that the UN plan would fail (Lundgren and Radetzki, 2009b; Bergström, 2009a, 2009c; Lomborg, 2009). Stockholm Initiative representatives said the coming fiasco would be a "lesson" for future politicians (Ahlgren et al., 2009). Lundgren, Radetzki and Nordin hoped that the Copenhagen negotiations would not lead to any binding agreement (Schück, 2009; Lundgren and Radetzki, 2009a, 2009b). This stance was the norm for Climate Sceptics, but very unusual in the climate debate.

"Climategate"

A few weeks before the Copenhagen conference something extraordinary occurred. Thousands of emails that climate scientist Philip Jones had sent or received since 1996 were made available after his computer was hacked. Jones was head of the climate unit (CRU) at the University of East Anglia in Norwich, which had contributed substantially to a number of IPCC climate reports. Research carried out over decades at the CRU had supported the case for anthropogenic climate change and this research contributed to the scientific consensus on which climate mitigation policies would have been based. Professor Jones' correspondence revealed his aversion both to Climate Sceptics and to other scientists who questioned the theory of anthropogenic global warming. In November 2009, email correspondence from the CRU at the UEA was uploaded to various websites. On 19 November, Anthony Watts broke the story of the emails in his blog, *Watts Up With That?* The term "Climategate" seems to have been used first on 20 November in a blog by James Delingpole, a writer for UK Conservative newspaper the *Daily Telegraph*. He made this his major blog topic for several weeks. The term Climategate carries a very powerful sense of wrongdoing. One series of emails in particular attracted widespread interest. One of the researchers who was accused of fraud and lying by Dellingpole was Michael Mann, a professor of Earth System Science at Pennsylvania State University. Mann was the main author of a historical temperature reconstruction (dating back to AD 1000 and known as the "hockey stick"), which had become highly influential among climate scientists, policymakers and the media. The hockey stick graph essentially showed an almost flat temperature curve from AD 1000 until the late twentieth century, when temperatures shot up. For a long time the hockey stick had been an icon for describing the warming that resulted from global anthropogenic climate change. Very famously, Al Gore used it in his movie. This fired the Climate Sceptic's questioning of the whole idea that burning fossil fuels was affecting the world's temperature; instead they argued that the temperature rise was due to natural variations in the Earth's climate. Within the global Climate Sceptic discourse the incident was immediately nicknamed Climategate, after the Watergate scandal, and was designated as irrefutable proof that the criticism of the IPCC had been correct (Lahsen, 2013b; Leiserowitz et al., 2013; Nerlich, 2010; Grundmann, 2013). The leaked correspondence was interpreted by leading representatives of the Stockholm Initiative as confirmation that the UN's climate scientists, not only Jones and his colleagues, had pressured scientific journals to prevent the publication of research they disliked; exaggerated global warming by manipulating temperature data; refused to provide their own data; and had used computer models in which a climate disaster was preprogrammed. The conclusion they drew was that Climategate fundamentally damaged confidence in the IPCC climate reports and decisively changed the conditions for the Copenhagen negotiations (Bern, 2009; Thauersköld Crusell, 2009; Goldberg, 2009)

Associate Professor Fred Goldberg repeated this argument when he expressed hope that politicians in Copenhagen would now come to realize that they had, "from day one been misled by the researchers, who are responsible for the IPCC reports": Climategate had displaced the scientific basis of climate negotiations and in this situation there was no reason whatsoever to hold the climate summit (Goldberg, 2009). It soon became evident that these hopes came to nothing. IPCC chief Rajendra Pachauri pointed out in his inaugural speech that the Copenhagen climate panel's conclusions rested on results from many independent research groups from around the world. UN Climate convention chairman Yvo de Boer, added that it was good that the issue of data had emerged, but that the process which led to the IPCC reports included input from 2,500 scientists and was more accurate than any other scientific project of its kind. Their assessment was that the scientific basis for UN negotiations remained stable. Climate Sceptic Bjørn Lomborg withhold that delegates in Copenhagen "quickly rebuffed" what he considered a research scandal (Lomborg, 2009).

Climate Scepticism after Copenhagen

The term Climategate dominated CNN's reporting during the first days of COP15 and set off an international dispute over the quality and trustworthiness of research on anthropogenically caused climate change and the scientists who produced it. Dubbed Climategate by Climate Sceptics and some in the media, the event generated considerable press attention across the United States and around the world, with articles and editorials published in major newspapers such as *The Washington Post*, and scientific journals and stories broadcast on major television and radio networks. Several books were also quickly written by Climate Sceptics in the US and France who used the controversy as proof that climate change was a hoax (Leiserowitz et al., 2012; Aykut et al., 2012). Climategate became the latest in a series of events and arguments that climate change sceptics used during a two-decade campaign to convince the world that climate change was not occurring (Oreskes and Conway, 2010). Six investigations largely exonerated the exposed scientists; they found no evidence of deliberate scientific malpractice and none put the blame on the climate researcher. As in the past, charges of corruption, unconditional faith and conspiracy did not hold up to close analysis, according to the investigators. None of the emails and files upset conclusions that had long prevailed. However, as in previous controversies, perceptions of the scandal took hold and this exaggerated the charges. The investigations did identify problematic aspects of their behaviour, including the tendency to resist the transparency of the data in order to support their scientific findings, the exclusion of the work of certain scientists in peer-reviewed journals and assessments based on extra-scientific considerations (Lahsen, 2009a; Leiserowitz et al., 2012; Nerlich, 2010; Grundmann, 2013).

After Climategate and the failure of Copenhagen, the situation changed dramatically. Actors in the Climate Sceptic discourse attributed the collapse to a UN process that for years had been unable to achieve consensus. No one within the Climate Sceptic discourse in Sweden lamented this failure, but it was also almost the only thing in the UN process they did not oppose (Bergström, 2009c). Later on, the US climate bill stalled in the Senate. Climategate and the failure of Copenhagen coincided with a widespread decline in public acceptance that global warming was happening, was caused by humans, and was a serious threat. A survey carried out by the University of Cardiff in September and November 2009 found a similar trend. This seems to show that Climate Scepticism was certainly strengthened by Climategate, even if it was not triggered by it (Leiserowitz et al., 2013; Nerlich, 2010). Framing the email conversations as a "gate" most probably contributed to this trend. The "gate" had first been used as a label during the Watergate scandal and has come to be used in any scandal involving some type of (suspected) cover-up by politicians. Research in the US suggested that Climategate deepened and perhaps solidified the change in public understanding of climate change. Climategate can also explain the erosion of public trust in scientists as sources of information on global warming after 2010 (Leiserowitz et al., 2013).

In France and the US, the situation after 2009 has been labelled as a third phase of the climate-change debate. The first phase was the carbon-war period of 1990–1998 with its dominating fossil-fuel imaginary. There followed a techno-market period with a carbon promise from 1999 to 2008 (Aykut et al., 2012; Levy and Spicer, 2013). This third period began with the Copenhagen failure and Climategate. In late 2009, two international controversies received substantial media coverage: Climategate and the revelation of errors in the fourth IPCC assessment report concerning the melting of Himalayan glaciers (Lahsen, 2013a). Domestic controversies in France were simultaneously given significant space in the media. These included debates resulting from the publication of a book called *L'Imposture Climatique* [*The Climate Fraud*] and the mobilization of authoritative geographers, peaking in a Climate Sceptic conference. A noteworthy change in France was that new actors and new themes gained access to the media after 2010, most notably scientists and intellectuals who contested claims about the consequences of climate change. Furthermore, sceptical voices had more frequent access to a wider range of media, such as newspapers, magazines and talk shows. Accordingly, climate controversies diversified, and ranged from the impacts of climate change to science–policy relationships, expertise processes, climate sciences, computer modelling, environmental ideology and appropriate climate-protection measures (Aykut et al., 2012).

In Sweden, Climate Scepticism had a very marginal place in the public mind until the Stockholm Initiative entered the scene. Between 2008 and 2010 it still seemed to have a limited influence on Swedish politics. The vast majority of politicians in Sweden said they took climate change seriously, in line with the vast majority of researchers, but perhaps this was not so after all. Jan Ericsson, a Conservative member of parliament promoted books on Climate Scepticism in his blog. In 2010, Ericsson, Christian democrat MPs Ingemar Vänerlöv and Lars Gustafsson, and Conservative MP Sven Yngve Persson invited members of parliament to a seminar with other Climate Sceptics. This event came a few years after Conservative parliamentarian Anne-Marie Pålssons' symposium with Lars Bern, a member of the Stockholm Initiative. In 2014 the Conservatives offered the former editor-in-chief of *Dagens Nyheter*, Hans Bergström, the opportunity to speak at a members meeting, a conversation that was applauded by Ericsson in his blog. In a parliamentary debate on 29 January 2013, the first Swedish political party to proclaim itself as Climate Sceptical emerged. The right-wing national populist Joseph Fransson claimed that the apocalyptic scenario that many painted in the climate debate was false. Fransson said this was "good news unless you are one of those who built up a lucrative career around fake climate science". Like other Climate Sceptics, the Swedish Democrats, a right-wing populist party, occupied a positivist approach to science: except in the case of climate science, which they viewed as a creation of politics and one which had originated from a totalitarian idea (Hultman and Kall, 2014).

Discussion

In three discourses the goal of the Copenhagen climate conference was a legally binding agreement with commitments to restrict emissions. The common starting point was the IPCC's major climate report from 2007, and the scenarios of future climate change outlined in it. The UN panel's declaration that, by 2050, the Earth's average increase in temperature could not exceed 2 degrees Celsius constituted a point of reference for all discourses, except for the Eco-socialists who said this level was politically negotiated and far too modest and the Climate Sceptics who claimed it to be scientific nonsense. The different discourses advanced very different demands for commitments, if any, in Copenhagen.

In the Industrial Fatalist discourse, Reinfeldt and Carlgren had long maintained that the Copenhagen conference was the last opportunity to stop a threatening development. They declared that commitments to reduce carbon emissions by 30 per cent in rich countries by 2020, compared to 1990 levels, and commitments by ability in developing countries, were absolutely necessary if the IPCC's two-degree target was to be reached. The Green Keynesian discourse agreed on the importance of the meeting, but criticized Reinfeldt especially for lowering expectations before the climate summit. The EU's negotiating tactics, where the Union's obligations were conditional upon others, were rejected because they rested on a belief that it was possible to negotiate with the climate. The proposed commitments on emission reductions were found to be completely inadequate. If the two-degree target could be reached it was assumed that rich countries would have to commit to reducing emissions by 40–50 per cent by 2020, and 100 per cent by 2050; whereas until 2020, developing countries would be allowed to talk about possible commitments to limit emissions without having to take any action. The latter was due to demands for climate justice and global economic fairness. Without global justice a climate protocol would never become real. It followed that the Kyoto process, in contrast to what the Industrial Fatalist discourse wanted, should be developed with two separate agreements. If the United States did not accept this, they could join later and not be allowed to block the entire UN process. Those in the Eco-socialist discourse took this a step further. Under their scenario, rich countries would have to reduce their carbon emissions by 100 per cent as soon as possible and shut down the fossil economy – a fundamental system change. For them Reinfeldt's tactics would result in a suicide pact, and the two-degree target was too risky. The carbon dioxide content of the atmosphere needed to be reduced immediately from 387 to 350 parts per million (in 2014 it is above 400). This requirement was communicated to the UN delegates through massive popular protests in Copenhagen. The Climate Sceptics rejected the two-degree objective, but for the opposite reasons: it was deemed unnecessary, costly and unrealistic; plus, its scientific base was entirely discredited. The global economic crisis with disastrous social consequences that Climate Sceptics predicted constituted a far greater threat than the increased concentration of carbon dioxide in the atmosphere. So any UN agreement on emission reductions which would prove to be futile should not be completed at all, according to the Climate Sceptic discourse.

The different demands on climate commitments constituted an accurate assessment of what was needed to reach an international consensus. To that extent, they represented a sort of lower limit. On the other hand, these multiple demands put pressure on UN delegates and created expectations for Copenhagen, which made the UN conference in Bali, two years earlier, fade by comparison. All the discourses postulated that it was in Copenhagen that the world's fate would be decided, no matter what the outcome.

When it was evident that a binding agreement would not be signed, all the discourses described it as a total fiasco. Proponents of the Industrial Fatalism and Green Keynesian discourses were especially disappointed: an attitude that permeated their discourses, albeit in different ways. In the Industrial Fatalist discourse their disappointment mainly concerned their perception that the UN negotiations had bogged down the proceedings. During Copenhagen negotiators focused on detail and procedural issues. This led to a sterile debate over two separate contracts instead of a common agreement, and ultimately gave birth to an agreement in principle without any liability. Despite all efforts, the roadmap to Copenhagen drawn up in Bali had led nowhere. Adherents of the Green Keynesian discourse expressed great disappointment that rich countries, especially the EU and the US, simply watched each other, and refused to accept their historical debt or take responsibility for their environmental footprint. The countries that could have led the way, by making ambitious climate commitments and ensuring the financing of climate actions in developing countries, chose instead to protect their national economic growth targets. This was described as a huge betrayal, especially of people in poor countries. Even within the Eco-socialist discourse, Copenhagen was a disappointment, but not a surprising one. The understanding here was that the UN process was totally dependent on global capitalism. What the climate summit illustrated, according to this discourse, was the inability of politics, at least within the UN framework, to confront and control private corporate interests. Moreover, the exclusion of dissenting voices from the Bella Center and the repressive and oversized police coverage that surrounded the climate negotiations reflected the fundamental lack of democracy and secrecy of the UN process in relation to people's expressions of opinion, according to this interpretation. With it came considerable frustration and anger over the privacy of citizens. The Climate Sceptics were not disappointed though; they wanted a breakdown in negotiations.

The rhetorical question raised by the Climate Sceptics was whether there really was a planned economy that Europeans wanted to reintroduce. They wanted the politicians in the Bella Center, and their plans, to be critically judged before the people of Europe were once again thrown into large-scale political, social, ecological and economic experiments with incalculable and potentially catastrophic consequences. What emerges is a very clear difference from the other discourses, which expressed hopes for the UN process, despite concerns that it was politically toothless. Somewhat inconsistently, the Climate Sceptic discourse showed the greatest faith in UN power to destroy the welfare of the entire planet, while on the other hand criticizing a powerful organization for being weak. The strongest contradiction existed between the Eco-socialist and Climate Sceptic discourses.

While the Eco-socialist discourse criticized the UN process because it took place within the capitalist GDP-growth ideology, the Climate Sceptic discourse questioned the process because it was based on planned micromanagement of the market, which was thought to be detrimental to the economy and environment. Both discourses claimed to speak on behalf of the public interest and developing countries, and against autocratic international policymakers. What the two discourses illustrated, by virtue of their strong antagonism, was that international climate politics produced profound differences that could not be solved by technical efficiency or the establishment of administrative and legal structures for handling the problem. Paradoxically and unintentionally, they shared a common cause in their fight against the efforts of Industrial Fatalism to conserve the capitalist market society. In this particular respect, they could also be said to have received support from actors articulating the Green Keynesian discourse.

The four discourses explained the failure in Copenhagen in completely different ways. The Industrial Fatalist discourse blamed the G77 countries' obstructions of the negotiation process and their insistence on maintaining the Kyoto Protocol as the main reason for failure. This argumentation was as follows: some countries, including the 130 who belonged to the G77, did not intend to contribute to a climate agreement, but instead used the negotiations to criticize global resource allocation and historical injustice. By refusing to cooperate, they could determine conditions for the consensus-oriented negotiations and thwart all constructive efforts to bring about a binding agreement. The conclusion was that these countries had "kidnapped" COP 15. In addition, Industrial Fatalists blamed the US and China for their passive approach; these two countries were not prepared to make commitments on a scale of those that the EU made. The EU was described in the Industrial Fatalist discourse as a rational, sensitive and caring actor that had been betrayed by its partners and disrespected by the children that it wanted to help. The prospect for agreement was destroyed from two directions.

In contrast, the Green Keynesian discourse saw the EU as the principal villain. The EU was trying to deviate from the Bali agreement to both negotiate the renewal of the Kyoto Protocol and a new separate contract that included all the UN countries. The EU's concentration on bringing about a new agreement had brought the entire UN process to an impasse. Although during the autumn of 2009 the G77 countries – on several occasions – declared that they would not accept a deal in which the Kyoto Protocol was not renewed after 2012, the EU became an ally of the US. This prompted several G77 countries to refuse to participate in a new climate treaty to replace the Kyoto Protocol. They feared that a new agreement would not be based on the principle that rich countries caused the climate problem and therefore had the responsibility to fix it, even though developing countries would have to cut emissions too. According to the Green Keynesian discourse, which viewed climate justice and global resource allocation as conditions for an effective climate agreement, it was not G77 countries who obstructed the negotiations in Copenhagen, but the EU. The G77 countries interpreted climate justice as meaning that rich countries would recognize their historical debt. In the Green Keynesian discourse this was inevitable and morally justified. The major problem in Copenhagen, according to this discourse, was that the rich countries had ignored the G77 countries' positions and importance as political subjects both before and during the negotiations.

In many ways, the Eco-socialist discourse shared this analysis, although the inability of the UN process to manage unsustainable economic growth was emphasized in a completely different way. As long as national growth objectives were superior to climate measures, there was no potential for achieving a new climate protocol ambitious enough to halt global warming. Eco-socialists declared that the UN, which operated within global capitalist conditions, could never handle the climate crisis; the outcome of the Copenhagen conference was inevitable. It was the product of a self-destructive economic system and illustrated the need for system change. The capitalist economic system showed itself once again to be incapable of any self-imposed limitations. Although the Climate Sceptics also pointed to the UN process as a major cause of the fiasco, they blamed the inertia of the planned-economy communist-oriented UN bureaucracy. The entire negotiation process was described as extremely inefficient. In their view, the development of energy technologies should be left solely to market and innovation dynamics.

The climate politics of the UK and US were characterized in a similar manner. Rogers-Hayden, Hatton and Lorenzoni portrayed the UK landscape as follows (for the US, see Levy and Spicer, 2013):

> Struggling against the dominant discourses of climate change and energy security are (a) a counter-hegemonic discourse of climate change as a societal issue resulting from unsustainable use of the Earth's resources; this can only be solved by implementing sustainable lifestyles including reducing the demand for energy; (b) a counter-hegemonic discourse of predictable supply issues in which greater diversity of energy supply is needed, including greater use of renewable energy. These two counter-hegemonic discourses come together to support a wider agenda in which reflection by society is needed, while energy demand is reduced, and energy supply diversity increased. This resulting discourse does not, however, necessarily exclude nuclear new build as an option for the UK; it is considered as an option within a larger long-term societal transition.
>
> (Rogers-Hayden et al., 2011)

The differing explanations within the four discourses also led to very different conclusions about how the UN process should be developed after Copenhagen. The Industrial Fatalist discourse demanded that the heterogeneous G77 countries should not be treated as a collective in ongoing UN negotiations. There were also voices commenting that some UN countries should be denied access to the negotiations because they devoted themselves to sabotage. Other proposals suggested that the 20 largest emitting countries create a new forum outside the UN framework. The Green Keynesian discourse emphasized instead that the pressure of civic public opinion on UN delegates must be intensified in all countries and that non-parliamentary environment and solidarity organizations needed to be integrated into the negotiation process in a completely different way. If that had been the case in Copenhagen, perhaps the collapse could have been avoided. Within the Eco-socialist discourse the expectation with regard to the continuation of the UN process was of considerably less interest. They emphasized the importance of the global climate movement, alternative conferences and international cooperation at the local level between popular movements in the global North and the global South. All these viewpoints highlighted the value of continued work on climate change, outside the commoditized UN process (e.g. Featherstone, 2013). The failure of the UN process was understood as the best that could happen since it was led by the Industrial Fatalist discourse. Climate Sceptics declared that the UN climate talks came to an end in Copenhagen because there was no science to support the talks.

In summary, the preparation for and the outcome of the Copenhagen climate conference meant that the four climate discourses made some changes to their positions. The climate talks in Copenhagen and the absence of agreement resulted in some convergence between the discourses that postulated that emission reductions must be made immediately. The IPCC's warning of an impending climate catastrophe and a shared disenchantment with the UN's inability to forge a consensus could have softened the discourse positions and forced a compromise. The Eco-socialist and Green Keynesian discourses, especially, become closer to one another owing to the issues of climate justice and the failure of political negotiations in Copenhagen. This culminated in a common critique of the economic system and a quest for a global environmental movement that could create pockets of change.

The years after Copenhagen have been very different from the years before. The peak of an attention cycle was reached regarding climate change and Climategate changed the public perception of the issue: since climate change had stayed at the top of media and political agendas for a couple of years, more controversial framing followed. As a high-profile issue, climate change produced media, scientific and political capital. Events such as Copenhagen and Climategate accelerated an ongoing process, as actors with other priorities, working methods and world views once again emerged and challenged the existing ownership structure of climate change. If we are to understand Copenhagen and the aftermath it is important to understand the way that social movements turned climate negotiations into antagonistic politics. The issue of climate justice signalled alternatives to the hegemony of Industrial Fatalism. When this played out, the discourse of Industrial Fatalism could not maintain its unity because it challenged actors from fossil-fuel dependent companies, governments and citizens. This antagonism clarified the unequal distribution of climate consequences and guilt (Featherstone, 2013). But the drop in mass media attention and the change in political priorities are harder to explain. It is exactly that question that occupies us in the concluding chapter.

References

"Höj rösten om klimatet", *Aftonbladet* 8/7 2009a.
"Vem bestämmer klimatmålen?", *Aftonbladet* 26/8 2009b.
"Betalar istället för att ta ansvar", *Aftonbladet* 31/10 2009c.
"Jorden utan ledarskap", *Borås Tidning* 20/12 2009.
"EU vill ha högre bud vid spelbordet", *Dagens Nyheter* 20/7 2009a.
"Fiasko för FN", *Dagens Nyheter* 20/12 2009b.

"Mål för uthålliga realister", *Dagens Nyheter* 12/12 2011.
"Snåla Europa", *Expressen* 13/9 2009.
"Sista given i klimatpokern", *Helsingborgs Dagblad* 16/8 2009.
"Pengarna på bordet, Carlgren!", *Östgöta-Correspondenten* 25/7 2009.
"Vilja är att kunna", *Sydsvenska Dagbladet* 7/9 2009a.
"Inga mirakel att vänta", *Sydsvenska Dagbladet* 13/10 2009b.
"Klimatekvation söker lösning", *Sydsvenska Dagbladet* 18/12 2009c.
"Berget födde en råtta", *Sydsvenska Dagbladet* 20/12 2009d.
"Tyngsta Spelarna har lagt sina bud", *Sydsvenska Dagbladet* 4/12 2009e.
"Historisk chans gick Kina förbi", *Uppsala Nya Tidning* 20/12 2009.
Åberg, L. "I väntan på apokalypsen", *Sydsvenska Dagbladet* 12/12 2009.
Ådahl, M. and Johansson, M. "Klimatmötet på väg mot fiasko", *Svenska Dagbladet* 13/10 2009.
Ahlefelt, A. "Hoppet står till en stark folklig opinion", *Kyrkans Tidning* 2009a:46, p. 11.
Ahlefelt, A. "Kyrkor mobiliserade i klimatkampen", *Kyrkans Tidning* 2009b:51, p. 20.
Ahlgren, G. "Åtgärderna mot koldioxid slösar bort vårt välstånd", *Svenska Dagbladet* 18/11 2009.
Ahlgren, G. et al., "Klimatlarmen har skapat en masspsykos", *Svenska Dagbladet* 31/7 2009.
Axelsson, L. "En vecka i COPenhagen", *Fältbiologen* 2009:4.
Axelsson, S. "Visa nu att du menar allvar, Stefan Löfvén", *Aftonbladet* 5/2 2012.
Axelsson, S. and Gustavsson, L. "Reinfeldt borde sätta press på USA", *Svenska Dagbladet* 12/11 2009.
Axelsson, S. and Lindberg, E. "Ingen tid att förlora", *Nerikes Allehanda* 29/11 2009.
Axelsson-Nycander, G. and Ekelund, T. "Sänk inte förväntningarna på klimatmötet i Köpenhamn!", *Borås Tidning* 20/11 2009.
Aykut, S. C., Comby, J. B. and Guillemot, H. (2012). Climate change controversies in French mass media 1990–2010. *Journalism Studies*, 13(2), 157–74.
Baltscheffsky, S. "Tiden är knapp för att nå klimatavtalet", *Svenska Dagbladet* 17/12 2009.
Bengtsson, J. "Kan de rädda planeten?", *Frihet* 2009:7.
Bergdahl, G. "Tänk om klimatmötet är på riktigt!", *Helsingborgs Dagblad* 19/12 2009.
Berglund, G. "Bakslag inför mötet om klimatfrågorna", *Helsingborgs Dagblad* 16/11 2009.
Bergström, H. "Besluta om vädret", *Dagens Nyheter* 16/7 2009a.
Bergström, H. "Global dimma", *Dagens Nyheter* 30/9 2009b.
Bergström, H. "Efter fiaskot", *Dagens Nyheter* 31/12 2009c.
Bern, L. "Dags att syna forskarbluffen", *Sydsvenska Dagbladet* 1/12 2009.
Bern, L. and Thauersköld, M. (2009). *Chill-out. Sanningen om klimatbubblan.* Hårda kulor förlag.
Berthelsen, A. "Bättre inget avtal, än ett fejkat", *Fältbiologen* 2009:4, p. 10.
Bildt, C. et al., "Vi har enats inför höstens klimatmöte i Köpenhamn", *Dagens Nyheter* 12/9 2009.
Björk, I. et al., "EU:s låga ambition kan sabotera klimatavtalet", *Göteborgs-Posten* 29/9 2009.
Björkström, S. "2dagar@BC", *Fältbiologen* 2009:4.
Blühdorn, I. (2011). The politics of unsustainability: COP15, post-ecologism, and the ecological paradox. *Organization and Environment*, 24(1), 34–53.
Borgnäs, K. "För en ekonomi bortom tillväxtjakten", *Tiden* 2009:6.
Borgström-Hansson, C. "Bil, biff och bostad är våra klimatbrott", *Aftonbladet* 16/12 2009.

Boykoff, M. T. (2011). *Who speaks for the climate? Making sense of media reporting on climate change.* Cambridge University Press.

Brors, H. "Enighet om klimatmål – men Kina bromsar", *Dagens Nyheter* 9/7 2009.

Brundin Danielsson, M. "Vad har hänt med klimatfrågan?", *Medmänsklighet* 2011:5.

Caballos, B. and Losman, B. "Ska vi lösa klimatproblemen duger inte sandlådegnäll", *Borås Tidning* 9/11 2009.

Carlgren, A. "Högst två grader varmare", *Nerikes Allehanda* 3/10 2009a.

Carlgren, A. "Köpenhamnsmötet kan alltjämt bli en milstolpe", *Dagens Nyheter* 16/11 2009b.

Carlgren, A. "Rädda regnskogen avgörande för klimatet", *Göteborgs-Posten* 5/12 2009c.

Carlgren, A. "EU:s press börjar bära frukt", *Västerbottens-Kuriren* 8/12 2009d.

Carlgren, A. and Västerteg, C. "Begränsad tillväxt ingen väg ut ur klimatkrisen", *Borås Tidning* 28/7 2009.

Chatterton, P., Featherstone, D. and Routledge, P. (2013). Articulating Climate Justice in Copenhagen: Antagonism, the Commons, and Solidarity. *Antipode*, 45(3), 602–20.

Edman, S. "Klimatkrisen avgörs i världens städer", *Göteborgs-Posten* 9/12 2009.

Ek, L. "Det här är Sveriges linje i samtalen om klimatet", *Dagens Nyheter* 1/12 2011.

Eklund, B. and Havén, S. "Vi måste vända världen rätt igen", *Miljömagasinet* 2009:52/53

Eliasson, J. "FN kan besluta om klimatet utan enhällighet", *Dagens Nyheter* 23/12 2009.

Eriksson, K. and Ölander, M. "Aktivisterna kan få revansch i Köpenhamn", *Expressen* 10/12 2009.

Esmailian, S. "Bördan skjuts mot u-länderna", *Arbetaren* 2009:44.

Falk, J. "Klimatet en rättvisefråga", *Dagens Nyheter* 22/10 2009.

Fälth, M. et al., "Fattiga kvinnor får betala klimatnotan", *Göteborgs-Posten* 15/12 2009.

Featherstone, D. (2013). The Contested Politics of Climate Change and the Crisis of Neo-liberalism. *ACME: An International E-Journal for Critical Geographies, 12*(1).

Forsberg, B. "Rika länders agerande förklarar misslyckandet i Köpenhamn", *Borås Tidning* 24/12 2009a.

Forsberg, B. "Fattinga tvingas vänta på de rika", *Nerikes Allehanda* 24/12 2009b.

Fröberg, J. "De pekas ut som skyldiga", *Svenska Dagbladet* 19/12 2009.

Goldberg, F. "Varför fuskar klimatforskare?", *Debatt, Sanningssökande, Mediakritik* 2009:5/6, s 5–13.

Grundmann, R. (2013). "Climategate" and The Scientific Ethos. *Science, Technology and Human Values, 38*(1), 67–93.

Halldin, M. "Därför kollapsade samtalen", *Dagens ETC* 2009:52, p. 13.

Henriksson, K. "Så förändrade han klimatet" *Expressen* 17/12 2009.

Holm, M. "Klimatmötet en stor besvikelse", *Dagens ETC* 2009:52.

Holmbäck, C. "Sverige får kritik för passivitet inför COP 15", *Arbetaren* 2009:38.

Holmin, S. "Idag är dagen före", *Fältbiologen* 2009: 4, p. 22.

Hultman, M. and Kall, A.-S. Klimatskepticism frodas på högerkanten, *Sydsvenska Dagbladet* 9/9 2014.

Hysing, E. (2014). A green star fading? A critical assessment of Swedish environmental policy change. *Environmental Policy and Governance, 24*(4), 262–74.

Johansson, M. et al., "Fredrik Reinfeldt, klimaträttvisa nu!", *Borås Tidning* 29/9 2009a.

Johansson, M. et al., "Klimatet måste få en prislapp", *Norrländska Socialdemokraten* 6/10 2009b.

Johansson, R. and Wallberg, P. "Hela världen såg hur värmen steg", *Helsingborgs Dagblad* 19/12 2009.

Jonstad, D. "Sista chansen att tvärnita", *Göteborgs-Posten* 22/11 2009a.

Jonstad, D. "Klimatfilm slår premiärrekord", *Fokus* 2009b:38.

Karlsson, L.-I. "Kris när Afrika pressade i-länderna", *Dagens Nyheter* 15/12 2009a.

Karlsson, L.-I. "Dödläget bröts några minuter i tolv", *Dagens Nyheter* 18/12 2009b.

Kihlberg, D. "Nu är det vår tur", *Fältbiologen* 2009:4, s 15.

Kjöller, H. "Kyligt i Köpenhamn", *Dagens Nyheter* 17/12 2009.

Knaggård, Å. (2014). What do policy-makers do with scientific uncertainty? The incremental character of Swedish climate change policy-making. *Policy Studies* 25(1), 22–39.

Kommittédirektiv (2014):53, Klimatfärdplan 2050 – strategi för hur visionen att Sverige år 2050 inte har några nettoutsläpp av växthusgaser ska uppnås.

Krüger, M. and Strömberg, Y. "Fult spel bakom klimatåtagandena", *Svenska Dagbladet* 17/12 2009.

Krüger, M. "Grön omställning skapar två miljoner nya jobb", *Göteborgs-Posten* 20/9 2009.

Lahsen, M. (2013a). Anatomy of dissent. A cultural analysis of climate skepticism. *American behavioral scientist*, 57(6), 732–53.

Lahsen, M. (2013b). Climategate: the role of the social sciences. *Climatic change*, 119(3–4), 547–58.

Landinez Wetterstrand, H. and Vennström, T. "De spelar med höga insatser", *Arbetaren* 2009.

Larsson, N.-A. "Klimatmötets stora poäng", *Göteborgs-Posten* 15/12 2009.

Leiserowitz, A. A., Maibach, E. W., Roser-Renouf, C., Smith, N. and Dawson, E. (2013). Climategate, public opinion, and the loss of trust. *American Behavioral Scientist*, 57(6), 818–37.

Levy, D. L. and Spicer, A. (2013). Contested imaginaries and the cultural political economy of climate change. *Organization*, 20(5), 659–78.

Lidskog, R. and Elander, I. (2012). Ecological modernization in practice? The case of sustainable development in Sweden. *Journal of Environmental Policy and Planning*, 14(4), 411–27.

Lillemets, A. and Schlaug, B. "Varva ner och dela", *Nerikes Allehanda* 23/10 2009.

Lindquist, K. "Mobiliseringen fortsätter", *Arbetaren* 2009:46.

Ljungbeck, O. "Medborgarna utsatta för det största bedrägeriet någonsin", *Kritiska EU-fakta* no. 115, 2009.

Löfgren, M. "Är en annan värld möjlig?", *Dagens Nyheter* 21/12 2009.

Lomborg, B. "Tomma löften räddar inte världen", *Sydsvenska Dagbladet* 14/12 2009.

Lönnaeus, O. "Köpenhamnsmötet riskerar bli fiasko", *Sydsvenska Dagbladet* 22/10 2009.

Lundgren, N. and Radetzki, M. "Handelskrig hotar efter Köpenhamn", *Sydsvenska Dagbladet* 2/12 2009a.

Lundgren, N. and Radetzki, M. "Räkna med klimatfiasko i Köpenhamn", *Aftonbladet* 25/11 2009b.

Machel, G. et al., "Afrika betalar dyrt för utsläppsfesten", *Aftonbladet* 14/12 2009.

Magnusson, E. "Reinfeldt tror mer på vilja än avtal", *Sydsvenska Dagbladet* 3/12 2009.

Malm, A. "Sömngångarvärld", *Dagens Nyheter* 17/12 2009.

Malmberg, J. "Låt dem inte komma undan med ett svek till", *Helsingborgs Dagblad* 9/12 2009.

Malméus, M. "Slutet på ny start för klimatrörelsen", *Arbetaren Zenit* 2009:52/53.

Malméus, M. et al., "Politiker löser inte klimatfrågan åt oss", *Nerikes Allehanda* 24/10 2009.

Martinez-Alier, J. (2012). Environmental justice and economic degrowth: an alliance between two movements. *Capitalism Nature Socialism*, 23(1), 51–73.

Martinez-Alier, J. and Alier, J. M. (2003). *The Environmentalism of the Poor: a Study of Ecological Conflicts and Valuation.* Cheltenham: Edward Elgar Publishing.

Matsson, C. "Visa ledarskap, Sverige", *Ordfront Magasin* 2009:4, p. 7.

Methmann, C. and Rothe, D. (2012). Politics for the day after tomorrow: The logic of apocalypse in global climate politics. *Security Dialogue, 43*(4), 323–44.

Morgan, J. "Europa måste visa ledarskap", *Svenska Dagbladet* 9/11 2009.

Myre, B. "Splittring tjänar ingen på", *Arbetaren* 2009:46, s 2–3.

Nerlich, B. (2010). 'Climategate': paradoxical metaphors and political paralysis. *Environmental Values, 19*(4), 419–42.

Nordin, H.-E. "En hotfull verklighet", *Nerikes Allehanda* 11/12 2009.

Nordin, I. "FN:s klimatpanel är inte vetenskaplig", *Svenska Dagbladet* 10/11 2009.

Nordström, N. "Ambulerande klimatcirkus", *Helsingborgs Dagblad* 10/12 2009.

Ohly, L. et al., "Solidaritet måste prägla avtalet", *Svenska Dagbladet* 12/12 2009.

Oreskes, N. and Conway, E. M. (2010). *Merchants of Doubt: How a Handful of Scientists Obscured the Truth on Issues from Tobacco Smoke to Global Warming.* New York: Bloomsbury Publishing.

Pehrsson, L. "Klimatmötet i FN utan framgång", *Dagens Nyheter* 23/9 2009.

Radetzki, M. and Lundgren, N. "En grön fatwå har utfärdats", *Ekonomisk debatt* 2009:5.

Rehnbergh, R. "I skuggan av klimatavtalet: Oljeindustri och stigande havsyta", *Fjärde världen* 2009:4.

Reinfeldt, F. "Nu måste USA och Kina följa EU i klimatfrågan", *Dagens Nyheter* 3/11 2009a.

Reinfeldt, F. "EU:s ledarskap har visat vägen", *Svenska Dagbladet* 21/11 2009b.

Reinfeldt, F. "Därför floppade vi på klimatmötet", *Aftonbladet* 23/12 2009c.

Reinfeldt, F and Barroso, J.M. "Klimatfrågan viktigast i L'Aquila", *Svenska Dagbladet* 8/7 2009.

Rockström, J. and McGlade, J. "EU:s klimatpolitik är ovetenskaplig och farlig", *Dagens Nyheter* 23/7 2009.

Rockström, J. and Wijkman, A. "Ett mirakel krävs i Köpenhamn", *Svenska Dagbladet* 7/12 2009.

Rockström, J. and Szombatfalvy, L. "Om medierna prioriterar klimatet lyssnar politikerna", *Dagens Nyheter* 14/12 2011.

Rogers-Hayden, T., Hatton, F. and Lorenzoni, I. (2011). "Energy security" and "climate change": Constructing UK energy discursive realities. *Global Environmental Change, 21*(1), 134–42.

Schlyter, C. "Klimatfiaskot brott mot mänskligheten", *Aftonbladet* 18/12 2009.

Schmidt, A., Ivanova, A. and Schäfer, M. S. (2013). Media attention for climate change around the world: A comparative analysis of newspaper coverage in 27 countries. *Global Environmental Change, 23*(5), 1233–48.

Schück, J. "Klimatlarmen sågas av tunga ekonomer", *Dagens Nyheter* 23/6 2009.

Sievers, J. "Professorn sågar klimatvetenskapen", *Östgöta Correspondenten* 7/12 2009.

Söderin, S. "Starten på en ny klimatrörelse", *Dagens ETC* 2009:49.

Svensson Smith, K. and Edman, S. "Att ta klimatansvar är en fråga om moral", *Svenska Dagbladet* 5/12 2009.

Swedish Government homepage (Accessed on 8 August 2014) Roadmap 2050 http:// www.regeringen.se/sb/d/15365.

Thauersköld Crusell, M. "Kalla fakta om het skandal", *Svensk Linje* 2009:4, s 34–35.

Törnvall, M. "Reinfeldt kräver tydliga miljömål", *Dagens industri* 23/9 2009.

Trafikverket (2013). *Nationell plan för transportsystemet 2014 – 2025.*

Walin, G. and Krause, P. "U-länder måste få öka utsläppen", *Aftonbladet* 2/11 2009.
Wallström, M. et al., "Förorenaren måste stå för notan", *Svenska Dagbladet* 23/7 2009.
Westlund, Å. "Håll rent på hemmaplan", *Västerbottens Folkblad* 21/7 2009.
Wetterstrand, M. "Reinfeldts attityd hotar klimatet", *Göteborgs-Tidningen* 1/12 2009.
Wijkman, A. and Rockström, J. (2013). *Bankrupting Nature*. London:Routledge.

7 Apocalyptic framing and conservative action?

A concluding discussion

For at least fifty years, climate-change debate has been part of the controversies concerning the global environment. In forms of anthropogenic global warming (AGW) and climate change, this notion has haunted human civilization since the middle of the enlightened 1960s. Since the establishment of the Intergovernmental Panel on Climate Change (IPCC), climate change has become a reoccurring issue that is high-profile, political, scientific and global. Sweden was part of this development through its organization of the first UN conference on global environment in 1972. It was also the first country to have a specific carbon dioxide tax legitimized by climate change and implemented in 1989. In the 1990s, Sweden entered a new age of environmental politics that was conceptualized as ecological modernization and characterized by managerial practices with regard to environmental problems, which were handled with new technology, carbon markets and green consumption. But climate change still was a spectre for this seemingly established political hegemony, and the period from 2006 to 2009 was to be marked by profound disagreements, all over the world, on the future of society.

The historical changes of the climate-change debate can be characterized in three phases. The first phase was a political awakening in which issues of sustainability were almost turned into transitional politics under the pressure of climate change and the environmental justice demands that led to the signing of the Kyoto Protocol. The emergence of the climate issue in the late 1980s posed a serious challenge to the fossil-fuel industry, which supports 85 per cent of the world's energy consumption. Regulatory controls on carbon and subsidies on cleaner technologies threatened economic profitability and the dominance of this energy intense sector over global politics. The rise of environmental organizations and the growing role of multilateral agencies presented the possibility of formulating transitional strategies (Knaggård, 2014). At the same time, growing public sensitivity to environmental issues augured a cultural shift. The aggressive response from industry to this perceived threat included the formation of issue-specific associations and lobbying towards politicians who challenged the science of climate change and pointed to the high economic costs of reducing emissions (Levy and Spicer, 2013; Aykut et al., 2012).

The second phase was characterized by a seemingly smooth consensus of hegemonic ecomodern managerial politics; it lasted until the years before Copenhagen, during which climate justice issues were once again put on the agenda. The ecomodern discourse gained support among politicians, business and environmental groups, forming the basis for a compromise structured around the promise of a gradual transition to a low-carbon economy through the creation of carbon dioxide markets and climate-friendly consumption that would not threaten existing energy companies. Large-scale business began to acknowledge the inevitability of emissions regulation, a rising price on carbon and new low-carbon technologies. By the beginning of the twenty-first century, the perceived balance of risks and rewards had shifted. In this changing landscape business and governments took steps to reduce their political and public relations costs by denying the evidence produced by climate science and opposing regulation. While most firms preserved their core strategies, they increasingly hedged their bets by making modest investments in low-carbon technologies and products and measuring and managing their carbon emissions (Levy and Spicer, 2013). A broad group of actors, from business to state agencies and environmental groups, became united on the ecomodern discourse, (Anshelm and Hansson, 2011) even portraying it as a new utopia in forms such as the hydrogen economy (Hultman and Nordlund, 2013) or bio economy (Birch, 2006; Schmidt et al., 2012; Levidow, et al., 2012) as well as the eco-efficient economy analysed in this book.

This managerial deadlock thus set the stage for Copenhagen, but the conflict was actually in evidence during the years before the meeting. Underlying disagreements were made visible again and intertwined with the rise in environmental climate justice solidarity groups all over the globe, who, together with scientists, concerned politicians and influential economists put climate change once again on the global agenda; this time more profoundly than ever before (Schmidt, Ivanova and Schäfer, 2013; Featherstone, 2013). In Sweden, as well as globally, the issue of global climate change was communicated as a matter of apocalyptic dimensions from the autumn of 2006 through to 2009. NGOs, scientists and global networks of environmental justice movements now influenced the political agenda at large. The Stern report on climate-change costs, the screening of Al Gore's film *An Inconvenient Truth* and the publication of the IPCC's fourth report on global climate change helped get it going (Sampei and Aoyagi-Usui, 2009; Lyytimäki and Tapio, 2009; Kurz et al., 2010; Reusswig, 2010; Schmidt et al., 2013). In response, conservative action was recommended by the dominating Industrial Fatalist discourse in order to cope with such dire predictions, in Sweden as well as globally (Swyngedouw, 2013a, 2013b).

This book has shown that between 2006 and 2009 the climate debate was intense and filled with disagreements. These disagreements challenged the neo-liberalization that had dominated Swedish environmental politics since the early 1990s. When climate change was interpreted as a call to rethink contemporary society's basic organization, Swedish society woke up to what was happening and politics was rediscovered as part of everyday life. We have analysed political actor's arguments in all kind of printed media, consisting of over 3,500 editorials, opinion pieces, political commentaries, books and major feature articles, and as a result we have been able to go beyond ordinary analysis of mass media or political science to examine how global warming, climate change and sustainability were described by leading politicians and commentators, thereby illuminating the antagonism that infiltrated climate change. An interesting and important pattern emerged that is only visible when conducting an in-depth study and interpretation of a large body of empirical material.

Market neo-liberalism was in government and hegemonic in almost all areas of political life in Sweden during this period. The Liberal–Conservative government was never seriously challenged when it implemented the transformation from citizen-owned infrastructures and institutions to privately owned market based solutions. Neo-liberalism in the form of New Public Management appeared simultaneously with claims to superior administrative skills that would represent the interests of all citizens. Suddenly this set-up was confronted by an environmental and climate debate which included strong ideological conflicts regarding concrete living conditions in a future climate-friendly society, both in Sweden and around the globe. Fundamental ideological frictions related to notions of what a "good society" is, how international justice should be understood and what our responsibilities towards future generations mean, generated highly divergent demands for political action and extensive social changes, far beyond anything that existing market mechanisms and innovation systems were capable of providing. The environmental and climate debate once again filled the whole of society with dystopian and utopian energies, and the strongest ideological confrontation appeared, for a few years, to be concentrated precisely on this issue.

Later, the dominant Industrial Fatalist discourse even made a pervasive effort to neo-liberalize the climate debate and narrow it down to the measures that would be most effective in the context of a market-liberal regime, as if there was a complete consensus on the goal. Conflicts regarding political values arose constantly and were emphatically created by alternative discourses that fought to take control of the climate debate. Green Keynesianism, Eco-socialism and Climate Scepticism challenged the Industrial Fatalist market-liberalism hegemony in their proposals for formulating the future design of society. But now, just a few years later, the situation looks totally different: as if anthropogenic climate changes were no longer occurring.

Copenhagen as the highpoint of attention and expectations

A review of articles from leading Swedish newspapers during the UN conference in Durban, in December 2011, showed that the tone of the climate debate had shifted radically during the two years after the Copenhagen negotiations; the movement towards taking necessary action at an international level regarding this issue had lost its momentum (*Dagens Nyheter*, 2011). Within the Industrial Fatalist discourse climate change was now downplayed. Climate change was no longer a question for human civilization, such that even the Conservative prime minister, Reinfeld, talked about it in 2008. The lowered attention globally was similarly remarkable (Schmidt, Ivanova and Schäfer, 2013). Copenhagen can thereby be described as the highpoint of an attention cycle that began in 2006 and most probably will return again. Copenhagen was described as a total fiasco regarding negotiations and was seen as a failure of international politics by all discourses except the Climate Sceptic discourse. Either the G77, the USA, China, the EU, or the whole political elite, was blamed. The contrast between what was going on inside the Bella Center and out in Copenhagen's streets and squares was striking. Those who believed in the UN process reacted negatively because of the poor results, and those who believed in the global social movement reacted negatively because they saw that the true action was happening outside of the UN. Indeed, the failure to sign a new protocol in Copenhagen exposed a profound crisis of environmental politics all over the world. Rather than producing a convincing strategy for reaching the IPCC targets formalized by the nations themselves, the negotiations revealed insurmountable discrepancies of interest between negotiating partners. The negotiations demonstrated that in terms of climate politics, an international community did not exist and that Europe, the self-proclaimed leader of global environmental politics, would neither be able to impose its particular understanding of the climate problem nor communicate its views about an appropriate counter-strategy to the whole world, since issues such as climate justice, technology failure and intrinsic environmental values were not recognized.

The five years after Copenhagen have seen a continuation in the rule of a Liberal–Conservative government in Sweden. Their main approaches have been to situate the climate change question in long-running studies and to emphasize Sweden's status as a frontrunner. The Liberal–Conservative government continues to testify that it act with urgency, but there have not been sufficient changes in legislation, regulation, taxation or subsidy to show its leadership in managing one of mankind's greatest decisions. On the contrary, Sweden has become a nation that is not achieving the environmental goals that it set for itself (Lidskog and Elander, 2012; Hysing, 2014). Instead of functioning as a true frontrunner, the Liberal–Conservative government has channelled the climate issue into the research system in the form of the Future Commission and the Roadmap 2050 programme. The government continues to present Sweden as already being an environmentally friendly country with decreasing emissions and a citizenry that is decreasing its ecological footprint. How could this seemingly paradoxical situation of the apocalyptic framing of climate change combined with conservative environmental actions be explained? Sweden is not unique (Blühdorn, 2011; Methmann and Rothe, 2012), but it may be one of the clearest examples of this apparently weird situation. We will discuss this situation with the help of ideas from the risk society, post-political theory and ecomodern utopias.

World risk society and self-confrontation

How can this whole process be explained? Was it the media's portrayals of dramatic international events that caused the controversy to flare up for a few years and then decline? Were climate politics in a void where repressed ideological differences could seek out and usurp space? Or, was it simply the case that the Swedish presidency of the EU, in relation to the geographical proximity of Sweden to Denmark and the globally acclaimed climate conference in Copenhagen, meant that the climate debate came to be imbued with an unusual seriousness and commitment? All of these factors probably contributed to the discursive battles that have been analysed. But, in accordance with the international research that we have referred to throughout this book, we believe it is worth placing the intensification of the conflict within the broader social process of the "world risk society" concept described by German sociologist Ulrich Beck. On the basis of his thinking, three basic explanations can be linked to global climate change. Climate change means increased social self-confrontation, reinforced subpoliticization and growing cosmopolitanism – three reasons why political disagreements intensified in the lead-up to the possible transition to a global society that could deal with climate change (Beck, 2009).

Beck's premise is built on the belief that modern industrial society's ability to control the risks it produces is on its way to an implosion. This will not happen as a result of industrial society's shortcomings, but rather as a result of its nearly limitless success. From Beck's perspective, climate change appears to be caused by unsubdued industrialization that systematically disregards ecosystems. Industrial capitalist society cannot do anything about the fact that the global economy is growing too fast, and at the expense of ecosystems, despite all the warnings showing that industrialized countries' continued increases in CO_2 emissions will result in a global climate catastrophe. In the framework of industrial capitalist society, climate change is thus perceived not as a catastrophic global risk, but as an acceptable risk with quantifiable side effects. The potential to impose substantial societal changes is overlooked. According to Beck there is an influential process of denial occurring in the midst of globalization. The risks are the product of deliberate decisions about the use of large-scale industrial technologies, and these decisions are made inside companies and government institutions that work on the premise that certain uncontrollable risks are inevitably associated with technological developments (Beck, 1992).

According to Beck, the increased number of serious self-inflicted risks increasingly undermines the operational logic of industrialized capitalist society because control can no longer be maintained in a credible way. Industrial society is forced to confront its self-produced risks and thus has been gradually transformed into a world risk society, because risks are no longer bound in time and space. In this context, it becomes increasingly clear that the threat of technological development can neither be calculated nor controlled. The self-defeating process of industrialization inevitably leads to increased social and political conflict. Industrial capitalist society is thus subject to institutional destabilization. When the self-generated risks start to dominate the public discourse, the political debate and private sector discussions have to confront a new situation. Industrial society, which previously created and legitimized risks, is forced to understand and criticize itself as a world risk society (Beck, 2009).

Beck further argues that a fundamental contradiction arises in contemporary society when it is forced to prioritize mega-threats created by itself, even though it lacks the ability to tackle them effectively while comprehensive institutional change is not allowed. Repeated failures to address environmental threats and fulfil the promise of security lead to a progressive social critique based in the fundamental inability to create suitable knowledge. The risks that were previously dismissed as side effects become a social and political problem that grows into an institutional crisis. State bureaucracies, politicians, business management, and research institutions attempt to establish criteria for what is safe and where nature's tolerance limits are, while, at the same time, global warming increases. It is, says Beck, therefore not the exceptions which are the true problems; it is the rules and regulations which leads to accelerated environmental degradation. He calls this phenomenon "organized irresponsibility" and stresses that it is revealed when unlikely events such as global climate collapse suddenly becomes likely. The large-scale risks inherent in current societies hold the possibility of self-annihilation and require effective political control; they contain a social and political explosiveness that will, sooner or later, compel profound social change. Industrial societies have hit a wall in terms of their solutions to this situation and they are being replaced by a world risk society whose contours are still emerging (Beck, 2009).

The climate debate studied here can be understood as an expression of the increased social and political conflicts that result from the self-defeating process of industrialization in capitalist societies. One reason that the climate debate became so intense and ideologically conflicted between 2006 and 2009 may be that the self-generated risks began to dominate the public discourse. A reconsideration of industrial society's claims to control became the heart of the political discussion; even the Conservative prime minister talked about climate change as a challenge for humanity. World risk society intrudes to this extent because the established society lacks the concepts and means to tackle the self-created climate crisis. In industrial capitalist society, this unavoidable self-confrontation leads to incipient attempts to understand societal risk in the context of a world risk society.

The Industrial Fatalist discourse seeks to thematize, understand and address self-generated risks through the capitalist institutions of industrial society. Its solutions are more of the same: increased, new and better technology, in-depth research, market mechanisms and political agreements on emission reductions, but absolutely no system changes, are presumed to be a workable recipe for overcoming the climate change threat. However, while this discourse rests on the assumption that climate change can be calculated by the IPCC and controlled through carbon markets and international treaties under the auspices of the UN, it also accommodates statements that it could soon be too late, if robust action is not taken promptly. This apocalyptic framing combined with conservative action dominates the global debates about climate change. The self-generated risks produced nothing like the pre-calculated spin-offs, but they are hazards that may well exceed any possibility of human control in a matter of decades, if countermeasures prove ineffective or impossible to mobilize. The dangers are expected to be serious and imminent so they are accorded considerable political significance. Thus, it appears that the dangers are inherent in systems that are articulated from within a world risk society horizon. Proposals for action still rest on industrial capitalist society's guarantees about rationality, security and control: and the risks in many ways are downplayed.

The increased degree of conflict with the Industrial Fatalist discourse that characterizes the Green Keynesian discourse grows out of the conviction that industrial capitalist civilization may well be about to destroy itself. In relation to the approaching disaster, and from a historical perspective, industrial society's trust in research, new technology and more market control appears as counterproductive, irresponsible and frivolous. What is understood as an urgent need is instead the transformation of contemporary industrial society, and the need for self-criticism and self-reformation. Green Keynesianism perceives that industrial society is creating global risks. In order to mitigate the increasingly probable disaster, far-reaching changes for transportation, energy production and consumption are required. If carbon emissions are to be reduced immediately, this must be forced by political regulation. The economic model also needs to be revised, the growth fetish discussed, consumption dematerialized and global resource allocation more fairly distributed. Industrial society will seal its own fate; international politics lacks the ability to tame the market. The global threat of climate change must therefore be given the highest priority and future society must be designed accordingly. This discourse draws its political strength from the realization that the transition to the world risk society has already begun and that industrial society's operational logic has become obsolete. Green Keynesianism issues assurances that the transition will not be shocking and that major structural changes can be implemented within the framework of the market economy. It does not have to mean fundamental changes in patterns of living, provided climate disaster can be arrested by powerful, binding international rules and national efforts to eliminate carbon emissions. This discourse still rests on an assumption that the mega-threat allows itself to be calculated, predicted and monitored using scientific models, and managed and controlled by balanced modifications of the socio-technical systems that form the basis of industrial capitalist society's expansion. Both the Industrial Fatalist discourse and the Green Keynesian discourse centre on ecological modernization as a form of politics in which capitalism and new technology are vital, even though choices of technologies and market instruments may divide them.

The Eco-socialist discourse is articulated as a critique of industrial capitalist society. The tangible threat of climate disaster is understood neither as firmly calculable, nor controllable. IPCC projections are only extrapolations of trends and there is no assurance that the ongoing climate catastrophe is not accelerating in an unpredictable and exponential way; tipping points are a real threat. This position is based in the belief that there is a fundamental inability to know exactly when disaster will occur, which calls for cautionary principles. No one has the right to act solely in their own interest when the existence of mankind is at stake. Yet, this is exactly what is going on in the world risk society and today's fossil-fuel economy. Stranded assets are not a problem, they are a necessity; we did not leave the Stone Age behind because we did not have gravel any longer. The entire industrial system, which rests on expansion through the exploitation of fossil fuels, must therefore be abandoned as soon as possible to ensure the planet's survival. This cannot be done within the framework of a capitalist economy, whose imperative is constant GDP growth, so the transition to democratic socialism or a localized self-sufficient economy has become inescapable. Only then can the necessary downscaling of production and consumption systems be achieved and the conditions for a fair distribution of the global resource allocation created. According to the Eco-socialist discourse there is no hope that the industrial capitalist system, through international carbon markets and negotiations, will be capable of modifying itself to the extent that global risks require. However, there is a hope that the climate crisis will force a form of politics that ensures a more viable future society. A fundamental system change is the only means of escaping the global hazards of climate change.

Each of these three discourses shows ways in which industrial modern society's self-generated ecological risks create social and political explosiveness. Simultaneously, there is a conservative movement in the form of Climate Scepticism which questions the whole science of climate change. This discourse articulates its own view of the apocalypse – that industrial societies will collapse because of the burden of policies implemented to save the Earth from climate change.

The inevitable demands for self-confrontation and self-criticism may help to explain why the environmental and climate debate is characterized by such strong ideological conflicts during the otherwise neo-liberal period examined here. The future of critical self-generated global threats forces an inquiry into the most fundamental political questions, particularly with regard to what a "good society" is; whether economic growth is a part of the solution or part of the problem; what constitutes an ecologically healthy relationship between politics and the market; how lifestyles and consumption patterns in the rich parts of the world affect climate; and whether global resources should be allocated equally. Between the years 2006 and 2009, when the world risk society horizon was becoming increasingly apparent, a fundamental political disagreement was articulated in the environment and climate debate. This is where the hardest battle over concrete future living conditions occurred.

Subpolitization and the necessity of a new world ethics

Beck asks why expectations of a climate disaster cause a reinvention of politics. His answer is that because the coming catastrophe can only be made present by imagining it as such, people cannot experience or study it to its full extent, apart from experiencing its devastating consequences in the forms of hurricane Katrina, altering seasons or rising sea levels. Beck says we need a new world ethic that considers the unknowable in connection to the concrete. These types of abstractions require visualization and planning to highlight the apocalyptic consequences of the climate threat. If the precautionary principle is taken seriously it assumes that what is unknown, but imaginable, must be prevented. The actors who develop the necessary new macro ethics are social movements and the global networks of solidarity movements. They have usurped the power to influence as a result of the contradictions that the industry and the administrative institutions for risk-management are entangled in. The contradictions become scandals when social movements reveal them. These social movements acquire political influence through actualizing the issues that political institutions ignore, such as how everyday life should be lived and how society should be organized in light of the global threat. Self-produced disasters cause both expectations and neglect, which means that state authority over science and the economy is questioned, not least when the failures of carbon markets and UN negotiations are highlighted. According to Beck this reduces the power of the state, while social movements increase their influence. Transnational actors working from below and extra-parliamentary challenges establish political organizations and interest groups through alternative descriptions of the problem. Climate problems open society to subpolitics, the politics that are disconnected from the formal political institutions. All spheres of life, from science and economy to everyday life and politics, must be renegotiated and rebalanced. Thus, the transformation of society will be increasingly subpoliticized and will occur independently of traditional political institutions. This means that social movements will acquire increasing influence as regards to setting the political agenda, but also that large corporations, lobbying groups, and scientific experts will increase their power over the portrayal of social conditions (Beck, 1997, 2009). The future is now on everyone's minds, according to Beck. These issues have not sprung from the regime's wisdom or from political wrestling in various parliaments – and certainly not from the power cathedrals of business, science or government. They have, despite stiff resistance from institutionalized forms of ignorance, been formulated by major and minor groups, organizations or networks. The subpolitical actors have struggled to gain a totally unlikely victory in terms of the questions on the political agenda (Beck, 1997).

The upsurge of subpolitics as a result of the increasingly serious threat of climate change may help to further explain the climate debate as well as the amplified conflict during the period we studied. Even if government representatives occupy prominent positions in the Industrial Fatalist discourse, positions are still forced by the subpolitical social movement's criticism of government neglect. In the summer of 2006, Fredrik Reinfeldt did not give environmental issues any great political importance, but one year later, when the alarm of an impending climate disaster permeated through the Swedish public, he identified climate change as a key issue for the future. However, it was not only critical subpolitical actors who influenced the government's stance. In the Industrial Fatalist discourse, Swedish trade organizations, business leaders, the Liberal press, wire editors, representatives of trade unions and Swedish economists became subpolitical actors. All these actors helped to articulate the issue of climate change as a matter of the utmost political importance in the context of industrial capitalist society's logic. While articulating the discourse of Industrial Fatalism they also paid great attention to describing climate change as a serious problem and claimed the situation could only be solved by new technology and sophisticated market economy mechanisms. Climate change was interpreted as indicating a temporary misconfiguration of the industrial capitalist system. The crisis was viewed as bolstering propositions and initiatives to facilitate calibration and fine-tuning using increasingly sophisticated methods, which also had the advantage of creating new markets. Suggestions of changing socio-technical systems, GDP-growth objectives, patterns of living, or industrial capitalist society as a whole were rejected. This neo-liberal and post-political approach constitutes the starting bid in the climate debate and it dominated the scene. In an ecomodern utopian way, this position strongly conserved the business-as-usual strategy, even if climate disasters had turned the issue into a controversial political challenge.

The urgency, importance and apocalyptic framing of climate change by the Liberal editorial writers and the powerful interest groups who were working from an Industrial Fatalist understanding of the climate problem simultaneously opened up the field to other subpolitical actors. A number of social movements and organizations strode into the battle for an alternative climate politics aimed at ecological reassessment. This Green Keynesian discourse was used mainly by actors who had been in the subpolitical realm for several decades such as the Swedish Society for Nature Conservation (SSNC), Greenpeace, the World Wildlife Fund (WWF), the Swedish Church, Diakonia and international solidarity groups, but also by newly formed organizations such as Climate Action and the Tällberg Foundation. Moreover, individual researchers, writers and journalists acted for a form of politics that represented the comprehensive, politically initiated transition of structures within the industrial capitalist society that generated the global risks. In-depth discussions on the design of contemporary and future society were mainly conducted outside of the decision-making assemblies and away from established institutions, within what Beck calls the "subpolitical". It was here that a strong political will and visionary energies gathered and established a firm foothold. It was along these lines of conflict that concrete plans for long-term global living conditions were drawn up. On the brink of climate catastrophe, the environmental movement, church organizations and international solidarity groups created or gave expression to the macroethics for a more balanced life, but they never rejected the rationality of industrial capitalism.

The Eco-socialist discourse maintained a greater distance from established political institutions. Groups such as Klimax, Climate Justice Now, Nature and Youth Sweden (Fältbiologerna) – and with regard to some issues, Climate Action – as well as magazines that covered societal critical debates, confronted all other discourses with far-reaching demands for changes in the economic system and relationships of global economic exchange. This was also manifested in protests, marches, petitions, direct actions, occupations and boycotts. Ultimately, it was about being able to clearly visualize and understand the implications of climate catastrophe and hence the necessity of radical change in systems and lifestyles, which would have to be adapted to the newly gained insights. Climate change was interpreted as the latest and most serious symptom of industrial capitalism's inherent self-destructiveness. This was not only because of the devastating evidence, but also the conditions of people – now, and in the future – across the globe. Climate change was, in the deepest sense, political and it was understood as the overarching question to which all others could be linked. The dominant discourse of neo-liberalism, was thought of as a political provocation in the light of challenges ahead. There was simply no question that was more politically and morally important than climate change. If it were taken seriously, it could show the way to a new, better, fair and sustainable society.

The Climate Sceptic discourse was also subpolitical. The Stockholm Initiative and a small number of researchers and industry representatives connected to it – without any support among the political parties in parliament up until 2010 – fought hard to counter the demands for government measures that had resulted from the successful establishment of the climate threat as a political problem. The belief that this was created on false scientific grounds and on the basis of hidden political motives, led actors in this discourse to proclaim how and why climate change had become, in their view, politicized in a certain way: that is, it had been kidnapped by an environmental movement with totalitarian goals. However, this meant that the political content of the climate debate was reinforced when conservative ideals of society were mobilized to confront the other discourses.

Ulrich Beck's thesis is that the climate problem – as a self-generated ongoing disaster that undermines science – the economy, and dominating politics, open the door to subpolitical efforts to bring about renegotiations in all spheres of society. We maintain that this can help to further explain why, during the period we studied, the climate debate was characterized by profound political differences, while political life in general seems to be dominated by neo-liberal hegemony. Latent political tensions were reactivated by subpolitical groups within the climate debate. It is not primarily parliamentary parties that are struggling with how the climate-friendly society should be portrayed, planned and realized, but organizations such as the Swedish Enterprise Organisation, the Swedish Church, the SSNC, Klimax and the Stockholm Initiative, as well as numerous individuals. It is these kinds of actors who can identify the climate threat and instigate new ways of imagining and the development of macroethics. They may also think ahead into the future and formulate moral standards of global responsibility. The dystopian and utopian energies take a route through subpolitics into the climate debate, and the reason that this happens is that the implications of climate change put everything at stake: the balance of ecosystems, global resource allocation, industrial civilization, material welfare, economic growth and even the survival of humanity. Through our close study of these political struggles, we can see that politics surrounds the issue of climate change even if, from a certain perspective, it does not look as if they are present.

Transnational risks and cosmopolitanism

A third reason that the climate debate became so conflicted may be the transnational character of climate change. Beck argues that the world risk society creates a historically unprecedented political situation, because no nation has an opportunity to independently manage its ecological issues while handling the problems that will affect the ability of society to survive. The global dynamics of the hazards collide with nationalistic perspectives and with the operating logic of the nation state as a political institution. Risks cannot be processed politically with the help of traditional institutions that are only capable of observing them. For Beck, the climate crisis is leading to the rejection of neo-liberal notions of a minimal state and demonstrates the need for transnational supranational political interaction. No actor can win on their own; all people, groups and nations are interdependent (Beck, 2009). Global risks therefore increase the influence of both states and civil movements, as new bases of legitimacy and means of action will be created for these actors, provided that they accept the transnational nature of the collaboration and are prepared to get to grips with complex interactions across borders. Global warming and other mega-threats lead, according to Beck, to a cosmopolitanism that emerges from below and is created by social movements.

These movements set the tone for global environmental politics at all levels. Global subpolitics circumvent national processes and institutions. This situation can lead to global alliances and a cosmopolitan society created to deal with the self-produced risks of a global industrial capitalist society. Cosmopolitan efforts to integrate the non-national interests in their decision-making will be met with resistance from the dominant nationalistic self-understanding. The belief that a nation has the right to jeopardize not only its own environment, but also that of other nations is still strong even though, through conventions such as the Kyoto Protocol and the Espoo Convention, it is becoming increasingly problematic; the need for transnational coordination and joint action is becoming increasingly urgent. A neo-liberal nationalistic logic that puts the world's fate in the hands of the individual consumer, Beck argues, has no prospect for dealing with the transition prompted by climate change (Beck, 2009). The idea that climate change demands global cooperation loads the Swedish climate debate with strong disagreements. It leads to disagreements about Sweden's international obligations, which are carved out more clearly here than in other matters. Few have denied political responsibility for the global situation, but perceptions of what this responsibility entails and how it should be handled have differed widely between the contending discourses and have raised fundamental ideological conflicts over values.

The Industrial Fatalist discourse understands cosmopolitanism as the solution to the problem of the climate crisis, as it requires supranational internationally coordinated efforts and legally binding agreements on the reduction of global carbon emissions. In this scenario, Sweden is put forward as a frontrunner and a good example to other nations. On its own, one country cannot do anything, but by adopting ambitious national emissions targets and taking an active role in the high politics of the UN, Sweden can show the way for other countries. All countries must assume their responsibilities; the EU and Sweden are described as the most progressive, insightful and responsible forces in this global cooperation project of unprecedented proportions. Through conditional promises of reductions made with other EU countries, Sweden can urge other countries to follow. This is how the country can contribute to a cosmopolitan solution to the climate crisis, which cannot be handled within the boundaries of nation states, according to the rhetoric of Industrial Fatalist actors. But when Industrial Fatalist actors changed from emphasizing the idea of becoming a frontrunner to portraying Sweden as already doing its fair share, this could be combined with a cosmopolitanism based on ideas of flexible mechanisms in a neo-liberal way. Introducing flexible mechanisms as solutions made it possible to carry out conservative actions while simultaneously describing the situation as apocalyptic.

A completely different interpretation of the inevitable cosmopolitanism is made within the Green Keynesian discourse. It emphasizes that the historical debt of Sweden and other rich countries, ecological footprints and moral duty should be the reason to push for a levelling of the global resource allocation. Sweden should be a real frontrunner and show leadership by example, not by using flexible mechanisms or redirecting development aid. Emission reductions along set national goals and international cooperation within the UN framework are at the centre of this discourse, the aim is to even out the loads placed on the atmosphere and ecosystems by all the countries of the world. This means that the rich countries must take responsibility for the global situation by immediately minimizing their emissions as a cautionary example. Sweden should work towards this through international negotiations and make an effort to ensure that rich countries assume responsibility for the global environmental threats that their own industrialization has caused. The belief that global political negotiations alone would achieve this aim was strong before Copenhagen, but severely limited afterwards. Afterwards it was understood that cosmopolitanism from below is needed. Cosmopolitan and global social movements must work together to put pressure on the politicians who represent their countries at UN negotiations, according to actors within the Green Keynesian discourse. Only through massive pressure from below, coming from united social movements from all countries (such as the network that Climate Action created), can politicians be made to act in accordance with humanity's long-term interests. In accordance with this approach, it is the NGOs and grass-roots public opinion rather than international politicians who represent an effective cosmopolitan stance.

Confidence in a UN-coordinated cosmopolitanism is almost completely lacking in the Eco-socialist discourse. It should be noted that not all of the actors within the Eco-socialist discourse are fully prepared to reject the UN form of cosmopolitanism, because so far no other internationally recognized partner organizations with the power of sanction has been found. But for the majority, it is not the UN, but rather a heterogeneous group of local social movements around the world that represent this cosmopolitanism. Hope and expectations are tied to their ability to create a global climate movement that can take climate politics to other forums, where local groups from different parts of the world can explain their concrete and specific experiences and lay the foundation for the cosmopolitan cooperation that climate change necessitates. The change must begin in everyday life and come from below: you must be the change you wish to see in the world.

Climate Sceptics also present cosmopolitan argumentations, but they make use of a totally different logic. They claim that climate change, and the relevant politics to handle it, will create chaos and make the world poorer. For them, the best way to create cosmopolitanism is through intensified trade that creates wealth both for the rich as well as the poor. They therefore dismiss the UN process. They will not hand over any emission reductions to markets because for them the climate threat does not exist and this means that there is no need for a cosmopolitan project based on environmental justice. Their focus on increasing national economic growth makes moral and fair cosmopolitanism a problem, especially if such a movement is based on solidarity with a goal of environmental justice. For them, cosmopolitanism is all about global markets, not shared cultural experiences and taking care of a common Earth. This nationalism and focus on Swedish industrial modernity becomes more evident when Swedish Democrats enter the parliament in Sweden 2010 and join the Climate Sceptic discourse.

The understanding that there is one common global threat for all people on Earth inevitably leads to the situation in which issues of international justice, moral responsibility and democratic influence arise. Thus, the reactivation of the Swedish climate debate reveals profound ideological differences. Conflicts over political values are at its very centre.

The climate debate and organized irresponsibility

The above discussion has attempted to point out some possible explanations for the way the climate debate progressed in Sweden between 2006 and 2009, a period characterized by profound ideological differences regarding what kind of society had the best potential to meet the crucial and ominous claim that climate change posed. Climate change is a global issue that subpolitical groups managed to put high up on the political agenda in various ways, while at the same time established and powerful actors co-created the climate debate situation. It is more difficult to explain why the intense debate on climate later became marginalized and incorporated into the public political discourse as part of the regular repertoire. Climate change has once again become an issue among others, a political management problem among many. Alarms have been silenced and the requirements of immediate social change have been put on hold. Even if the fire in the basement is larger than ever, people are seeking silence and covering their eyes. Given that global carbon emissions continue to rise and Swedish emissions have now been recalculated by the state environmental boards as being 15–20 per cent higher than in 1990, if outsourced emissions are taken into account, it is very important to explain this negligence of the climate change problem, both in Sweden as well as all over the world.

Based on the material analysed, it is almost impossible to answer the question of why this debate has changed so dramatically, without falling prey to naive speculations about a kind of exhaustion in mass media; that alarmism caused a rebound effect when the predicted chaos seemed to disappear; that the air went out of the critical opinion balloon when the high expectations of the Copenhagen summit ended in nothing; or that the economic recession and the financial crisis, with attendant mass unemployment in the US and Europe, thwarted all attempts to actualize a discussion about relevant climate-change policies. Such temporary circumstances might, of course, have contributed significantly to reducing screams to a faint murmur. To what extent is hard to determine; and these different explanations also fall prey to being part of pre-designed explanations, while none of them take into account that attention cycles of this kind have happened before and are very much part of the success of subpolitical groups.

The turnaround could also be given a more theoretical explanation with the help of Ulrich Beck's concept of "organized irresponsibility". Although the world risk society allows itself to be self-confrontational, climate challenges are still mainly handled in accordance with industrial capitalist societal performance frameworks and operational logic. The social and political contradictions of global mega-risks remain largely concealed as long as industrial society's simple and linear rationality categorizes and controls the demands of such risks: this is facilitated is by organized irresponsibility (Beck, 2009). This means that within nation states it is impossible to hold any one entity legally responsible for the threatening effects of decisions that affect the climate, but also that the fragmentation of the legal areas and the absence of legal regulation between nation states makes it possible both for the states and for other stakeholders to ignore the global risks. In other words, global warming is legitimized by inflexible rules and the absence of regulations. This allows all climate commitments to be made voluntarily and also permits the actors who prioritize economic growth or profitability at the expense of effective climate protection to continue to do so. The Copenhagen climate summit laid bare a clear situation of organized irresponsibility, and national governments' unwillingness to let the knowledge from climate change affect economic interests. The hope of a common roadmap that was born in Bali was quenched efficiently in Copenhagen. COP 15 was not just another in a series of failed climate conferences, but demonstrated in a brutal way the immense scale of this structural problem despite the ambitions that were declared.

How is it possible to have apocalyptic framing and conservative action simultaneously?

As discussed earlier, only two years after Copenhagen a remarkable turnaround had occurred. The climate-change debate had spawned widespread reactions. Climate denial was resurgent around the world. The oil industry renewed its public campaign to support industrial modern solutions of more and more fossil fuels such as shale gas, which was described as the new energy future (Levy and Spicer, 2013). Climate change was once again presented by the dominant actors as an environmental issue among several others, and it did not dominate the agenda as before (Schmidt et al., 2013). The reverberation of Copenhagen and "Climategate" was used for the resurgence of climate denial and a restructuring of the cultural politics of climate change in the US, the UK, Sweden, France and other countries. Levy and Spicer discuss this:

> [T]he proponents of climate denial, including the Tea Party in the US, have successfully tapped into populist anger rooted in economic insecurity and a perception that political elites are out of touch. The claim

that climate change is a hoax used to justify an expansive regulatory state, higher taxes and funding for scientific elites, had been floating around right-wing political fringes, but the recession appears to have provided a material context in which this discourse could thrive.

(Levy and Spicer, 2013)

Levy and Spicer also present popular cultural examples: the 2010 Super Bowl ads for car brands Dodge ("Man's Last Stand") and Audi ("Green Police") which capture the spirit of, "gendering environmental concerns by mocking submissiveness to women and the intrusiveness of the 'green police' nanny-state" (Levy and Spicer, 2013). In 2011, opinion polls in the US and the UK showed a dramatic jump towards doubt and denial regarding climate change, with white working-class conservative males in the US exhibiting the highest rates of denial in the aftermath of Copenhagen, Climategate and the more forceful lobbying by the fossil-fuel industry (McCright and Dunlap, 2011). To conclude, the elements described above combined to lower interest in climate issues among the mass media, citizens and politicians.

Post-political apocalypse forever?

The current climate-change debate, both in Sweden and across the world, is very different from the way it was before Copenhagen. In Sweden, climate change has been channelled into long-running research studies by the Liberal–Conservative government. They maintain images of Sweden as a frontrunner, but from having a comic apocalyptic framing which suggests that flawed humans have the capacity to mistakenly influence the end of the world, the narrative has slightly changed towards a tragic apocalypse, which portrays global warming as a matter of ill-fate as the logic of adaptation spread.

This forces our analysis to take into account how this apocalyptic framing can function together with conservative inclinations to do nothing. Erik Swyngedouw has been one of the most prominent scholars arguing that climate change and other environmental issues have been constructed in a consensual post-political way that includes them as problems for neo-liberal managerial politics (Swyngedouw, 2007, 2010). He argues that climate change has been made into a "carbon consensus" that shapes the issue into managerial and large-scale technological tasks. This puts the focus on how to reduce carbon emissions in the atmosphere rather than on societal discussions about how to transition the economic and political institutional arrangements away from a fossil-fuel dependent economy. Swyngedouw proclaims that: "At the symbolic level, apocalyptic imaginaries are extraordinarily powerful in disavowing or displacing social conflict and antagonisms. Apocalyptic imaginations are decidedly populist and foreclose a proper political framing" (Swyngedouw, 2013b). In a similar vein, Ingolfur Blühdorn discusses how climate politics and the failure at Copenhagen clearly show how environmental politics has turned and is locked into a politics of unsustainability.

A politics of unsustainability is defined as simultaneously recognizing the urgency of radical political change while at the same time expressing an extraordinary unwillingness and inability to implement such a change. According to Blühdorn, this situation includes a certain normalization and mainstreaming of the environmental crisis as well as the suppression of visions of an ecologically and socially reconciled society beyond the pathologies of modern consumer capitalism (Swyngedouw, 2007, 2010; Blühdorn, 2011). The process of channelling climate change into the investigation machine is a practice of post-politics in Sweden. This practice was the outcome of a very heated debate, not an outcome of the fact that climate change was described as apocalyptic, and the debate might open up again when the apocalyptic framing once again takes centre stage. In our empirical study we claim that the situation is actually the reverse to that put forward by other post-political scholars: we claim that apocalyptic framing makes radical and democratic politics possible and it is only by living within it that political change is possible.

The dominant version of apocalypse in Sweden between 2006 and 2009 actually provides a comic challenge from which people may learn, grow, and adapt; the comic version is open-ended. Furthermore, comic variations of the apocalypse present the apocalyptic telos in a non-totalizing way, again with the effect of amplifying human agency. Within the opposite, tragic variation of the apocalypse, climate-change politics is viewed as the demise of humanity. In Sweden, Climate Sceptics are the only ones portraying the situation in this way, and they are talking about the outcomes of climate politics, not climate change. The comic apocalyptic frames of Industrial Fatalism, Green Keynesianism and Eco-socialism, promote human agency as the cause of climate change. The comic apocalypse promotes humanity as mistaken, rather than sinful. As such, it allows space for bringing disparate communities together. Humans may be inspired to take steps to change because they have been told that it is a possibility. We agree here with Methmann and Rothe (2012) as well as Foust and O'Shannon Murphy (2009) that the kind of climate-change politics that emerges from apocalyptic framing is not determined, as Swyngedouw tends to say and be understood. In the comic apocalypse, humans can take action and this is the discourse that actually dominates the debate on global climate change. Even though the hegemonic discourse of climate change eradicates differences across the globe and presents humanity as a universal sufferer (Swyngedouw, 2010), this does not dismiss antagonism, it actually makes politics in the form of climate justice even more likely. Engaging with antagonistic forms of contentious politics suggests that post-political accounts of climate-change politics are partly not based on empirical studies and tend to marginalize different forms of climate-change politics that are being shaped. Any post-political consensus after Copenhagen is an active process achieved through the disciplining work of repressive economic, policing, rhetorical and judicial frameworks. The apocalypse is here and we need to embrace it as it opens up the opportunity for radical democratic politics.

For us, this signals one of the key achievements of mobilizations before and at the Copenhagen meeting. They did not necessarily live up to the expectations of some commentators, but they did create a significant challenge to the dominant discourse in terms of articulating climate justice as a core element of climate politics. This was achieved through the consistent prioritizing of issues of climate justice, constructing climate-change politics in directly antagonistic ways and positioning climate change in relation to the economic crisis (Featherstone, 2013). This is something that tends not to be recognized when our global state of being is theorized (Swyngedouw 2010, 2013). Mobilizations before and within Copenhagen suggest that forms of contentious politics shape more generative geographies of antagonism and more diverse modalities of contestation than is acknowledged by post-political theorists. The apocalypse is not present in the dominating discourse today and neither is climate change as a question of civilizational dimensions.

Overlooked utopian components in post-political ecomodern times

If we now have one part of the explanation for our current situation, that is, how the apocalypse can actually be presented as two sides of the same coin – given that the comic apocalypse creates space for action, while the tragic variation conserves the situation as it is – we still have to understand how both these processes work together. Blühdorn proposes that in the new post-political phase, the aim of changing the social order and societal practices in such a way that they become sustainable has been supplemented and even overtaken by the unspoken but defining practice of how to maintain social structures and lifestyles that are known to be unsustainable. The main aim for the dominating discourse in the aftermath of Copenhagen is, according to Blühdorn, how to defend what industrial modernization has achieved against "environmental refugees and environmental justice movements, without appearing openly xenophobic, selfish, and perpetuating gross global injustice" (Blühdorn, 2011). What needs to be explained, according to Blühdorn, is how this politics of unsustainability can be achieved and maintained; we think that one clue is to critically examine nationalism as expressed through frontrunner images and visions of the future, such as the eco-efficient economy. The politics of conserving an unsustainable state has been discussed in terms of an ecomodern utopia in which new large-scale technological solutions such as nuclear, CCS (carbon capture and storage) and climate engineering are loaded with positive associations, including clean water, controlled emissions and the conservation of the Earth's atmosphere (Hultman, 2013; Anshelm and Hansson, 2014). We think it is fruitful to look for one explanation of this maintaining of the unsustainability in the overlooked utopian components of post-political times. We have mentioned post-political scholarship, but it tends to leave out the importance of emotional and identity politics. However, we want to understand and critically examine the success of the post-political consensus not only in terms of technocracy, management or to what extent it "elimates fundamental conflict or elevates it to antithetical ultra-politics" (Swyngedouw, 2010), but also how Liberal–Conservative politicians, companies and organizations elaborate on the idea of the ecomodern utopia in order to gain hegemony.

In the ecomodern discourse that became dominant from the 1990s onwards, environmentalism abandons the idea of limited expansion and criticism of mastery over nature and humans. Instead ecomodern proponents seek ecological sustainability via changes in liberal–capitalist attitudes and institutions rather than replacing it with something else (Huber, 2004; Mol, 2001). The ecomodern discourse wanted to bring about major changes in energy and environmental policy throughout the countries of the OECD (Organization for Economic Cooperation and Development) and the world. Environmental problems were changed from being threats to civilization, which demanded radical system-wide changes, to being mostly under control and soon to be solved. The private sector changed its rhetoric and was now described as a locomotive that would handle both economic and environmental crises. The ecomodern discourse enabled economic growth to be placed squarely at the centre of the environmental debate, as the concept of sustainable development allowed for the claim that there was no conflict between economic growth and environmental problems. In fact, it was declared that environmental problems actually fostered growth, innovation and competitiveness (Lundqvist, 2000, 2001). In the ecomodern discourse that underlies sustainable development strategies at all levels in the OECD countries today, environmental conservation and economic growth are held to be compatible (Hajer, 1995; Mol and Sonnenfeld, 2000). But institutional change with ecological sustainability as its goal has been simultaneously implemented by large energy companies (e.g. Vattenfall), influential political bodies (the EU), politicians in countries that emit large quantities, such as the US (Bush and Schwarzenegger), who all propose large-scale technical solutions to the problem and say that technological fixes are part of a larger vision of the future. The ecomodern discourse contain both an institutional side and a technocratic side, and both are promoted with environmentally friendly messages, proposals and images.

The ecomodern utopian concept allows us to understand the strong emotional attachment to big technologies such as nuclear power, CCS, climate engineering and the hydrogen economy, and how these attachments shaped a technological ideal during this period of apocalyptic framing (Hultman and Nordlund, 2013; Anshelm and Hansson, 2014). Climate change inside this ecomodern utopia was no longer something frightening that the environmental movement and researchers could use to threaten the base of industrial modernity; instead, climate change was embraced as a new opportunity to create large-scale socio-technical systems. This could be exemplified with the proposal of the hydrogen economy. The most interesting aspect of the huge expectations of the hydrogen economy – and perhaps the one with the most emotional appeal – was the frequent use of the water metaphor. Water was described as the energy resource as well as the only emission of such economy. In the first EU study on the hydrogen economy, a drop of water illustrated how energy was tapped from nature's own circulation system, used to the benefit of society and then given back to nature again simultaneously as coal; in the report this was described as baseload for the system (Hultman, 2010). The water metaphor, which has the capacity to touch people on a very deep emotional level, was used to describe the circulation of energy in industrialized societies trying to recreate themselves as environmentally friendly. The water metaphor illustrated a cycle that was represented as nature's own solution to the energy issue. Historians Manuel and Manuel stress that a utopia is characterized by being "not a sleepy or bizarre vision, but one that satisfies a hunger or stimulates the mind and the body to the recognition of a new potentiality" (Manuel and Manuel, 1979:29). The extensive use of the water metaphor in marketing hydrogen and fuel-cell technology is remarkably allusive in the policy documents, especially since the energy sources were planned to be of fossil heritage. As such, it is a symbol that speaks not only to people's rationality but also to their emotions. Scholars who have studied utopias suggest that although the authors describe them with rational arguments and scientific authority, a utopia must also touch the audience emotionally (Hultman and Nordlund, 2013).

Another example is of CCS, connected to fuel cells as an intrinsic part of a hydrogen economy. When Vattenfall's CEO, Lars G. Josefsson, was awarded Time magazine's prize "European Hero" and described as "Mr. Clean" for his way of dealing with climate change through the building of CCS test facilities (Buhr and Hansson, 2011), this was an example of the emotional technical sublime at play in the very heart of ecomodern utopia. CCS was presented as a solution to climate change in the IPCC reports in 2006. The following year, the EU adopted it as a core solution to climate change (Hansson, 2012). Large socio-technical inventions were presented as making it possible to have our cake and eat it too. As one of the single largest creators of carbon dioxide emissions in Europe, and owned by the Swedish citizens as a state energy company, Vattenfall tried to hide their faults by storing emissions in the ground. The case of Vattenfall illustrates clearly the displacement strategies of ecomodern utopia: on the one hand the image of clean and green is highlighted and connected to the strong emotions attached to progress, economic growth and expansion; on the other hand, the proposed technology does not deal with the problems, it only displaces them. Instead, what seems to be happening is that different countries, companies and citizens send emissions to other locations, and bury them to be dealt with at another time. Emissions are thus displaced from countries such as the Netherlands, the USA, Sweden and Japan to countries such as China and India (Rothman, 1998).

New or modernized nuclear plants were presented as another solution, both globally and in Sweden, and were a fundamental part of the ecomodern utopian argumentation of "carbon-free" technological solutions. The upsurge of beliefs in nuclear power was termed the "nuclear renaissance" by its proponents, and was the other type of large-scale socio-technical solution that was suggested as a solution to climate change (Teräväinen et al., 2011). Nuclear power was more evident in the Swedish debate than CCS because of the comparative lack of coal and gas in the Swedish energy system. Nuclear was thus widely proclaimed by the Industrial Fatalist discourse as a probable technology for the future, paving the way for continuous economic growth and reduction of the CO_2 emissions. The underlying argument in the Industrial Fatalist discourse was that Sweden was a frontrunner country because it combined lowering emissions and enduring economic growth, and that every country should do as Sweden was doing by putting its money on having at least 30 per cent of nuclear power in its total energy mix.

We see that the post-political condition shares similarities with discussions about ecological modernization and ecomodern discourse in the way that politics has been turned into beliefs and practices of markets, green consumption and new technologies. But only having an understanding of the political reports, laws or regulations misses a central aspect in the ecomodern discourse: namely, that there is a strong emotional connection to large-scale solutions that create conservative actions. When actors within the Industrial Fatalist discourse are creating strong images of Sweden as a frontrunner and making economic growth and the lowering of carbon emissions simultaneously possible through an eco-efficient economy, ecomodern utopia is at work. Concurrently, the Liberal–Conservative government is displacing issues of climate justice, use of natural resources and consumption-based accounts of carbon emissions, and political commentators are shaping an inevitable road ahead away from the fear of earth floors. In ecomodern utopias, the overall development of society is merely extrapolated from the present to the future, with some technological fixes added. What is central to these is a call to hasten the pace of change in order to keep up with the catastrophe ahead. The pace of technological change has to increase, but the social structures and power relations must remain intact. Throughout history, other versions of utopia have been characterized by a heavy reliance on technology, while detailed descriptions of it are, paradoxically – and notably – absent. Instead the focus shifts towards the favourable benefits it would provide, such as efficient industrial processes, clean waste (or none at all), the absence of noise and a harmonious state (Hultman and Nordlund, 2013).

The vital argument of this analysis of Sweden as the frontrunner in creating an "eco-efficient green economy" is that utopianism of one form or another permeates all types of environmentalism, whether radical or reformist; the particularly conservative utopianism set in motion by the Industrial Fatalist discourse makes it possible to frame climate change as apocalyptic while proposing conservative actions. This ecomodern utopianism was particularly present during the run-up to Copenhagen, when the Industrial Fatalist discourse articulated a vision of the future based on an eco-efficient economy alongside the image of Sweden as a frontrunner country. With such a powerful and repetitive description of Sweden as an environmental frontrunner with an eco-efficient economy, the Industrial Fatalist discourse was able to simultaneously describe the situation as apocalyptic and maintain conservative politics.

A conservative ecomodern utopia

There is, however, an overlooked utopian feature in the environmental ecomodern discourse. To date, there have been numerous studies about the history of environmental politics, especially with regard to how ecological modernization came into being, as well as research about its spread in different areas (e.g. Mol and Sonnenfeld, 2000). But very few analyse the visionary and utopian aspects that may explain how any such approach to politics can gain so much acceptance when it is described as a salvation from contemporary problems that are presented as apocalyptic. The ecomodern utopia's combination of the desire for a lost paradise with the promise of heaven meant that its proponents could argue that the chance for humanity to be saved was imminent. There is a clear determinism in the Industrial Fatalist discourse, which becomes visible when every critique is brushed away with arguments of backwardness, earthen floors and poverty and puts the elements of time and progress in the hands of Liberal–Conservatives. These types of utopian ideas can be described as "millenarianism". The millennial good time restores something of the glory of a Golden Age, but it is also described as being at the end of time. Millenarianism is historically associated with Christianity's messianic message. This has created a dynamic dimension to the forward-looking determinism that encourages the acts of a selected few (Kumar, 1991), which is similar to the way that Sweden is described as being the frontrunner in climate-change politics. A green economy or eco-efficient economy is a partial critique of the present society, a critique based on scientific language. The solution can be seen as a form of millenarianism in the sense that those in government create a distinct actor network that infuses hope and creates a way out of the dilemma. The hope is infinite since it offers the prospect of the ultimate society, in the form of an eco-efficient economy. In line with the ecologically modern discourse, an "eco-efficient economy" is presented as an utopia that launches a couple of technological fixes, which means that contemporary society does not need to change fundamentally.

Although the description of an utopia always contains a critique of the prevailing society, it need not necessarily be a total alternative to it (Kumar, 1987). An eco-efficient economy can instead be described as the opposite: a conservative utopia. Society is merely extrapolated from the present to the future, with some technological fixes added. Such utopias are characterized by the existence of a great faith in technology, although detailed descriptions of technology are left out. The direction that the society is moving towards is not altered although the pace of change is said to be increased (Segal, 1986). The image of conservative utopias is made attractive as a result of their effectiveness, purity, absence of noise and harmonious conditions. The government would be left to the experts, not citizens, which would create effective communities (Segal, 1986). The analysis of Sweden as a frontrunner and the ideal eco-efficient economy demonstrates that the understanding of utopia as a system-change is not valid. Such a limited understanding of utopia tends to reduce the possibility of certain types of utopias; conservative utopias might be dismissed from analytical scrutiny. In the case of the eco-efficient economy, it is not about changing existing institutions, behaviour or power relations, even if utopia in many other cases contains the call for radical change.

Climate change is a much contested field. We find that during the period that we studied, the dominant discourse, Industrial Fatalism, was heavily attacked for not being able to manage the problem; simultaneously this discourse invested strong emotions in the image of Sweden as a frontrunner country while making the lowering of carbon emissions and continued economic growth a possibility, through an eco-efficient economy. By framing climate change as a problem for humanity, actors within the Industrial Fatalist discourse matched their deep-anchored faith in large-scale technologies, such as nuclear power, with comic apocalyptic scenarios in which they were in control. The comic apocalypse was co-created with human solutions presented in a powerful way. Industrial Fatalist actors presented themselves as being able to manage both the problem and the answer. This proposed solution was halted – to a large extent, globally – after Germany decided to abandon nuclear power and Japan stopped all nuclear operations after the Fukushima disaster; at the same time, the UK and Finland were prominent examples of the opposite (Wittneben, 2012). In Sweden, as of 2014, the Liberal–Conservative government still supported the plan to swap old nuclear power plants for new ones and continue the dependency on uranium supplied by Ukraine and Russia.

The post-political situation in which apocalyptic framing can occur simultaneously with conservative action is possible because the apocalypse, through its comic presentation, is made governable by humans and is met concurrently by big emotionally embedded planetary engineering solutions that offer the assurance that the industrial capitalist world's ecological system can handle climate change.

Epilogue

Engaging with antagonistic forms of contentious politics suggests that post-political accounts of climate-change politics are not based on empirical studies and tends to marginalize the different forms of climate-change politics being shaped. Any post-political consensus that came into existence after Copenhagen was an active process achieved through the disciplined work of repressive economic, policing, rhetorical and juridical frameworks. It is not difficult to understand that the years after Copenhagen created despondency among those who stressed the need for fundamental social change, while at the same time creating hopes for an alternative society. If the substantial mobilization that took place before the COP 15 did not lead to anything, how could future large-scale protests pave the way for a radical transformation of society? On the other hand, a new cosmopolitan climate-change movement was born that will continue to have an impact in the long run. In all likelihood, the confrontation between critical and utopian energies and the tangible experience of organized irresponsibility contributed to a slowdown of the climate debate. Judging by the history as told here, there can hardly be any doubt that new global environmental crises may lead to new ideological conflicts and an escalation in conflicts of value. The differences and the need for extensive fundamental changes in industrial structures, as articulated between 2006 and 2009, will be reactivated again. What is at the moment only smouldering will once again be flaring up if even the most modest predictions made by climate scientists become real. Antagonistic politics are surely lurking behind the contemporary style of post-politics. The years between 2006 and 2009 were hardly an exception, but were probably rather a modest premonition of what is yet to come.

References

"Mål för uthålliga realister", *Dagens Nyheter* 12/12 2011.
Anshelm, J. and Hansson, A. (2014). The last chance to save the planet? An analysis of geoengineering advocates'discourse in the public debate. *Environmental Humanities.*
Aykut, S. C., Comby, J. B. and Guillemot, H. (2012). Climate change controversies in French mass media 1990–2010. *Journalism Studies, 13*(2), 157–74.
Beck, U. (1992). *Risk Society: Towards a New Modernity.* London: Sage Publications.
Beck, U. (1997). *The Reinvention of Politics: Rethinking Modernity in the Global Social Order.* Cambridge: Polity Press.
Beck, U. (2009). *World at Risk.* Cambridge: Polity Press.
Birch, K. (2006). The neoliberal underpinnings of the bioeconomy: the ideological discourses and practices of economic competitiveness. *Genomics, Society and Policy, 2*(3), 1–15.
Blühdorn, I. (2011). The politics of unsustainability: COP15, post-ecologism, and the ecological paradox. *Organization and Environment, 24*(1), 34–53.
Buhr, K. and Hansson, A. (2011). Capturing the stories of corporations: A comparison of media debates on carbon capture and storage in Norway and Sweden. *Global Environmental Change, 21*(2), 336–45.
Featherstone, D. (2013). The contested politics of climate change and the crisis of neo-liberalism. *ACME: An International E-Journal for Critical Geographies, 12*(1).
Foust, C. R. and O'Shannon Murphy, W. (2009). Revealing and reframing apocalyptic tragedy in global warming discourse. *Environmental Communication, 3*(2), 151–67.

Hajer, M. A. (1995). *The Politics of Environmental Discourse: Ecological Modernization and the Policy Process.* Oxford: Clarendon Press.

Huber, Joseph (2004) *New Technologies and Environmental Innovation.* Cheltenham: Edward Elgar Publishing.

Hultman, M. (2013). The Making of an Environmental Hero: A History of Ecomodern Masculinity, Fuel Cells and Arnold Schwarzenegger. *Environmental Humanities*, 2, 83–103.

Hultman, M. and Nordlund, C. (2013). Energizing technology: expectations of fuel cells and the hydrogen economy, 1990–2005. *History and Technology*, 29(1), 33–53.

Hysing, E. (2014). A green star fading? A critical assessment of Swedish environmental policy change. *Environmental Policy and Governance*, 24(4), 262–74.

Knaggård, Å. (2014). "What do policy-makers do with scientific uncertainty? The incremental character of Swedish climate change policy-making." *Policy Studies* 25(1), 22–3.

Kumar, K. (1987). *Utopia and Anti-utopia in Modern Times.* Oxford: Blackwell.

Kumar, K. (1991). *Utopianism.* London: Open University Press.

Kurz, T., Augoustinos, M. and Crabb, S. (2010). Contesting the "national interest" and maintaining "our lifestyle": A discursive analysis of political rhetoric around climate change. *British Journal of Social Psychology*, 49(3), 601–25.

Levidow, L., Birch, K. and Papaioannou, T. (2012). EU agri-innovation policy: two contending visions of the bio-economy. *Critical Policy Studies*, 6(1), 40–65.

Levy, D. L. and Spicer, A. (2013). Contested imaginaries and the cultural political economy of climate change. *Organization*, 20(5), 659–78.

Lidskog, R. and Elander, I. (2012). Ecological modernization in practice? The case of sustainable development in Sweden. *Journal of Environmental Policy and Planning*, 14(4), 411–27.

Lundqvist, L. (2000) "Capacity-building or social construction? Explaining Sweden's shift towards ecological modernization." *Geoforum* 31, 21–32.

Lundqvist, L. (2001) Implementation from above: The ecology of power in Sweden's environmental governance. *Governance: An International Journal of Policy and Administration*, 14, 319–37.

Lyytimäki, J. and Tapio, P. (2009). Climate change as reported in the press of Finland: From screaming headlines to penetrating background noise. *International Journal of Environmental Studies*, 66(6), 723–35.

Manuel, F. E. and Manuel, F. P. (1979). *Utopian Thought in the Western World.* Cambridge, MA: Belknap Press.

McCright, A. M. and Dunlap, R. E. (2011). Cool dudes: The denial of climate change among conservative white males in the United States. *Global Environmental Change*, 21(4), 1163–72.

Methmann, C. and Rothe, D. (2012). Politics for the day after tomorrow: The logic of apocalypse in global climate politics. *Security Dialogue*, 43(4), 323–44.

Mol, A. P. J. (2001). *Globalization and Environmental Reform. The ecological modernization of the global economy.* Cambridge, MA: MIT Press.

Mol, A. P. J., and Sonnenfeld D. A. (2000). Ecological Modernisation Around the World: an introduction. *Environmental Politics*, 9(1), 3–14.

Reusswig, F. (2010). *The new climate change discourse: A challenge for environmental sociology* (pp. 39–57). Netherlands: Springer.

Rothman, D. (1998). Environmental Kuznets curves – real progress or passing the buck? A case for consumption-based approaches. *Ecological Economics* 25(2), 177–194.

Sampei, Y. and Aoyagi-Usui, M. (2009). Mass-media coverage, its influence on public awareness of climate-change issues, and implications for Japan's national campaign to reduce greenhouse gas emissions. *Global Environmental Change, 19*(2), 203–12.

Schmidt, A., Ivanova, A. and Schäfer, M. S. (2013). Media attention for climate change around the world: A comparative analysis of newspaper coverage in 27 countries. *Global Environmental Change, 23*(5), 1233–48.

Schmidt, O., Padel, S. and Levidow, L. (2012). The bio-economy concept and knowledge base in a public goods and farmer perspective. *Bio-based and Applied Economics, 1*(1), 47–63.

Segal, Howard P. (1986). The Technological Utopians. In Corn, J. (ed.) *Imagining Tomorrow: History, Technology, and the American Future*. Cambridge, MA: MIT Press.

Swyngedouw, E. (2007). Impossible/undesirable sustainability and the post-political condition. In Krueger J.R. and Gibbs D (eds) *The Sustainable Development Paradox* (pp.13–40). New York: Guilford Press.

Swyngedouw, E. (2010). Apocalypse forever? Post-political populism and the spectre of climate change. *Theory, Culture and Society, 27*(2–3), 213–32.

Swyngedouw, E. (2013a). Apocalypse Now! Fear and doomsday pleasures. *Capitalism Nature Socialism, 24*(1), 9–18.

Swyngedouw, E. (2013b). The non-political politics of climate change. *Acme, 12*(1), 1–8.

Teräväinen, T., Lehtonen, M. and Martiskainen, M. (2011). Climate change, energy security, and risk – debating nuclear new build in Finland, France and the UK. *Energy Policy, 39*(6), 3434–42.

Wittneben, B. B. (2012). The impact of the Fukushima nuclear accident on European energy policy. *Environmental Science and Policy, 15*(1), 1–3.

Index

Åberg, Lars 146
Alfsen, Knut H. and Eskeland, Gunnar 25, 36–7
anthropogenic climate change: Climate Sceptics on 100, 103, 110, 112; climategate and 154–6; historical debate 3, 169–70; *see also* apocalyptic climate change; climate change
apocalyptic climate change: as alarmist 107–8; climate change as global war 91–2; comic 43, 91–2, 100, 110, 131–2, 185; comic to tragic transition 184; and conservative inaction 184; global media coverage of 23–4; overview of 169; and political conflict/change 8–9, 81; as post-political 184–6; tragic 110–11, 113, 184, 185; *see also* anthropogenic climate change
assistance aid 138–9
Axelsson, L. 150
Axelsson, S. and Gustavsson, L. 136, 140
Azar, Christian 58, 68, 106

Bali, UN climate conference 41, 121, 135
Barosso, José Manuel 124, 126
Beck, Ulrich: Industrial Fatalism, term 19; organized irresponsibility 182–3; risk society concept 7, 172–4; subpolitization 176–7, 179; transnationalism 179–80; *World at Risk* 4
Berggren, C.*et al* (2007) 71, 72
Bergström, Hans 106, 129, 150–2, 153, 157
Bern, Lars 104, 107, 151, 152, 157
Berthelsen, Alexander 150

Bildt, Carl 123, 126
Bloch, E. 94, 184
Blühdorn, Ingolfur 8, 184–5, 186
Boer, Yvo de 155
Bolund, Per 55–6
Borgnäs, Kajsa 146
Brandell, D. 89
Brännlund, Runnar 37
Brazil 66, 101, 127, 128
Bush, George W. 43, 81

capitalism, critiques of 83–5, 93–4, 144–8
carbon consensus 184
carbon emissions: economic growth and 20–1, 30–1, 32, 59–60, 144–7; limits on and impact on developing countries 152–3; personal allowances 90–1; sale of, SSNC 87; underestimation of, Sweden 60–1; *see also* emissions trading; greenhouse gas emissions
carbon management: within ecomodern discourse 2; personal allowances 90–1; within post-political discourse 8
carbon markets 2, 91, 127
carbon rationing 90–1
carbon taxes 108
Carlgren, Andreas: commitment to binding international agreement, Copenhagen Summit 41, 42, 122–3; consumer-led ecological consumption 28; eco-efficient green economies 126; emissions and economic growth link 31; role of EU in global negotiations, Copenhagen summit 123, 124; Sweden as international role model 32; technological solutions 25
Carvalho, A. and Peterson, T.R. 4

For Product Safety Concerns and Information please contact our
EU representative GPSR@taylorandfrancis.com Taylor & Francis
Verlag GmbH, Kaufingerstraße 24, 80331 München, Germany